TAKING SPACE SERIOUSLY

Taking Space Seriously

Law, Space and Society in Contemporary Israel

ISSACHAR ROSEN-ZVI
Haifa University, Israel

Routledge
Taylor & Francis Group
LONDON AND NEW YORK

First published 2004 by Ashgate Publishing

Published 2017 by Routledge
2 Park Square, Milton Park, Abingdon, Oxfordshire OX14 4RN
711 Third Avenue, New York, NY 10017, USA

First issued in paperback 2017

Routledge is an imprint of the Taylor & Francis Group, an informa business

British Library Cataloguing in Publication Data
Rosen-Zvi, Issachar
Taking space seriously : law, space and society in contemporary Israel. - (Law, justice and power series)
1.Minorities - Legal status, laws, etc. - Israel
2.Minorities - Legal status, laws, etc. - Israel - Case studies 3.Minorities - Israel - Social conditions - Case studies 4.Ethnicity - Israel - Case studies 5.Citizenship - Israel 6.Jews - Israel - Identity 7.Israel - Politics and government
I.Title
346.5'694013

Library of Congress Cataloging-in-Publication Data
Rosen-Zvi, Issachar.
Taking space seriously : law, space and society in contemporary Israel / Issachar Rosen-Zvi.
p. cm. -- (Law, justice and power)
Includes bibliographical references and index.
ISBN 0-7546-2351-3
1. Territory, National--Social aspects--Israel. 2. Citizenship--Social aspects--Israel. 3. Segregation--Israel--Case studies. 4. Segregation--Law and legislation--Israel. 5. Local government--Law and legislation--Israel. I. Title. II. Series.

KMK2055.R67 2003
340'.115'095694--dc22

2003058292

ISBN 13: 978-1-138-26404-5 (pbk)
ISBN 13: 978-0-7546-2351-9 (hbk)

Contents

Acknowledgments

This book began as a dissertation submitted to Stanford University. I had the privilege of working with three great legal scholars, Thomas Grey, Lawrence Friedman and Richard Ford, as my advisors. Tom Grey's wisdom and extensive knowledge in every realm of jurisprudence was an invaluable source of knowledge and his comments on my drafts were encouraging as much as they were helpful. Rich Ford, whose ground-breaking scholarship in the areas of political geography and local government law was the inspiration for my own work, provided me with important insights and guided me to the right path when I went astray. Lawrence Friedman, whose pioneering work in the areas of legal history and law and society paved the way for scholarship such as mine, provided me not only with intellectual stimulus but also with true friendship. I cannot imagine my time at Stanford without him. Lawrence was also kind enough to help me transform the dissertation into a book. Renato Rosaldo, who taught at the Cultural and Social Anthropology Department at Stanford University, contributed to my anthropological understanding of the conception of space. Ariel Porat of Tel-Aviv University's Law School, a teacher and a friend, read and made very useful comments on parts of my book. And Austin Sarat who assisted me in finding a home for the book.

Writing can be a very lonely experience. I was fortunate to have many friends and colleagues who made my writing odyssey not only an experience of intellectual growth, but also a very enjoyable one. I am especially thankful to Kathy Eade who read and edited countless drafts of this book. Noa and Hemi Gefen, Yoav Samet, Rachel Kolodny, Yuval Nov and many many others offered me their friendship and helped me through some tough times. San Francisco and New York have always been a source of comfort.

The exceptional staff of the Stanford Law Library was truly more than any researcher can ask for. I am particularly indebted to Paul Lomio, David Bridgman, Troy Cook, Kelly Kuehl, Sonia Moss and Erica Wayne, who did not spare any effort to locate and bring me every source I needed for my book. I am also grateful to Anat Liberman of Tel-Aviv University's Law Library who helped me track down particularly tricky references, and to my brother, Assaf, who assisted me in finalizing the bibliography. Their help is immensely appreciated.

Finally, this book could not have been possible without the important support of my family. My wife and best friend Vered, who has always stood by me and also skillfully prepared this book for printing. My precious daughter, Ronnie, whose endless joy and ability to appreciate the wonders of life taught me a lot about living a happy life full of magic. My mother Miriam, the great matriarch of our family, whose unconditional love and support were an invaluable source of strength. And last but not least, my four brothers—Benaya, Yishai, Assaf and Avri—who were always there for me when I needed them.

The book is dedicated to my late father, Ariel Rosen-Zvi, a wise, affectionate and brave man, to whom I owe more than I can ever express in words, who taught me to live a full and meaningful life in a world fraught with tensions and complexities. I miss him greatly.

Chapter 1

Introduction

Our journey begins with two legal cases involving spatial transgression. The first case, *Hakim v. Minister of Interior,*[1] takes us some fifty years back to the early years of Israeli statehood. In 1944, Subhi Farah Khuri, a Palestinian citizen, left Mandate Palestine lawfully to pursue his studies at the American University in Beirut. Throughout the time he studied in Lebanon, Khuri regularly came back to Palestine to visit his family. In 1948, following Israel's declaration of independence and the ensuing war between Israel and the Arab countries, the territory of Mandate Palestine was occupied by the Israeli armed forces. When in 1950 Khuri attempted to return to his village, which was by then under Israeli sovereignty, he was caught by a military patrol and transferred back to Lebanon which, upon Israel's independence, had become an enemy state. His mother Na'ima, an Israeli citizen by virtue of residency in Mandate Palestine, asked the state authorities to grant her son Israeli citizenship, but her request was denied. Hakim challenged the decision in court, arguing that her son, being a Palestinian citizen who lawfully lived outside the country temporarily, should not be punished for the change of sovereignty and asked the Supreme Court to instruct the State of Israel to register her son as an Israeli citizen. The Court refused to grant the requested relief, asserting that no remedy would be provided to a person who chose willfully to reside in an enemy state.

The second case, *Sheinbein v. Attorney General,*[2] took place almost fifty years later in a place very far from Palestine. In 1997, Samuel Sheinbein, a seventeen-year old American-Jew from Maryland strangled to death Alfredo Tello and then charred and dismembered his body. Before the police were able to apprehend him, Sheinbein fled to Israel. State prosecutors from Montgomery County, Maryland, where the murder occurred, sought to extradite Sheinbein to the United States where he was facing charges of first-degree murder.[3] The Israeli Ministries of Justice and Foreign Affairs strongly supported the extradition of Sheinbein, who was born and raised in the United States, had never visited Israel before, had no relatives in Israel and did not speak any Hebrew. The Supreme Court, however, denied the extradition request. The Court held that Sheinbein, being an Israeli citizen by virtue of his father's birth in 1944 in what was then Mandate Palestine, could not be extradited. The Court rejected the Attorney General's argument that as a condition for its application the Extradition Act requires that some bond exist between Sheinbein and the State of Israel other than being a Jew. Any Israeli citizen, stressed the Court, regardless of his or her bond to the state, is non-extraditable. The Court supported its decision by pointing to the legislative history of the Extradition Act, which demonstrated that although the Act employed the neutral concept of citizenship to denote those who had a 'right' not to be extradited, the real intention of the legislature was to benefit Jews thus collapsing the distinction between the notions of citizenship and ethnicity.[4]

These two cases illustrate a dominant contradiction that structures Israeli polity and society and will occupy us throughout this book. Although far apart in time and place, the two cases illustrate the complex interplay of space and society that characterizes Israel. Israel as a political entity is characterized by a profound paradox. On the one hand, Israel has a strong notion of geographical boundaries and the ubiquitous sense of territorial borders, borders of a small state surrounded by enemies that constantly threaten it. The border, both as a metaphor and as an actual geographical place, helps mold the collective consciousness of Israel (Kemp, 2000). On the other hand, Israel is guided by the logic of ethnicity and genealogy, which can be traced back to early Zionist thinking. Israel is the home of the Jews and as such its political definition transcends geographical boundaries. As put by Edward Said, 'Israel is now the only state in the world that is not the state of its citizens but of the whole Jewish people wherever they may be' (Said, 2000, p.190). The quintessential example of this is the Law of Return that grants any Jew automatic Israeli citizenship upon arrival to Israel.[5] In other words, there is an inherent discrepancy between two conceptions of space, both constitutive of Israeli collective identity—the political space of the liberal-democratic state and the political space of the Jewish nation.

In a recent article, Richard Ford pointed to a historical transition from a tribal to a territorial conception of political space: 'As late as the fifteenth century... [s]pace was understood only in concrete terms of or in relation to the plan of the divine. In premodern Europe, what appears to modern eyes to be territorial communities were in fact simply groups united by kinship, common interests and customs... The ruler of a nation was king of a people, not a territory' (Ford, 1999, pp.872–873). Modern sovereignty, argued Ford, an offshoot of feudalism, replaced the genealogical with the territorial as its subject, and as a result 'the title of the sovereign evolved from *King of the Franks* (a people) to *King of France* (the territory)' (Ford, 1999, p.873).

Israel's history of space and its interrelations with the emergence of Israeli nationalism do not fit into this neat evolutionary model. Israel retains a strong notion of territorial sovereignty, but, at the same time, also holds on to tribal sovereignty, which results in an inherent and constant problematization of the usually unproblematic link between identity and place (Gupta & Ferguson, 1997). This state of ambiguity is reflected in many social spheres, law being just one of many. This study focuses on the production and representation of space in the legal sphere, but treats law—loosely considered as the operations of legal texts, courts and various other legal agents—as one social arena in which the politics of space is enacted and negotiated. Legal arenas and practices are, then, only a site or useful device for thinking about the relationship between space and society.

This book is a socio-legal essay on the historical production of political space. Its purpose, in a nutshell, is to map out and understand the different ways in which the state deals with various social groups through the mechanisms of space. This is done by looking at three case studies, involving three social groups in Israel's multicultural society, in which the different roles played by political space in legal analysis are revealed and analyzed. The book then proceeds to uncover the unifying logic underlying the disparate legal treatment of political space, brought to light in the case studies, and to propose a reform of local government law that attempts to achieve greater social equality through a conscious reorganization of political space.

The first chapter of the book examines the spatial dimension of school desegregation with regard to the largest ethnic subgroup within Israel's Jewish society—the Sephardim or Arab-Jews. It argues that the attempt to desegregate schools within the current system of local government, which is characterized by an unequal division of political space, is an exercise in futility. This chapter asks how is it that school segregation continues to be so widespread despite several decades of governmental attempts to desegregate schools. It concludes that one of the main reasons for the perpetuation of school segregation is that the conspicuous reality of ethnically-based residential segregation, which forms the foundation for school segregation, is left completely outside the scope of policy-making initiatives and judicial scrutiny. The inability to recognize the link between residential segregation and school segregation is tied to the way local government law is currently structured. State law draws the borders of school districts to match local government boundaries, and requires all children to attend schools within the district in which they reside. Segregated local governments escape, in turn, scrutiny by judges and policymakers due to two widely held misconceptions: one that assumes that political boundaries have no effect on the distribution of political power and economic resources (space as transparent), and another that assumes that political boundaries delineate natural and primordial communities (space as opaque). These two misconceptions lead the courts and the policymakers to believe that segregated residential patterns are beyond the proper scope of legal analysis and policy reform. It is in this way that space functions as a central organizing principle, at the same time that it completely disappears from analytical purview. The first chapter concludes by proposing a structural reform of the school system—consolidating all school districts within a metropolitan region into a unified school district—that would foster ethnic integration and increase pluralism in the educational system.

The second chapter of the book focuses on the Bedouin-Arab minority and the recurrent attempts by the Israeli government to settle them in seven segregated planned townships. It explores the various spatial mechanisms employed by state and local governments to concentrate the Bedouin within segregated localities and incorporate them into the regional economy as an urban underclass. These mechanisms include land expropriation, urban planning, public services and territorial jurisdiction. The chapter explores the crucial role played by the legal system in legitimizing a combined scheme of land expropriation, economic exploitation and spatial segregation. Legal agents and institutions assisted in confining the Bedouin to impoverished localities, enforcing a strict policy of segregation, and attempting to cleanse certain areas of undesired Bedouin presence. These attempts were justified by a discourse of 'cultural difference' that rationalizes these practices as a spatial reflection of a natural and prepolitical difference between cultural communities. In striking opposition to the disappearance of space from legal analysis when Arab-Jews were involved, in the case of the Bedouin space played a conspicuous role in legal analysis. The courts invoked and reinforced jurisdictional boundaries that separate the Bedouin from Jewish localities as a spatial marker of the natural cultural difference between the two social groups. The chapter then criticizes progressive scholars from the left, who, by uncritically embracing the discourse of cultural difference, assisted in the production and dissemination of a 'fetishism of difference', which is necessary for legitimizing the state's segregative policies. The chapter concludes with a reform proposal, offered as an alternative to the current segregationist policy toward the Bedouin. The reform proposes a regional, rather than local, integration of the Bedouin within the metropolitan area, which would serve to eliminate political disempowerment and enhance economic development in an atmosphere hostile to integration on the local level in both the Jewish and the Bedouin communities.

The third chapter of the book addresses attempts by the ultra-Orthodox community to carve out an autonomous enclave in the city of Jerusalem. It argues that the efforts of the ultra-Orthodox community to prohibit traffic on the Sabbath in streets that border neighborhoods which are heavily populated by the ultra-Orthodox are part of a continuous effort to delineate the boundaries of an 'ultra-Orthodox territory'. This chapter focuses on the response of the legal system to such attempts to achieve geographical separatism by examining a landmark Supreme Court decision—the Bar-Ilan Road case—which involved a successful political campaign of the ultra-Orthodox to prohibit traffic on the Sabbath on a major highway in Jerusalem that crossed ultra-Orthodox neighborhoods. The doctrinal arguments made by the Court are analyzed in an attempt to trace the politico-philosophical premises and the conceptions of space underlying them. The chapter concludes by proposing that unlike the previous two case studies which were characterized by a clear and unambiguous treatment of political space—either ignoring space as lacking any political significance in the case of the Arab-Jews or imposing space on a social group by assuming it has a natural and prepolitical meaning in the case of the Bedouin—in the ultra-Orthodox case no uniform treatment of political space can be distilled from the case law. Some Justices 'see through' the ultra-Orthodox territory, failing to appreciate its political salience and view only the individual citizens that inhabit such territory. Other Justices acknowledge the existence of a 'communal sphere' of the ultra-Orthodox, an intermediate entity between the traditional private and public spheres, and argue that it deserves deference because it is a manifestation of a local political community.

The fourth chapter ties together the three case studies. It attempts to provide a unifying logic for the place of space in legal analysis by situating space within a broader historical, political and sociological context. The case studies demonstrate that political space is treated differently, and that different conceptions of space organize the courts' analysis, depending on the social group involved. In the case of the Arab-Jews, political space was totally ignored. It was misconceived by the courts as transparent; lacking any political significance or consequences of its own. In the Bedouin case, the opposite was true. Space was resurrected in order to reify and justify a political community, and to ground its boundaries in a political space that was misconceived as opaque, thus having a natural and prepolitical meaning. In the case of the ultra-Orthodox, political geography played an ambiguous and indeterminate role and the legal discourse oscillated between the spatial notions of transparency and opacity.

Chapter four attempts to explain this disparate treatment of political space. Israel's politico-spatial map, it is argued, can be traced back to early Zionist thinking and, accordingly, the differential treatment of space can also be explained as an offshoot of Zionism. The conceptual vision of space governing Israeli polity and society has evolved through a dialectical interaction between the Zionist-Self and its various Others. Ethnically, racially and religiously identified spaces were produced through positioning the Others of Zionism—primarily the Arabs, but also Arab-Jews and the ultra-Orthodox—as the antithesis of the Self; the modern European Jew. This chapter aims to critically explore the way such received ideas within the Zionist ideological paradigm have shaped and reinforced different spatial notions with regard to different social groups. The Bedouin, as part of the Arab minority, are the ultimate Other of Zionism, which defines itself as against an imagined orient. The distinctiveness of the Arab Other is predicated on the seemingly unproblematic assumption that Others occupy naturally discontinuous spaces. The Arab-Jews, on the other hand, despite their Arab cultural identity—the marker of their difference from European Zionism—are ideologically part of the Zionist Self, and are therefore required to assimilate into the Zionist body-politic by ridding themselves of any Arab characteristics. As part of the Zionist nation-building project, segregated Arab-Jewish spaces, although very common due to both state policies and individual choices, were discursively integrated into the larger space of the Jewish nation-state. Consequently, ethnically identified spaces within the nation-state were misconceived as politically insignificant—a mere administrative convenience—and thus disappeared from sight. Lastly, the ultra-Orthodox retain an ambiguous status within Zionist thinking. They have elements of both the Self (as Jews of European origins) and the Other (as enemies of Zionism), and what is more they cannot, and in any case would not, be assimilated. This conceptual ambivalence is reflected in the treatment of the ultra-Orthodox space—some include the ultra-Orthodox within the Zionist-Self thus conceiving of their space as transparent, others exclude them from the national whole and accordingly treat their spaces as opaque.

The final chapter of the book, chapter five, attempts to mend the segregated system of political space and the 'separate and unequal' distribution of political power and economic resources that accompany it by proposing a reform of local government law. Local governments are significant to the study of political space because an important source of segregation is the autonomous political subdivision. After accounting in the first part of the chapter for the historical roots of contemporary local government structure and describing in detail its operative legal mechanisms as well as its political and social shortcomings, the second part lays out various theoretical models of local governance and examines their respective strengths and weaknesses. In the third part, I propose a few concrete reforms that attempt to mediate the characteristic conflict between local parochialism and centralized bureaucracy. I argue that the locus of 'local' decision making must be the metropolitan area, which is, in present times, the significant political and economic unit. At the same time, cities should retain a reduced, yet meaningful, power to shape their environment.

Although Israel is the focus of this book, its theoretical implications reach beyond Israel's territorial boundaries. Israel is a paradigmatic case of how a multiethnic nation-state, with a hegemonic ethnic group, deals with the various social groups that comprise it through the mechanisms of space. Israel as a case study can impart an important lesson about the role played by political space in the oppression and subordination of ethnic and racial minorities, and the potential political space has, if thoughtfully reformed, to empower and liberate them.

Notes

1 H.C. 24/52, *Na'ima Nasir Hakim v. Minister of Interior*, 6 P.D. 638.

2 Cr.A. 6182/98, *Samuel Sheinbein v. Attorney General*, Takdin Elyon 99(1) 1225.

3 Philip Shenon, 'Murder Suspect Who Fled U.S. Agrees to Plea Bargain in Israel', *New York Times*, 25 August, 1999.

4 MK Menachem Begin, later the Prime Minister, who was one of the amendment's initiators, defended the bill in the Knesset, stressing that the main justification for the amendment was the fear, based on the long history of anti-Semitism, of harm to Jews for being Jews per se. 'We have to be very careful', said Begin, 'about extraditing Jews into the hand of foreigners.' 79 D.K. 1453 (1977) (9 February, 1977). Several months later, when the bill was cast for the final vote, the chairman of the Knesset's Legislation, Constitution and Law Committee, MK David Glass, presented the bill to the parliament saying:

> The central argument for the rule [that citizens could not be extradited] is that the concept of citizenship entails the right to be adjudicated and punished by the state of citizenship. To that we must add the special complicated and delicate situation that Jews in foreign countries are subjected to. Despite the atmosphere of freedom and equality that characterizes most of the countries, it is better that when the firm hand of the law is called for, this hand would be an Israeli hand, because it is reasonable that Israeli judges will follow the rule 'Israel [read here as a Jew] although he had sinned is still Israel [a Jew]' (81 D.K. 1032 (1977)).

When the question of the definition of citizenship was raised both in the parliament and in its committees, the answer was unambiguous: 'As long as...we espouse the legal principle that every Jew in the world is potentially an Israeli citizen and by immigrating to Israel (making Aliyah) he can acquire or even automatically acquires Israeli citizenship—how can we distinguish between a new Israeli and an old or veteran Israeli?' (Address to the Knesset by MK Benjamin Halevy, 80 D.K. 547 (1977)). And also '[t]he principle that every Jew in the world is potentially an Israeli national is not a technical notion. It was evolved from the principle of freedom of immigration to Israel, as a Jewish-Zionist principle, for which we fought for many years' (Protocol of the Knesset's Legislation, Constitution and Law Committee, 2 November, 1977, p.9).

5 This state of affairs, which totally collapses the notions of territoriality and ethnicity, stands in striking opposition to the common situation among nation-states in which '[o]ne...cannot become a British subject simply by deciding to move to the United Kingdom' (Ford, 1999, p.844).

Chapter 2

Invisible Spaces: The Case of the Arab-Jews

'Parents, researchers, courts, and others interested in school desegregation for the last four decades have noted almost unanimously that school desegregation and residential segregation are inextricably entwined' (Denton, 1996, p.795).

This chapter will demonstrate how law's failure to account for political geography plays a crucial role in perpetuating the educational inequality between Arab-Jews[1] and European-Jews in Israel. Its main argument is that attempts to desegregate schools from within the current system of local government, which is based on an unequal division of political space, is an exercise in futility.

The Israeli public education system, administered by the Ministry of Education, is very complex, reflecting the segmented nature of Israeli society and, in fact, reinforcing it. It consists of two fully segregated subsystems: one for the Jewish majority and the other for the Arab minority. These subsystems differ in language of instruction, as well as in other aspects of the curriculum.[2] Within the Jewish subsystem, there are two additional subsystems: general public schools and religious public schools. Religious public schools enjoy pedagogic autonomy and are administered by a separate division in the Ministry of Education. Private education is almost exclusively of a religious nature. The ultra-Orthodox sector has full control of its own private education system, which is financed by the state but not supervised by it. Private education in the Arab subsystem is mainly Christian (Goldstein, 1980a; Gavison, 2000).

This chapter deals only with ethnic segregation in Jewish public schools, ignoring altogether the institutionally mandated segregation between Arab and Jewish schools. Segregation between Jewish and Arab schools is desired not only by the Jewish majority but also by the Arab minority that attempts to use the school system as a vehicle of cultural autonomy. As a result, no meaningful political group advocating desegregation currently exists in Israel.

Ethnicity in Israel

Israeli Jewish society is rifted along many axes, among them religion, political affiliation and class. The most fundamental division, however, is that between the two large ethnic categories—Arab-Jews and European-Jews.[3] This division is reflected in various socio-economic and political indices. Arab-Jews belong, on the whole, to lower socio-economic classes, tend to be 'traditional' in the religious sense, and to vote for right-wing parties, while European Jews belong to the middle and upper-middle classes, tend to be more secular and to support the left-wing parties.[4] Since the establishment of the State of Israel, and even before, Jews of European origin have enjoyed a higher socio-economic status than Jews of Middle Eastern and North African origins. These differences can be seen, for example, in contrasting levels of income, education and occupation (Gonen, 1985). In order to understand the origins of this ethno-class stratification, a brief historical background is necessary.

The Zionist movement—the Jewish nationalist movement striving for separate statehood—originated in Europe in the late nineteenth century as a reaction to widespread anti-Semitism, and developed throughout the twentieth century. At the end of the nineteenth century, European Jews (also known as Ashkenazim) were confronted with economic displacement and collective discrimination in a continent that was becoming increasingly nationalistic. After several rounds of suggestions for a solution for the 'Jewish question', Zionism finally focused on Palestine, the ancient Land of Israel which was at the time a region within the Ottoman Empire, as the future homeland of the Jewish people. Zionist ideology found its realization in immigration to Palestine and later to Israel. The first wave of Jewish migration to Palestine, known as the First Aliyah, occurred between 1882 and 1903; the immigrants came mainly from Czarist Russia, following the Ukrainian pogroms. Four migration waves from both eastern and western European countries followed prior to the establishment of the State of Israel.[5] When the State of Israel declared its independence in 1948, it had a population of about 670,000 of which approximately 90 per cent came from Europe and only ten per cent from other parts of the world, including the Arab countries (Schmelz et al., 1991). Immigrants from Arab countries began to come en masse only after the establishment of the State of Israel, following an outburst of anti-Jewish sentiment in the Arab countries.[6] By the time the first wave of Arab-Jewish immigrants arrived, the key positions in all the political, social and cultural institutions were occupied by European-Jews and the Arab-Jewish immigrants (also known as Mizrahim) encountered a cohesive and centralized socio-political system controlled by a strong Ashkenazi establishment (Ben-Zadok, 1993).

This Ashkenazi establishment, influenced by European orientalism and a genuine fear of the 'Levantinization' of the country, was scornful of the new immigrants from the Arab countries. The Arab-Jewish immigrants were stigmatized as primitive, ignorant, uneducated, and superstitious and their Arab culture was treated as inferior to the enlightened European culture.[7] The more fortunate immigrants were settled in existing villages or towns, but the majority of them were sent to 'transit camps' (Ma'abarot) located on the fringes of various localities and later also to New Towns built in remote locations throughout the country, mainly in the Southern and Northern frontiers. Both the Ma'abarot and the New Towns were built hastily and without appropriate economic infrastructure. As a result, many of the new immigrants found themselves unemployed for long periods of time, living in great poverty on the fringes of society. Those who found employment worked either as construction workers for the government or as agricultural workers for the Jewish National Fund and the Kibbutzim (Segev, 1986). When jobs were created beginning in the late 1950s, they consisted mainly of low-paying, manual labor positions in labor-intensive industries such as food and textile. As a result of these social and political processes, 'by the late 1950s, the ethnic-class division was formed', with the European-Jews largely associated with the growing middle-class and the Arab-Jews counted overwhelmingly among the ranks of the working class (Ben-Zadok, 1993; Lipshitz, 1998).

The socioeconomic gap, which originated in structural inequality, did not substantially diminish in later years. Surveys conducted during the1980s confirmed that 'the gap between the [Arab-Jews] and the Israelis of European and American origins is not closing but indeed widening, at least in certain respects' (Peled, 1990, p.348). Historical patterns, in which Arab-Jews are concentrated in low status occupations while European-Jews dominate the high status occupations, persisted and in general European Jews rank higher on socio-economic indices than Arab-Jews (Nahon, 1993; Ben-Zadok, 1993). A recent survey by the Israeli Central Bureau of Statistics (2000) confirmed once more the socio-economic gap between the ethnic groups.

This chapter explores one instance in the history of ethnic relations in Israel: the integration (or desegregation) reform—a governmental initiative intended to remedy the educational inequality between European-Jews and Arab-Jews by promoting school integration.

Integration in Education: Chronicle of a Failure Foretold

Let us begin at the end. In 1992, Shimshon Shoshani, the former director general of the Education Ministry, published a policy statement in which he announced a moratorium on the efforts to achieve school integration in the Tel-Aviv metropolitan area. Shoshani asserted that the integration reform, which was designed to remove inequality in education and equalize the conditions of schooling for all segments of society, had failed and should be replaced by a 'parental choice' program (Tel-Aviv Department of Education, 1992). This declaration came as a surprise to no one. A year earlier the Kashti Commission (1991), a ministerial commission appointed in 1989 to investigate the status of 'distinctive schools',[8] declared that there was an explicit trend toward social separation and segregation, and away from integration. Several years earlier, in 1988, a newspaper article revealed that, in spite of the ongoing integration efforts, Arab-Jewish students remained in segregated classes and that there was little interaction between them and the Ashkenazi students from higher socio-economic strata.[9]

But let's go back to the beginning. Integration reform was the product of increasing displeasure with the schooling conditions of Arab-Jewish students. As early as the late 1950s, it became apparent that educational inequality was both widespread and deeply entrenched (Swirski, 1999). In 1956, Moshe Smilanski, a scholar and an official in the Ministry of Education, submitted a report to the Minister of Education that documented the failure of public education for Arab-Jewish students. Smilanski (1957) reported that Arab-Jewish students accounted for less than 20 per cent of all Jewish high-school students and that by the twelfth grade they constituted only 7.8 per cent of all Jewish twelfth graders. When confronted with these figures, Israeli educators and state officials attributed these dismal statistics to the presumed intellectual inferiority and cultural backwardness of Arab-Jewish students (Swirski, 1999).

Nevertheless, the fact that Arab-Jewish students were doing so poorly aroused considerable concern among Israeli politicians. Because they were convinced that the source of the problem was the intellectual inferiority of Arab-Jewish students, Israeli educators and politicians opted for the official institutionalization of differential education and introduced lower level educational standard and special programs designed specifically for Arab-Jewish students. In the process a new concept was introduced in the educational discourse 'students in need of special nurture' (Teunei Tipuach). Until 1994, the definition for students in need of special nurture was explicitly ethnic: 'the son or daughter of a father who is a Jew of African or Asian origin and who had a low level of schooling and a large family' (Algrabli, 1974). In 1963, the Ministry of Education established a Ministerial Center for Schools for Students in Need of Special Nurture to develop specialized curricula, teaching methods and books. Students designated as 'in need of special nurture' were assigned reduced portions of the required material, generally just the basics. Special nurturing schools expanded within Arab-Jewish localities very rapidly:

> [By] 1977, 41 per cent of all Jewish elementary school pupils, and 37 per cent of all junior high school pupils, were defined as teunei tipuach. Since teunei tipuach were, by definition, Mizrahi children, and as Mizrahi children constituted between 50 per cent and 60 per cent of the school population, this meant that the majority of Mizrahi pupils were defined as functionally incapable of coping with the regular program of studies (Swirski, 1999, p.180).

Another innovation that accompanied the creation of special nurturing schools was the massive increase in the number of students educated in vocational high schools. In 1965, the Ministry of Education began to send students—primarily Arab-Jewish students—to privately administered vocational schools with the purpose of doubling the population of these schools, a goal that was achieved within five years. Unsurprisingly, the vocational schools became effectively Arab-Jewish schools, a fact which had a detrimental effect on Arab-Jewish students. 'In 1970, of the 9,077 high school graduates who achieved matriculation diploma, the prerequisite for university entrance, only 273 (2.7 per cent) were graduates of vocational high schools' (Swirski, 1999, pp.182–183; Shavit, 1984).

In 1968, after several years of deliberations, the Israeli parliament (Knesset) approved a major restructuring of the school system, recommended by a ministerial committee. The old structure consisted of eight years of compulsory elementary school and four years of high school. Under the reform, elementary schooling was reduced to six years, followed by a three-year mandatory junior-high school and a three-year high school. According to Shlomo Swirski (1999), integration was introduced as part of the school reform in a very incidental manner. The reform infuriated a group of Arab-Jewish parents from Jerusalem neighborhoods contiguous to a middle-class Ashkenazi neighborhood in which one of the best high schools in Israel was located. These parents demanded that their children be admitted to elementary schools in a neighboring 'registration district' so that they would have the chance to study in the prestigious high school. State officials presented the proposed reform as a rejoinder to these parents' demands. Since a new regional junior high school system, they argued, had to be built and would be attached to existing high schools, ethnic integration on the junior high-school level was bound to take place. Although ethnic integration was not the major preoccupation of the reform's architects—it was emphasized as a major goal of the reform. Ultimately, integration 'was to become the identifying label of the entire restructuring program, changing the elitist image of the [reform] in its wake' (Swirski, 1999, p.193).

Attempts to obtain parliamentary approval for the reorganization of the school system provoked a heated public debate that resulted in a political compromise. Instead of endorsing integration through legislation, as suggested by the Ministry of Education, the Knesset passed a recommendation urging each local government to adopt the integration reform. The only requirement dictated by the Knesset was that within ten years integration would be universally implemented in all local governments, under the supervision of the Ministry of Education (Chen & Addi, 1995).

The end of this story, as already noted, is not a happy one. Although in most local governments integration is still the official policy, in reality efforts to integrate have been abandoned. This is, at least partially, a response to the frustration experienced by educators and policy makers when they realized the persistence of segregation. The integration reform clearly failed to achieve its goals. Educational inequality, which the reform was designed to remedy, is endemic and continues to persist today. A survey by the Israeli Central Bureau of Statistics (1998) documented the profound gap between the educational opportunities of Arab-Jews and European-Jews: while 51 per cent of the European-Jewish population pursue university or other post-graduate degrees, only 16.7 per cent of the Arab-Jews pursue any kind of university or other post-graduate degrees. And compared to the 42 per cent of Arab-Jewish students who drop out of school during junior-high, only 22 per cent of their European-Jewish counterparts drop out of school.

The Role of the Supreme Court in the Integration Reform—The Official Story

The Supreme Court assumed a leading role in the integration efforts. When the Ministry of Education, in cooperation with the local governments, began to implement the reform, they were confronted with widespread opposition from European-Jewish parents who fiercely opposed integration. Middle class parents in many urban localities and the kibbutzim organized vocal, and occasionally violent, demonstrations against the integration reform and, as a last resort, appealed to the Supreme Court (Swirski, 1999).

In a series of decisions the Supreme Court rejected the arguments of European Jewish parents challenging the integration policy and requesting the Court to exempt them from the obligation to send their children to integrated schools. While the Court was not unsympathetic to their pleas, it almost always supported integration by disallowing European-Jews to flee integrated school districts. Stephen Goldstein (1995) documented the dramatic shift in the Supreme Court's attitude toward student placement following the Knesset's endorsement of school integration. Whereas prior to the integration reform the Supreme Court was receptive to petitions by parents asking to prevent the administrative assignment of students to particular schools, after the Knesset adopted the integration policy, the Supreme Court changed course and embraced a clear commitment to integration preferring it over the right of parents to choose their children's school.

The Supreme Court's first decision to implement the integration reform was delivered in 1971. In *Kramer v. Municipality of Jerusalem*,[10] a group of parents from an upper-middle-class neighborhood in Jerusalem filed a petition to have the Court declare the policy of enforcing the integration reform invalid. The petitioners' children were among the top students in their elementary schools and their parents desired that they continue their studies at the University School, a private school that brings together students with the highest performance levels in Jerusalem. The local authority, on the other hand, wanted these children to continue their studies at Denmark School, a newly established junior high school integrating students from various neighborhoods in the city. In order to make sure that integration efforts were not thwarted, the director of the city's education department sent a letter to the University School administration informing them that the city would not approve admission to the University School of students who were scheduled to attend Denmark School. As a result, the University School refused to consider applications by these students. The parents of students who were refused admission to the University School filed a petition with the Supreme Court, arguing that the local education authority unlawfully interfered with their constitutional right to choose their children's school and that the local authority was in error in trying to deprive them of their rights on the basis of the needs of the integration reform, which had never been legislated into law. The petitioners further argued that their right to choose an educational institution for their children was a fundamental right, equal in weight to the right to choose a vocation or a trade, and thus could not be restricted except by an express statutory provision.

In a lengthy decision emphasizing the importance of the integration reform the Supreme Court rejected the petition. At the outset of the Court's opinion the Justices stated that the petition before them was extremely significant to the public and fateful to the future of education. After setting forth the facts, the Justices went on to describe the social importance of school integration:

> The orderly implementation of the educational reform is of paramount importance. When the chairman of the Knesset's Education and Culture commission brought the recommendations of the special committee for the examination of the educational structure to the Knesset's approval, he noted and emphasized that every educational reform is, by its nature, a public-political-educational decision. 'As to our country, reducing the gap among the children of Israel—is a national goal of the highest importance.'

The Supreme Court concluded that it would not permit any actions that might frustrate the orderly implementation of the educational reform.

The decisions that followed *Kramer* confirmed the Supreme Court's support for integration. In *Kozlovski v. Regional Council Eshkol*[11] the Supreme Court affirmed a decision by the local authority refusing to provide busing for students attending a segregated school outside their school district. In *Ramat Raziel Council*[12] the Supreme Court affirmed a decision by the local authority not to transfer students between schools within the same school district. The Court stated that the decision of the local authority to implement integration and prevent 'Ashkenazi flight' was reasonable. In *Hayun v. Herzliya*[13] the Supreme Court rejected the claim that local authorities were obligated to register students in schools that are closest to their residence. The Supreme Court emphasized that such an interpretation would frustrate the policy of school integration. Finally, in *Sarig v. Minister of Education*,[14] delivered in 1989, the Court summed up its long-standing support for the integration reform stating:

> The insistence of the education authorities on their duty to implement the integration policy and their constant objection to allowing deviations from the principles of this policy has always gained the unreserved approval of this Court. In Kramer it was first recognized that education authorities, both state and local, are permitted to take into account integration, which is intended to socially integrate people from different classes and ethnic origins, in allocating students to educational institutions. In many cases since, the integration policy considerations trumped the arguments and complaints of parents asking to send their children to educational institutions to their liking ... it seems that nobody can dispute the importance of integration as a 'fundamental principle in the education policy'.[15]

Even the most vehement critic of Israeli educational policy, Shlomo Swirski (1999), acknowledged the affirmative role the Supreme Court played in supporting school integration.

Yet the question remains, why did integration efforts go astray? The political, administrative and judicial branches supported the integration reform. Local governments, in cooperation with the Ministry of Education, adopted and implemented it. What, then, went wrong? 'How can one explain,' as one perplexed commentator asked, 'the insignificant achievements in comparison to the large investments which have been made?' (Chen, 1980). The failure is especially puzzling given the favorable structural conditions in Israel. Unlike the situation in many countries, in Israel students cannot transfer from public school to private school without the permission of state authorities. As a result, the state's control over education and the ability to promote integration is relatively high (Goldstein, 1980b).

The failure of the integration reform is, of course, a complicated story and cannot be attributed to one factor alone. The orientalist and paternalistic attitude of teachers, students and others in the education system undoubtedly had a detrimental effect on integration (Rash et al., 1977; Swirski, 1999). The widespread opposition to integration by middle class Ashkenazi parents also contributed to its failure. It is my argument, however, that the most important explanation for the failure of integration is structural rather than psychological. Ignoring political geography in both policy making and legal analysis has played a large role in perpetuating the structure of ethnic segregation in the school system. By overlooking the ubiquitous presence of 'ethnically identified spaces'—physical spaces primarily associated with and occupied by particular ethnic groups—and failing to appreciate the link between widespread residential segregation and educational segregation, the legal system paved the way for the reproduction of both types of segregation. Under such conditions, even the most well received school integration proposal would have been an exercise in futility.

The Place of Education: An Exercise in Critical Legal Geography

Israeli Education Law

The Israeli educational system is based on a delicate balance of power between local and state agents. Education is provided by statutory special purpose districts—local education authorities (LEA)—in close cooperation with the Ministry of Education. The division of labor between local and central authorities, loosely prescribed by law, is that the central government is responsible for setting the policies, norms and standards for education, the execution of which is the domain of local authorities. For the most part, the LEA's function is to provide the physical means and conditions (such as facilities' maintenance and student registration) that allow the state to carry out its responsibilities in the field of education (Naor et al., 1978; Kalchheim, 1988; Ben-Elia, 1995).

Territoriality is a fundamental element in the definition of the LEA as a legal entity. Each LEA is required to supply education only to students residing within its school district (Goldstein, 1995). As the Supreme Court recognized:

> One of the accompanying conditions of the definition of a 'local education authority' ... is that it is tied to a particular and defined territory ... The 'territoriality' principle as part of

the definition of 'local education authority' was established time and again in the rulings of this court.[16]

The territorial jurisdiction of each LEA (a 'school district'), defined by the Compulsory Education Act, coincides, in most cases, with local government boundaries. The law further instructs LEAs to divide their school districts into smaller units called 'registration districts'. Their discretion in drawing registration district boundaries is, however, restricted by law. The single most important restriction mandates that registration districts must be small enough so as to ensure that the distance from any student's residence to the school she is registered in shall not exceed two kilometers; and in the case of fifth graders and higher—three kilometers ('two-kilometer rule'). The only exception to this rule is if the physical characteristics of the school district do not enable its implementation. In such cases, the LEA may form larger registration districts on the condition that it supplies busing for those students registered in schools located more than two or three kilometers (as the case may be) from their place of residence.

When the Knesset approved the integration reform it was politically impossible to repeal the existing laws. Therefore, the Ministry of Education had to deal with the fact that the existing laws remained in place and had to rely on the good will of local governments and favorable interpretation by the courts.

The Role of the Supreme Court in the Integration Reform Revisited

The Supreme Court, as we have seen, perceives itself and is perceived by many as having played a progressive role in promoting school integration. The reason, I submit, that the Supreme Court can be so perceived is related to the type of petitions heard by the Supreme Court, and is not related to the effects of its decisions. The overwhelming majority of the cases heard by the Supreme Court were attempts by European-Jews to traverse jurisdictional boundaries in order to flee integration. In such cases the sealing up of jurisdictional boundaries, prohibiting the flight of European-Jewish students from integrated school districts, promoted the image of the Supreme Court as the 'white knight' of school integration. The hermetic closure of local jurisdictions, when applied universally, is, however, a double-edged sword. The dire consequences of such a policy were apparent in *Afgin v. Netanya*,[17] the only published case involving Arab-Jewish students trying to cross jurisdictional boundaries in order to avoid segregation.[18]

The facts of the Afgin case are as follows: Abigail Afgin was the principal of a school for students 'in need of special nurture' (Teunei Tipuach) located in Emek Hefer, near the city of Netanya. As is clear from the above discussion, special nurturing schools are, in fact, homogeneous Arab-Jewish schools. Despite their geographical proximity, Netanya and Emek Hefer constituted two separate school districts, administered by different LEAs. Afgin decided that for 'educational reasons' it would be best for her students to study in a school in the nearby city of Netanya. She applied to the LEA of Netanya and managed to obtain its approval for the transfer of her students to a school in its jurisdiction. After the children had been registered, the LEA realized that the students were 'in need of special nurture' and revoked its consent, claiming that the school was not equipped to deal with such students. Afgin filed a petition with the Supreme Court, requesting the Court to issue a decree forcing the LEA of Netanya to admit the students to the school in which they were already registered.

In a brief opinion the Supreme Court dismissed the petition. The Court stated that since no regulations existed involving the transfer of students from one school district to another, it was impracticable to require an LEA to admit students from another school district. The only way to transfer students between school districts is to obtain the consent of both the LEAs, and such consent should be granted only after thorough deliberations and with good justification. Therefore, even if the LEA of Netanya had known at the time of registration that the students were in need of special nurture, it was allowed to withdraw its consent in the absence of a legal obligation to admit the students. The Supreme Court was equally persistent in protecting the integrity of registration districts and strictly applied the two-kilometer rule.[19]

The result of such legal rules, as interpreted by the courts, is a school system divided into many small, discrete and autonomous school districts, whose jurisdictions coincide with local government boundaries. These school districts are divided in turn into yet smaller units, creating in fact an elaborated system of 'neighborhood schools'. The detrimental social and political consequences of this system will be critically examined after we have laid out both the theoretical framework underlying our discussion of political space and the social reality which is its backdrop. We now proceed to the theoretical discussion.

Suspended in Space: School Districts between Opacity and Transparency

> Space as we experience it is in many ways the product, and not the fixed context, of social interactions, ideological conceptions, and of course, legal doctrine and public policy (Ford, 1994, p.1859).

There is no self-conscious legal conception of space, Richard Ford (1994) wrote, opening his discussion of the (mis)conceptualization of space in legal analysis. 'Legal boundaries are often ignored because they are imagined to be either the product of aggregated individual choices or the administratively necessary segmentation of centralized governmental power' (Ford, 1994, p.1857). Borrowing his theoretical framework from philosopher Henri Lefebvre (1991) and critical geographer Edward Soja (1989), Ford (1994) asserted that legal doctrine on local government oscillates between two conflicting misconceptions of political geography—opaque and transparent—which, although contradictory, are similar in their consequences. These misconceptions of space are responsible, according to Ford, for the judicial failure to examine local jurisdictions, and for their neglect to consider the effect of boundaries and space on segregation.

The misconception of space as transparent treats local jurisdictions as geographically defined delegates of centralized power, an administrative convenience without autonomous political significance (Ford, 1994). Under the transparency misconception spatiality is reduced to a mental construct (Soja, 1989). 'We "see through" political geography, failing to see its political salience' (Ford, 1994, p.1859). Space is understood as insignificant and without political consequences of its own.

The alternative misconception of political geography—space as opaque—treats local jurisdictions as autonomous entities that deserve deference because they are manifestations of local political communities, unmediated democratic sovereignties. Unlike the transparency misconception, in the case of opacity 'we cannot "see inside" political space to perceive the social institutions that define and comprise it' (Ford, 1994, p.1858). Instead of seeing space for what it is, namely a product of social interactions and practices, under the opacity misconception 'space is perceived as inert, primordial', a result of 'natural' forces such as the economic market, aggregated individual preferences and physical topography. As a result, space is perceived as 'having a natural and pre-political meaning' (Ford, 1994, pp.1858–1859).

The consequences of the two misconceptions of space are similar. They both prevent the courts from perceiving the social consequences hidden behind the territorial jurisdiction of local governments and thus help sustain racial segregation, though for different reasons. While the first account avoids examining the potentially segregated character of local jurisdictions by denying them any legal or political significance and labeling them as mere agents of state power; the second account avoids scrutiny by referring to local governments as self-validating political communities that are beyond the reach of the state. In other words, 'political space does the work of maintaining racially identified spaces, while reified political boundaries obscure the role of political space and represent it either as the delegation of state power and therefore inconsequential, or as natural and therefore inevitable' (Ford, 1994, p.1876).

Local government in Israel: Opaque or transparent? Oscillation between the opacity and transparency misconceptions of political geography similarly characterizes the Israeli legal doctrine of local government. The official status of local governments is that of mere delegates of state power with very little political power of their own (Elazar, 1988; Ben-Zadok, 1993; Vinograd, 1998). The status of local governments in Israel, stressed David Deri (1994), is that of 'subcontractors' of the central government, lacking independent power.

Closer analysis reveals a more complex picture than the one described above. The overburdened central government is unable to carry out its oversight duties, thus leaving local governments extensive leeway for independent action (Elazar & Kalchheim, 1988; Kalchheim, 1997). The result is a great discrepancy among local governments. Strong local governments, especially those located in the geographic and economic center of the country, are able to achieve relative autonomy from the central government, while the peripheral and weak localities are totally dependent on the central government both financially and administratively (Inbar & Choshen, 1994; Kaspi, 1994).

The notion of local governments as mere delegates of state power is also the official legal doctrine of local government (Vinograd, 1998). The courts consider local governments administrative tools of the central government for the supply of municipal services to local communities, whose jurisdictions are entirely the product of administrative convenience.[20] Thus, the courts refused to interfere with decisions of the central government that involve defining the jurisdictional boundaries of local governments, asserting that this is to be decided on at the sole discretion of the state government.[21] But although it seems that the legal conception of local government falls neatly under the transparency paradigm (namely, local governments are nothing but political subdivisions of the state created for convenience sake for the purpose of exercising such governmental powers as may be entrusted to them), this is not entirely true. A close look reveals that the epistemological status of local governments is more complicated than appears at first glance. Legal analysis oscillates between the two contradictory conceptions of local political space.

The oscillation between the opaque and transparent conceptions of space is illustrated in *Sa'ida v. Minister of the Interior*,[22] in which conflicting conceptions of space were invoked to legitimize a ministerial decision to annex the territory of an unincorporated Bedouin village into a neighboring Bedouin local government. The village of Um-el-Ganem was an unincorporated Bedouin village located in geographic proximity to the incorporated village of Shibly. The residents of the two villages belonged to two rival Bedouin tribes. In 1992, the Minister of the Interior issued a decree annexing the territory of Um-el-Ganem into the jurisdiction of the local council of Shibly.[23] The residents of Um-el-Ganem, who objected to the annexation because of the long term rivalry between the two villages, petitioned the Supreme Court arguing that the decree was void, as it was issued without explicit legal authority and without consulting them first. The Supreme Court rejected their argument, reaffirming its long-held position that the discretion of the Minister of the Interior to create and alter jurisdictional boundaries is almost absolute. The Supreme Court also emphasized that the annexation of the unincorporated village to an existing local council was designed to ensure a better supply of municipal services such as water, sanitation, planning and education, which are harder to supply to an unincorporated community. In other words, the spatial annexation was portrayed by the Supreme Court as an administrative convenience, in accordance with the transparency misconception. The Supreme Court, however, did not stop there, but went on to provide yet another rationale for upholding the annexation of Um-el-Ganem to Shibly: Um-el-Ganem 'is a Bedouin village with a population of 900 people and Shibly is a Bedouin village as well, populated by 2,500 residents. The cultural and social background of both villages is identical. The geographical and demographic proximity enables the future consolidation of the two villages into one village'. The Supreme Court shifted from a transparent to an opaque conception of political space. The annexation was justified not only as an administrative convenience but also as a reflection of a preexisting political community united by a similar cultural and social background. The Supreme Court accepted, then, the notion of local boundaries as demarcating autonomous political units without noticing that such a formulation, if taken seriously, would limit the discretion of the state in drawing local boundaries.

In conclusion, the legal doctrine of local government rests on two conflicting misconceptions of political space—opaque and transparent—which correspond to two conflicting conceptions of local governance. On the one hand, the courts perceive local governments as merely administratively convenient delegates of state power and therefore treat their territorial boundaries as politically inconsequential. On the other hand, the courts also view local governments as reflections of preexisting political communities and therefore treat their jurisdiction as natural and self-validated. In both cases the result is similar: the political space of local governments is reified and the social consequences of their territorial jurisdiction are left unexamined; they are perceived to be beyond the scope of legal scrutiny.

Bundling of powers/spaces: The spatiality of school districts Neither the transparency nor the opacity misconceptions of space alone can account for the legal treatment of school districts' jurisdiction. This is not to say that the courts scrutinize the way these jurisdictions were created. On the contrary, despite an unambiguous recognition by the courts that 'territoriality' is a central component in the definition of LEA, they failed to examine how these territorial jurisdictions came into being and to consider the effect of school district boundaries on ethnic segregation. The lack of judicial scrutiny, I submit, is a direct result of the way local government law is currently structured, which uses local government boundaries to define the boundaries of the various school districts in the country. Legal political geography, argues Richard Ford (1994), consists of three primary elements, two of which are the jurisdictional boundaries that define a government or entity and the power and rights of the entity vis-à-vis land and individuals within its boundaries. The Israeli legal regime created school districts—LEAs—and vested them with the power to provide educational services to all people residing within each of their respective jurisdictions but at the same time set the boundaries of school districts to coincide with local government boundaries. The result is that, although the LEA is formally a separate legal entity, in fact local governments are vested with complete authority over education (just like other city services such as sanitation, water supply, business licensing etc.). This bundling of powers/spaces—the grouping together of a package of jurisdictionally linked services that could feasibly be separated (Kelman, 1987; Ford, 1999)—strips the LEAs of any and all independent spatiality. Local education authority as a spatial entity disappears, becoming a mere power of the local government, and as such the jurisdiction of school districts becomes unquestionable, more so even than the jurisdiction of the local governments on which they are built. 'It is absolutely compelling, as it is hopelessly arbitrary' (Ford, 1999, p.850). The jurisdiction of school districts is always already decided as part of the jurisdiction of the local governments and therefore need not be brought to consciousness. School district jurisdictions are both transparent and opaque at the same time. On the one hand, they are transparent in the sense that we 'see through' them, failing to see their political salience, indeed failing to see them at all. We cannot challenge the boundaries of school districts independently, but we must instead challenge the jurisdiction of the local governments to which school districts are bundled, even though the two jurisdictions might serve different social purposes. On the other hand, the jurisdiction of school districts is also opaque in the sense that it prevents us from 'seeing inside' the jurisdiction to perceive the social institutions that define and comprise it. Opacity, in other words, hindersany questioning of the social and political origins of the boundaries of local governments that define the school districts' boundaries. The result is that, since the territorial origins of local governments are exempt from judicial scrutiny—justified, as they are, by either administrative convenience or popular sovereignty—school districts, segregated as they may be, are never questioned.[24]

The 'hide and seek' between the boundaries of school districts and local governments is exemplified in the case of *Nir v. Be'er Ya'akov*.[25] In this case, a group of Ashkenazi parents who wanted to flee integrated schools registered their children in schools outside their school district—the LEA of Be'er Ya'akov. After their request to transfer their children to another school district was refused by the LEA, they filed a petition with the Supreme Court, requesting it to declare that their neighborhood—Talmei Menashe—constituted a separate school district and therefore the LEA of Be'er Ya'akov had no jurisdiction over them. Due to the way local government law is currently structured, instead of focusing on the educational needs of Talmei Menashe and asking whether it should or should not be awarded the status of a separate school district, the discussion was focused on the nature of the local government. The petition was mainly an attempt to convince the Court that Talmei Menashe was a cooperative settlement (Moshav), deserving the status of an independent local government (which would automatically entail an independent LEA). The petitioners' argument was that the people living in Talmei Menashe constituted a political community distinct from Be'er Ya'akov and therefore Talmei Menashe should have jurisdictional sovereignty over its members. The Supreme Court correctly dismissed the petition but for the wrong reasons. After examining the formal legal requirements for obtaining the status of a cooperative settlement, the Supreme Court found that Talmei Menashe did not meet the criteria for a separate local government but was, in fact, a neighborhood which was, territorially and administratively, part of the local government of Be'er Ya'akov. Therefore, the Court concluded, Talmei Menashe was subject to the jurisdictional authority of the LEA of Be'er Ya'akov.

The consequences of the bundling of powers/spaces are very harmful. School district jurisdiction disappears as a politically suspect factor; these jurisdictions are taken for granted and ignored by the courts. This leads, in turn, to a perpetuation of historically imposed segregation and, at the same time, enables the courts to perceive (and thus also misrepresent) themselves as advocates of integration. The following section explores the detrimental effect that results when the jurisdictions of local education authorities are insulated from judicial scrutiny, given the social reality of ethnically homogeneous local governments and the unequal division of space that characterize Israeli society.

The Urban Geography of Ethnicity: Patterns of Residential Segregation

One cannot understand the social geography of local governments in Israel today without understanding the basic patterns imprinted on that geography by public housing during the era of mass immigration and the large-scale housing construction of the 1950s (Gonen, 1995). Until recently, all Israeli governments, past and present, have espoused a policy of population spatial dispersion. The need for such a policy was a result of the polarized spatial distribution of the Jewish population in the late 1940s. On the eve of independence, approximately 80 per cent of Israel's Jewish population, who were predominantly European Jews, lived in the central regions (Tel-Aviv, Haifa, and the Coastal Plain lying between them), 7.5 per cent lived in the northern region (the Galilee), and 10 per cent in the area around Jerusalem. The southern region was practically devoid of Jewish presence (Lipshitz, 1998). In order to take effective possession of the northern and southern regions, driven by both Zionist ideology and what was seen as 'security' reasons, early Israeli governments viewed population dispersal as a national goal of the highest priority (Segev, 1986). It was precisely at this juncture, in the early 1950s, that mass immigration from the Arab countries took place. More than one million immigrants came to Israel during this decade, mostly from Arab countries in North Africa and the Middle East. Some 700,000 immigrants arrived in the first five years of independence (1948–1953), doubling Israel's population, and 500,000 more immigrated in the following five years. Most of these new immigrants came with only meager economic resources (Kallus & Law-Yone, 2000).

Public housing became the principal instrument of the government's geographical policies in the 1950s. State agencies were in a position to direct the hundreds of thousands of people searching for housing to places chosen by the government. Since the choice of location was driven by the governmental aim of dispersing the population, public housing was constructed rapidly in many parts of the country with little attention to transportation systems, employment opportunities and economic infrastructure (Gonen, 1995). Two major spatial dispersal policies guided the construction of public housing: one was the establishment of New Towns and agricultural settlements in the periphery of the country; the second was using deserted property in former Arab towns, and building housing projects on the fringes of existing cities (Gonen, 1995). These policies led to the concentration of many Arab-Jewish immigrants in both the country's periphery and the urban periphery and thus 'inadvertently served as an instrument of residential segregation by class and ethnicity' (Gonen, 1995, p.3). In the sections that follow we discuss the two spatial dispersal policies.

The country's periphery In order to accommodate the new immigrants, some 300 small cooperative settlements (Moshavim)[26] and more than 40 urban localities, known as 'New Towns', were built. About half of them were established on the geographic periphery of the country—the Galilee in the north and the Negev in the south—which, prior to the arrival of these new immigrants, contained no significant Jewish population. As a result, the inhabitants of most of the New Towns—up to 90 per cent in some towns—were Jews of North African and Asian origins (Schmelz et al., 1991; Lipshitz, 1998).

The New Towns and Moshavim were hastily built, without any adequate transportation system or economic infrastructure. Thus they were unable to provide employment for the large number of new immigrants and, consequently, many new immigrants were unable to find jobs. When jobs were created in the late 1950s and early 1960s they consisted mainly of jobs in labor-intensive industries such as farming, textiles and quarrying, low-wage jobs that required minimal skills. As a result, 'a spatial correlation rapidly developed between social class and ethnic affinity' (Gonen, 1995, p.2). Arab-Jewish immigrants became locked into the lowest economic strata of Israeli society. As a result, the Israeli geographic periphery also became the socioeconomic periphery (Lipshitz, 1998).

The ethnic homogeneity and economic inferiority of the New Towns and the rural settlements did not diminish over the years. Amiram Gonen (1985; 1998), analyzing ethnic residential patterns within Israeli urban localities in 1985 and then again in 1995, stated that 'analyzing ethnic residential patterns in the New Towns is of little significance, since they tend to be ethnically homogeneous, with an overwhelming majority of persons in the Asia-Africa category' (Gonen, 1985, pp.25–26).[27]

The urban periphery Ethnic residential segregation patterns in the urban areas were affected by two main factors: the Israeli-Arab national conflict and its aftermath, and the locations chosen for public housing projects in the urban areas. These two factors influenced the evolving social map both of Israeli cities and metropolitan areas and thus require some elaboration.

1. Arabs Leave, Jews Enter: Residential Segregation in Metropolitan Areas
   Residential separation between Jews and Arabs has characterized the urban areas since the inception of Zionist immigration to Palestine. The national conflict between the Arabs and the Zionist Jews, which became increasingly sharp from the late nineteenth century on, had an enormous impact on urban residential patterns. At the turn of the century, urban Arabs and Jews lived mostly in separate neighborhoods and even separate cities, though there had been a certain measure of residential coexistence in mixed cities such as Haifa, Jerusalem and Jaffa. Beginning in the early 1920s, when the conflict between the two groups intensified, there was increasing residential

disengagement which followed sporadic outbreaks of violence. Towns with small populations of Jews lost them entirely to Jewish towns or to mixed towns with sizable Jewish populations, and Arab neighborhoods in mixed cities lost their entire Jewish population. Toward the late 1940s, as the British Mandate came to an end, Jews and Arabs resided completely apart either in different cities as in the case of Tel-Aviv and Jaffa, or in separate neighborhoods as in the case of both Haifa and Jerusalem (Gonen, 1995).

The 1948 war between Israel and the Arab countries, which followed the establishment of the Jewish state, dramatically transformed the urban landscape. During the war, most Palestinian-Arabs either fled or were transferred from Israel, leaving behind them an abundant supply of land and houses made available for Jewish urban and rural development. The Israeli government, confronted with the need to house the mass-immigration of the early 1950s, decided to use these resources and embarked on a massive urban resettlement project (Gonen, 1995). The government settled impoverished Jewish immigrants from the Arab countries and European refugee camps in former Arab cities and neighborhoods. As a result, these neighborhoods, regardless of the social status of their former Arab residents, became largely low status residential areas within the newly formed ecology of cities. The former Arab towns and neighborhoods built prior to the twentieth century were usually physically deteriorated and lacked modern infrastructure; they soon turned into pockets of poverty (Gonen, 1995). The European-Jewish immigrants, who had better connections with the Ashkenazi establishment, generally managed to obtain housing in better areas, leaving the former Arab towns and neighborhoods for the Arab-Jews. The result was the development of a clear pattern of residential segregation between Arab-Jews and European-Jews on a regional-metropolitan level. This is true for many of the Israeli metropolitan regions. In the Tel-Aviv metropolitan area the ethnic division of space between northern and southern cities is quite conspicuous. The northern and north-eastern cities and towns absorbed relatively small proportions of the immigrants during the post-1948 influx, while the southern cities, many of them former Arab towns, overwhelmingly house Arab-Jewish immigrants. The ethno-spatial division is reflected in socio-economic indices; the social and economic status of southern (Arab-Jewish) cities of the metropolitan region are lower compared to the northern (European-Jewish) cities. A similar pattern of residential segregation can be observed in both the Haifa and Jerusalem metropolitan areas (Gonen, 1995).

2. Chocolate Suburbs, Vanilla Cities: Residential Segregation in the Cities

The same patterns of ethnic segregation that emerged on the regional-metropolitan level also developed on the local-municipal level. As described above, the former Arab neighborhoods in the mixed Arab-Jewish cities were populated overwhelmingly by Arab-Jews, which resulted in spatial segregation between European-Jewish and Arab-Jewish neighborhoods within these cities. Residential segregation, however, emerged not only in the mixed cities but also in Jewish cities that grew out of the Moshavot (such as Petah-Tiqwa, Kfar-Sava, Rishon Leziyyon and Herzliya).[28] This was both because of the middle class preference for inner urban living and the supply of areas available for low-income public housing projects, which was outside the urban centers.

The Jewish European middle class that arrived in Palestine prior to the establishment of the state preferred residential locations offering proximity to the economic, social and cultural opportunities in the center of the cities. Except for a few marginal cases of middle-class suburban development, the urban fringe was left to the lower and lower-middle classes that could not afford the high cost of living which characterizes the inner urban areas (Gonen, 1995).[29] In the first decade of statehood, as a response to the mounting housing shortage brought about by the massive waves of immigration from the Arab countries, huge scale construction of public housing was initiated. Public housing projects had to be built quickly and as inexpensively as possible given the limited resources then available, thus catering largely to the lower income immigrants group (which consisted of a large majority of Arab-Jews), providing them with dwellings of less than average size, and with few amenities (Gonen, 1995). It was almost impossible for the housing agencies to achieve the goal of rapid, low-cost construction within the developed areas of the cities. Land values in the inner cities were high and rapidly rising and landowners were not in a hurry to sell their land. Moreover, land parcels within the built up areas of the city were relatively small and usually owned by numerous proprietors, rendering the assembly of large tracts of land a difficult and time-consuming task. By contrast, on the fringes of the cities, often several miles away from the built up areas, large tracts of publicly owned land were readily available for housing construction. As a result, public housing projects were overwhelmingly constructed on the remote fringes of many of the existing Jewish cities and towns (Gonen, 1975; Gonen 1995).

The massive construction of housing for immigrants radically transformed the ecology of Israeli cities. While the growth of urban areas prior to 1948 was gradual and contiguous, the leapfrog nature of urban development in the 1950s and the 1960s turned many Jewish towns into highly dispersed urban areas (Gonen, 1995). Much like the former Arab neighborhoods and towns, many public housing projects evolved into concentrations of Arab-Jewish populations. Some developed as such from the outset, while others reflected the effects of out-migration of European-Jewish households.[30] To sum up, in contrast to the situation in North America, as well as cities in many other Western countries, the combination of Ashkenazi middle-class residential preferences and state housing projects produced a concentric (core-periphery) residence pattern in which middle-class European-Jews are concentrated in the inner cities and low-income Arab-Jews live mainly in suburban areas on the margins of the cities (Gonen, 1985).

3. The Middle Class Spread to Suburbia

Developments in later years did not substantially affect the division of the Israeli urban scene into ethnically identified residential areas, although they did leave their mark on the urban social geography. The internal migration of Arab-Jews from the poverty-stricken New Towns and rural settlements to the urban center, which took place in the 1960s as part of the general accelerated urbanization process that occurred in the country, did not affect the basic 'Ashkenazi-core Mizrahi-suburb' residential pattern. The internal migrants, the majority of whom were poor, could not afford to live in the inner cities, settling instead in the poor suburbs (Schmelz et al., 1991).

Since the early 1970s, the European-Jewish middle class has shown a growing interest in suburban and exurban living. Open space, privacy, and a quiet and unpolluted environment have increasingly come to be considered preferable to the urban lifestyle. Improvements in the transportation system and rising levels of car ownership contributed to the growing willingness of the middle class to trade accessible, inner urban locations for low density living on the fringes of the city and even further (Gonen, 1995). Evidently, suburbanization tendencies among the Israeli middle class were not motivated by a desire to flee integration, as was the case in many North American cities, since Israeli inner cities were and still are largely European-Jewish middle-class havens. On the contrary, those middle class urbanites who sought suburban living encountered obstacles associated with the lack of available residential land on the urban fringe as well as the social composition of the population already living there, which consisted mainly of Arab-Jews. These obstacles prevented the substantial development of new neighborhoods in the suburbs and led those members of the middle class seeking suburban living to resort to several other ways to achieve their goal of low-density living. One solution was to build new suburban towns, another was to settle in small exurban towns far beyond the suburban fringe, and a third one, quite limited in scale, was to join existing rural communities (Gonen, 1995). All these alternatives were consciously designed to maintain homogeneous residential neighborhoods free, as far as possible, of Arab-Jewish population. Elaborate mechanisms were developed to ensure ethnic homogeneity, such as 'resident screening procedures' to select 'appropriate' candidates,[31] and the redrawing of local government boundaries in a way that separated the middle class suburban and exurban settlements from the poorer Arab-Jewish and Arab local governments in the same region (Yiftachel, 1998). As a result, despite ethnic mixing in some suburban neighborhoods, the sprawl of the middle class into suburbia and the exurban areas tended to reproduce residential ethnic homogeneity.

In conclusion, high levels of ethnically based residential segregation in Israel have existed since the establishment of the state, continue to be high, and can be expected to remain so in the foreseeable future.

The Persistence of Segregated Education: The Role of the Legal System

With this understanding in mind, we can appreciate the severe distortions that result from neglecting to recognize the importance of political geography in legal analysis. Residential segregation is the missing link in prior attempts to understand the failure of integration reform. Given the social reality of ethnically identified spaces, the spatial structure dictated by law, which uses local government boundary lines for school districts, inevitably reproduces segregated education by requiring all children to attend schools within the segregated district in which they reside. The policy makers and the courts, confused by the bundling of powers/spaces of school districts and local governments, implemented the integration policy with virtually no attention given to the way ethnic groups are divided geographically. The ethnic segregation of entire neighborhoods and even localities failed, despite its conspicuousness, to appear on their radar screen. The law, however, creates political geography even as legal doctrine denies its relevance. By relying on local government boundary lines to define school districts, the legal system trapped Arab-Jewish students in segregated schools and supported the division of Israeli society into distinct ethnic groups.

Both the courts and the policy makers failed to appreciate what sociologist Nancy Denton claims is now common knowledge, that 'school segregation and residential segregation are inextricably entwined' (Denton, 1996, p.795). Segregated urban schools are built on the basis of residential segregation. This interrelation between residential segregation and school segregation becomes even stronger when segregation is along municipal boundaries. As a result, 'failing to link housing and education implicitly accepts segregation as a policy matter' (Powell, 1996, p.761). More attentiveness by Israeli courts and legislators to the unequal social division of space, within which the reform was implemented might have led them to adopt legal rules and policies that fostered integration instead of thwarting it. This argument is supported by the 1993 Annual Report of the Israeli State Comptroller, which stated that the official policy of socially integrated schools does not apply to 20 per cent of the local governments and 60 per cent of the students. The enormous gap between the large number of local governments implementing the reform and the low number of students affected by it is due to the homogenous nature of the majority of local governments and thus also the majority of school districts (State Comptroller, 1993; Ben-Elia, 1995).

The role of the Israeli Supreme Court in perpetuating segregation is similar, in many ways, to the role played by the United States Supreme Court in perpetuating segregation in the United States. The Israeli Supreme Court's ruling in *Afgin v. Netanya* is in many ways similar to the American Supreme Court decisions in *Missouri v. Jenkins*[32] and *Milliken v. Bradley*.[33] In Jenkins the Supreme Court invalidated a federal court desegregation order that attempted to induce desegregation across jurisdictional lines. And in *Milliken* the Supreme Court held that busing as a remedy for a proven pattern of de-jure racial segregation in metropolitan schools could not expand to include predominantly white suburban school districts. Similarly, in *Afgin* by sealing school districts' boundaries and refusing to allow students from segregated localities to cross-jurisdictional boundaries, the Supreme Court in fact perpetuated segregation. Notwithstanding this similarity, the consequences of the bundling of space are more harmful. While the persistence of residential segregation and its effect on school segregation is acknowledged by the United States Supreme Court, although not remedied,[34] for the Israeli Supreme Court residential segregation is completely invisible. Therefore, the Israeli Supreme Court, unlike its American counterpart, can perpetuate school segregation while at the same time perceiving itself as an enthusiastic supporter of integration.

Before we attempt to envision a legal alternative to replace the one currently in place, it might be helpful to examine two more spatial-legal mechanisms that played a role in derailing the integration reform.

Spatial Tricks: How to Evade Integration in Heterogeneous Local Governments

We have seen thus far that the integration reform took place within a highly segregated environment. Residential segregation in both the large metropolitan areas and the New Towns is very common and, as a result, school integration, if attempted from within these localities, is unlikely to succeed. In rural areas, however, the situation is somewhat different. Local governments in the rural regions are usually 'regional councils', lumping together under their jurisdiction a large number of small rural settlements (mostly kibbutzim, Moshavim and immigrants' Moshavim, but also exurban settlements). While most of the individual settlements that comprise the regional councils are fully segregated, the regional councils themselves are usually quite heterogeneous.[35] Since the jurisdiction of school districts track the boundaries of the local government, which in this case is the regional council, the school district is theoretically heterogeneous, consisting of students from all the different settlements. The two-kilometer rule does not apply, in most cases, due to the territorial magnitude of regional councils, which makes busing the only solution. The failure of the integration reform even within heterogeneous regional councils and the role played by the legal system in this failure require explanation.

Kibbutzim: The hollow hope One of the elements that could have provided at least a partial rejoinder to the spatial segregation in the northern and southern regions, where many of the New Towns are located, were the kibbutzim (Israeli collective settlements). kibbutzim are rural settlements, based primarily on agriculture and more recently also light industry, which are geographically scattered throughout the country and were, at the relevant time, relatively affluent. The kibbutzim have an extremely small percentage of Arab-Jews in their population (Schmlez et al., 1991). One explanation for this, representing the official Zionist view, is that 'the kibbutzim ... had been set up by European

Jews imbued with socialist ideals that were alien to most of the new immigrants. Hence these existing localities did not attract many new immigrants especially those of Asian-African origin' (Schmelz et al., 1991, p.24). A more plausible explanation, however, is that the kibbutzim were elitist settlements, controlled by the Ashkenazi establishment, and were extremely reluctant to accept Arab-Jews as members of the collective. This explanation is consistent with the widespread and vocal opposition within the kibbutzim to the integration reform (Swirski, 1999; Chen & Addi, 1995).

By virtue of their geographical dispersal, the kibbutzim could have served as agents of successful integration in the northern and southern regions of the country. The reason it did not happen is once again related to the way legal doctrine was spatially structured.

Over the years the kibbutzim managed to retain control over their school system, which is well known for the high-quality of its education. The Compulsory Education Act provides that, with respect to a kibbutz, the kibbutz's secretariat is the local education authority with jurisdiction over people residing within its territorial boundaries.[36] This is justified by the need to accede to the 'different educational-ideological needs of these settlements'.[37] The kibbutzim also have an autonomous subdivision within the Ministry of Education which allows them administrative independence. As a result, the kibbutzim have complete control over their schools, including whether or not to participate in the integration reform. Their decision to keep their schools homogeneous should surprise no one. The fact that they justified this decision using collectivist ideology is cynical to say the least.

The Supreme Court's rulings reflect mixed feelings about the refusal of the kibbutzim to take part in the integration reform. In some cases, the Court revealed its frustration and disappointment with such refusal. In other cases, however, the Supreme Court seemed sympathetic to the decision of the kibbutzim not to participate in the integration reform, as justified by their distinctive collectivist values and different way of life.

Distinctive and supra-regional schools A second phenomenon detrimental to school integration in heterogeneous local governments is the rise of supra-regional distinctive schools and programs. Distinctive schools, also called 'magnet' or 'experimental' schools, are public schools offering distinctive curricula, such as arts and sciences. The Kashti Commission (1991), a ministerial commission appointed to investigate the distinctive schools, reported that there are about 40 distinctive schools in operation countrywide enrolling between 10,000 and 15,000 students which represent about 2 per cent of the entire student population. Distinctive schools are supra-regional institutions that have no jurisdictional restrictions on enrollment but instead use stringent screening mechanisms to pick their students such as personal interviews, group interaction observation and IQ testing. Unsurprisingly, the overwhelming majority of the students enrolled in these schools belong to the Ashkenazi middle-class (Swirski, 1999).

The legal framework for supra-regional distinctive schools and programs is found in the Registration Regulations. The Registration Regulations, as amended in 1975, authorize local education authorities, subject to the approval of the Ministry of Education, to declare a school in its jurisdiction as a 'school not subject to the [integration] reform'. The Regulations further provide local education authorities with the authority to declare schools and programs within their jurisdiction as supra-regional schools and programs. These two regulations combined to allow for the establishment of supra-regional schools and programs that are exempted from the integration reform.

When the issue of supra-regional schools and programs came before the Supreme Court in *Sarig v. Minister of Education*,[38] the Court turned a blind eye to the goals of integration in order to accommodate the distinctive schools. In *Sarig* the Ministry of Education declared the opening of a supra-regional distinctive program in environmental and Eretz-Israel studies in the agricultural high school of Ein Karem. The program was designed to attract students from all over the country. The Ein Karem school was within the jurisdiction of the Mate Yehuda regional council, which had under its jurisdiction another high school, Harey Yehuda, to which most of the students were registered. The environmental and Eretz-Israel studies program evoked a lot of interest and dozens of students enrolled in it. The candidates were screened and tested and eventually thirty-nine students were accepted in the program, thirty-eight of whom were from affluent villages in the jurisdiction of Mate Yehuda. When these results were published, the regional council of Mate Yehuda, as well as the teachers and parents of students in the Harey Yehuda high school, demanded that the program be canceled. They argued that the students accepted in the distinctive program were the best students from the more established European-Jewish localities in their jurisdiction, thus taking the best students from the regional Harey Yehuda high school. The Harey Yehuda high school, they argued, had been integrating students from settlements of various socio-economic levels and the new program would undermine these integration efforts. The Minister of Education acceded to their demand and cancelled the program. The program, he explained, was designed to promote integration by attracting a heterogeneous body of students from all over the country, not to promote segregation by 'stealing' the best students from the integrated regional high school. The parents of the students enrolled in the program challenged the Minister's decision in court.

The Supreme Court overturned the Minister's decision. It framed the ministerial decision to open the program as a 'governmental promise' which could be retracted only in the event of a change in circumstances. And since no 'change in circumstances' had occurred during the time period between the decision to open the program and the decision to call it off, the Court found the Minister's decision unreasonable and thus illegal. According to the Court, the frustration of the program's integrative goals due to the identity of the students enrolled in it hardly amounted to a change in circumstances.

The Court went to great pains to dismiss the evidence presented by the Ministry of Education to prove that the opening of the distinctive program would be detrimental to the integration reform. In order to justify its decision, the Court did not hesitate to cast doubt upon the data provided by the experts of the Ministry of Education and to question the professional integrity of the experts. Toward the end of its decision the Court conceded, however, that even if it had been proven that the opening of the program had a negative impact on integration, this would not have changed the Court's decision. In conclusion, the Court, when faced with an opportunity to support integration, chose instead to endorse segregated programs thereby thwarting integration even in heterogeneous regional councils.[39]

Governmental policies and the reproduction of segregated education The segregation that we currently experience would never have emerged without both explicit and implicit public policies, and would not continue without a legally maintained structure designed to perpetuate it. Segregated education is a direct result of state policies of population dispersal, maintained and reproduced by a legal structure that fails to appreciate the link between residential segregation and school segregation.

Justice Thurgood Marshall in his dissent in *Milliken* predicted that any attempt to desegregate public schools wholly from within the segregated city was doomed to failure. History proved him right. Similarly, any attempt to desegregate Israeli schools from within the existing system of segregated local governments is an exercise in futility. The only way to remedy these historical wrongs is to recognize the role of political geography in perpetuating such wrongs. The implicit assumption of the Court that political geography has no relevance in legal analysis has enabled the power of geography successfully to conceal the geography of power (Gupta & Ferguson, 1997). The last part of this chapter will broadly sketch out an alternative legal regime that takes the widespread residential segregation into account, thus identifying the missing link between residential segregation and school segregation.

Toward a Spatial Reform of the Israeli School System

School desegregation is a controversial issue. Some opponents of desegregation argue that it is nothing but a euphemism for the assimilation of subordinated groups into the dominant culture (Shetrit, 1999b). Others believe that educational, as well as social, separation reflects the choice of all relevant communities that should be respected by the state (Gavison, 2000). This chapter does not contribute to this debate. Despite its undeniable importance, the issue is beyond the scope of this book. My limited argument is that, to the extent that we do support integration, the failure to take into account political geography inevitably leads to the failure of any integration efforts. In other words, no integration reform in education can succeed without being at the same time a consciously spatial reform.

Moreover, the discourse about integration, as currently framed, is not only ineffective, it is also harmful. Through this discourse the structure of inequality is both reproduced and legitimized. It removes the responsibility for the failure of the educational reform, and thus also the obligation to correct it, from the state and the Ashkenazi elite. Supported by the Supreme Court, the government can argue that it did all that it could to integrate Arab-Jewish students and imply that the continuing educational gap should be blamed on the Arab-Jews themselves. The integration discourse threatens a return of the old rhetoric which implies that Arab-Jews are intellectually and culturally inferior, and therefore do not deserve the same caliber of education as European-Jews.

To Bundle or Not to Bundle

The failure of the integration reform, as currently conceptualized, stems primarily from the failure to account for the crucial link between residential segregation and school segregation. School segregation is maintained and reproduced by legal rules that treat education as a power vested in local governments, thus bundling school districts with the largely segregated local governments. There are two ways to solve this problem: one is unbundling—removing education from local governments; the other is keeping the bundling in place, but instead reforming the structure of local governments. In both cases the result should be the same—an end to segregation.

Unbundling of spaces: School districts as special purpose districts The only way to reform the school system in a manner that would foster integration, without restructuring local government law in its entirety, is to peel off education from the powers vested in local governments, thus giving it spatiality of its own. In other words, if we were to construct an analytic model that links residential segregation and segregation in education, the first step would be to dissociate local education authorities from local governments, creating independent school districts. The territorial jurisdiction of segregated local governments should not be the basis on which school district boundary lines are drawn. By simply redrawing school districts boundary lines we can open public schools to diversity. There is nothing sacred about the coupling of school districts and local governments. In the United States, for instance, more than 75 per cent of school districts are not contiguous with any other local boundary and only about one in ten school districts tracks city boundaries (Frug, 1998; Bollens, 1957). Eliminating the geographical linkage of school districts and local governments will open the possibility, now remote, of redrawing the jurisdictional boundaries of school districts in a spatially conscious way that fosters integration among different ethnic groups.

But why peel off education alone? What justifies preferring education to other powers, such as land use, fire, sanitation or welfare services, which are also vested in local governments? Without a doubt, unbundling the whole package, creating a special purpose district for every power now vested in local governments would be inefficient and harmful. There is, after all, a good reason why 'the jurisdictional "market" always bundles' (Ford, 1999, p.844).

This question is not easy to answer. Land-use regulation and the power of zoning in particular, are crucial powers that could be used to create a more heterogeneous residential environment; and these powers are vested in local governments. Public services such as sanitation, despite their apparent marginality, are also important in changing attitudes toward the environment. Unclean streets are seen as a sign of a bad neighborhood and therefore, some scholars contend, lower the general level of behavior wherever they are found. Some go as far as arguing that 'improved sanitation contributes to crime prevention' (Frug, 1999, p.209). While I believe in reforming the structure of local government, there are good reasons, both theoretical and practical, for distinguishing education from other powers vested in local governments that justify treating education differently without unbundling the whole municipal package.

From a theoretical standpoint, education, as the United States Supreme Court in *Brown v. Board of education* put it, 'is perhaps the most important function of state and local governments'.[40] In school, wrote John Dewey, the philosopher of education, 'each individual gets an opportunity to escape from the limitations of the social group in which he was born, and to come into living contact with a broader environment' (Dewey, 1916, p.24). The educational experience influences more than what the individual knows and the way she thinks about the world; it is the primary vehicle for the reproduction of society itself (Frug, 1998; Frug, 1999). The harm caused by segregated school systems stems directly from the important role education plays in a nation's life. Justice Thurgood Marshal in his dissent in *Milliken v. Bradley*,[41] stated, 'our nation, I fear, will be ill served by the Court's refusal to remedy separate and unequal education, for unless our children begin to learn together, there is little hope that our people will ever learn to live together'.[42] The policy grounds for treating education differently, preferring it to other powers vested in the local government, lies in the fact that education is judged by many to be the most important of all governmental undertakings (Bollens, 1957).

Moreover, since residential segregation and school segregation are inextricably intertwined and the homogeneity of schools has a profound impact on housing choices, redrawing the boundaries of school districts with the explicit purpose of diversifying them, might have an impact on current patterns of residential segregation by eliminating one of the strongest incentives to form ethnically homogeneous neighborhoods and local governments (Orfield, 1996).

There are also practical reasons that lead me to believe education is a good candidate for a special purpose district:

1. Political Feasibility
   While school segregation has been on the public agenda for many years driving policy makers to look for a solution, the structure of local governments and particularly the issue of residential segregation has continuously been swept under the table.[43] Therefore it might be politically more feasible to convince legislators to initiate a reform that only affects schools. As Eran Razin (1994) argues,

'Organizationally, prospects for the establishment of large metropolitan municipalities or for large scale amalgamation are as small as ever. Such reforms ... lack political feasibility... the more viable alternatives consist of more flexible organizational structures for cooperation and coordination within the fragmented system. These include single-purpose bodies, forums for coordination and cooperation, and joint corporations' (Razin, 1994, p.19). In addition, the control local governments currently retain over education is quite limited in nature. The Ministry of Education is officially responsible for setting educational policies and standards, while the role of local governments is merely to implement these policies. As a result, it might be politically more plausible to persuade local governments to give up their limited control over education than to convince them to forgo other powers.

2. Structural Feasibility
   The state's ability to eliminate residential segregation is quite limited despite its crucial role in creating it. The state created the initial conditions for residential segregation but the mechanisms perpetuating it are much more complex. They include legal rules and jurisdictional structures that undermine desegregation and which reinforce private choices influenced by racism, economic infrastructure and a desire for ethnic clustering. It is impossible to distinguish private choices clearly from governmental imposition of residential segregation 'since government helped to create the context in which the private choices occur' (Ford, 1997, p.1388). On the other hand, the state has a great deal of control over education due to the centralist structure of the Israeli education system and therefore the ability to effectively desegregate schools.

3. Financial Feasibility
   In contrast to most other municipal services that are financed by local governments from their own resources, education is largely financed by the central government (Sharkansky, 1997). The percentage of the education budget that comes from the Ministry of Education is often as high as 75 per cent, while local governments contribute only 10 per cent (the remainder comes from various sources that include parents and non-governmental agencies) (Kalchheim, 1997; Harmelekh Report, 1992). Therefore, assuming responsibility over education would not impose a significant additional financial burden on the central government.

Stripping local governments of the power of education and creating instead discrete school districts has been proposed before not as a solution for school segregation but in order to overcome the economic inefficiencies that stem from the small size of Israeli local governments. Inbar and Hoshen (1994) recommended the creation of new entities, educational regions, comprised of several local education authorities that do not track local government boundaries. Since their proposal was motivated by economics rather than social equality, it was based on the good will and cooperation of local governments. 'The aggregation into "educational regions"', argued Inbar and Hoshen, 'has to be flexible. ...The educational regions are not intended as super-authorities but are based on coordination, cooperation and mutual support among the local governments' (Inbar & Hoshen, 1994, pp.125–126). The formation of regional education authorities was also proposed in the Harmelekh Report (1992), issued by an inter-ministerial commission established to look into the financing of education and welfare services by local governments. The Harmelekh commission, however, proposed the creation of such regional authorities only as a preparatory step to complete privatization of education. Due to the voluntary and transitory nature of these proposals, the chances that they would result in school desegregation are not very high.

Regional governments and metropolitan school districts Given the prevalent core-suburb patterns of residential segregation, metropolitan school districts which would be built into a new system of regional governments might be the only way to solve the endemic problem of school segregation. The urbanization process Israel has been undergoing since the 1960s facilitates a transition to metropolitan governance.

1. Metropolitan School Desegregation: The American Experience

   Metropolitan school integration has been shown to be both feasible and durable in a number of large metropolitan areas in the United States (Orfield, 1996; Powell, 1996). Metropolitan-wide desegregation strategies that crossed municipal boundaries have been more successful at promoting and maintaining a greater level of integration than city-wide approaches. This is because they address the issue of 'white flight' in that they make it difficult for families to escape integrated schools by moving to homogeneous residential areas. Metropolitan school districts reduce the link between segregated housing and schools by creating one metropolitan-wide school district in which everyone belongs regardless of where one lives (Powell, 1996).

   The most obvious difference between a metropolitan school district and the typical neighborhood school system which divides the metropolitan area into many separate school districts is that the former constitutes a single unit of school governance that provides public education for all sectors of the community. The children of the wealthiest and the poorest sectors depend on the same large institutions, supported by the same tax-base and, as a result, have a vital interest in its success. People cannot shop among school districts. They cannot flee to a more homogenous school district without leaving the metropolitan region entirely and therefore they must guarantee the success of the existing school district (Orfield, 1996).

   Since 1971, various metropolitan areas in the United States have pursued a metropolitan-wide desegregation policy. An example of successful metropolitan-wide desegregation can be found in the case of Charlotte, North Carolina. The city and suburbs of Charlotte were combined in the early 1970s into one large county-wide school district implementing mandatory desegregation policy across municipal lines. In the mid-1990s, despite its continuous policy of metropolitan-wide school desegregation, the Charlotte school district was gaining more white students both numerically and proportionally and in 1995, local voters overwhelmingly defeated candidates supporting the partial dismantling of desegregation (Orfield, 1996).

2. Metropolitan Desegregation in Israel: Can it Work?

Israel's geography facilitates a transition to a metropolitan-wide desegregation scheme. It also makes busing practical. Israel is a small country with a relatively dense network of roads in its inhabited areas (Schmelz et al., 1991). Unlike the United States in which geography oftentimes poses a real barrier to implementing school desegregation, in Israel the distances between local governments are very short. Thus, for instance, the distances between the four large metropolitan regions are: Tel-Aviv and Jerusalem—39 miles; Tel-Aviv and Be'er Sheva (the largest city in the southern district)—70 miles; Tel-Aviv and Haifa (the largest city in the Northern District)—56 miles. Within the metropolitan areas themselves distances between the different local governments are naturally much shorter. Therefore, school desegregation within these areas is a viable option.

Due to the legal structure of local governments, school desegregation is currently possible only in the few heterogeneous urban local governments and regional councils and, as we have seen, it is usually frustrated even in these few cases. Creating metropolitan-wide school districts has the potential of substantially reducing school segregation in Israel. In conclusion, there are strong reasons to think that metropolitan school districts with strong desegregation plans can develop powerful and effective local schools that are well linked to major institutions, thus offsetting some of the racial and economic polarization existing in Israel.

3. Transforming the Conception of Local Autonomy

The establishment of metropolitan school districts, although a huge step forward, is not enough to eliminate the existing educational inequalities entirely. The socioeconomic inequality among the various metropolitan areas and the existence of segregated local government outside these metropolitan regions would still pose a problem. More particularly, the northern region is not as affluent as the central region and the southern region is poorer than both the central and northern regions. Even the European-Jewish population of the southern region, although on average better off than the Arab-Jewish population, is still economically inferior to its counterparts in the Tel-Aviv or Haifa metropolitan areas. Therefore, a more comprehensive solution must be sought, a solution that would alter the rules governing the allocation of resources among local governments, redistribute wealth across jurisdictional boundaries and favor the poorer regions. Such a solution will be discussed in the last chapter of the book.

Unfortunately, the Israeli school system is heading exactly in the opposite direction. In the last decade, following the failure of the school integration reform, the power of parents and communities in the educational system has been strengthened and their involvement and influence are felt in areas such as defining and selecting registration districts, as well as in setting the educational agenda (Kaspi, 1994). Moreover, this proposed spatial reform will not solve the acute problem of inequality among the various ethnic groups in Israel, nor will it by itself solve the problem of inequality in education. Getting students in the front door of better schools is only the first step. Whether or not they enjoy the full benefits of desegregation depends on fair treatment within the schools, the attitude of the teachers, 'grouping' policies and many other factors. If schools continue the current practice of dividing students into 'ability groups' that keep all the Arab-Jewish students in slow classes, segregation will be perpetuated despite any spatial reform. Spatial reform is, however, a necessary first step in a long journey toward an integrated school system that fosters plurality and equality.

Conclusion: The Fallacy of Transparent Spaces

This chapter explored the spatial dimension of school desegregation. It argued that the failure of the school integration reform to achieve its goals was due to the failure of both the legislature and the courts to take political geography into account in their analysis. The puzzling phenomenon this chapter examined is that the conspicuous social reality of residential segregation, which is the bedrock for school segregation, completely disappeared from legal analysis. The result has been very detrimental to Israeli society. A segregated school system that reproduces hierarchies has been perpetuated and legitimized as natural and inevitable.

The origin of the judicial inability to appreciate the link between residential segregation and school segregation lies in the legal structure of local government. Local government law bundles the power/space of education to local governments by using the territorial jurisdiction of local governments as the basis on which school district boundary lines are drawn. This legal structure restricts Arab-Jewish students to segregated school districts yet allows legal agents to continue to perceive themselves as promoting school desegregation.

Notes

1 Different terms are used concurrently to refer to Jews of North African and Middle Eastern origins (mostly from Arab and Muslim countries), the most prevalent of which are Sephardim or Mizrahim, translated in English as Oriental Jews. Some Oriental-Jewish activists identify themselves as Arab-Jews, a definition that is considered an oxymoron by a large segment of the

Jewish population who sees the 'Jew' as the Other of the 'Arab', and therefore cannot conceive of an Arab-Jewish identity. As part of the Western-Ashkenazi Jewish category, I questioned the appropriateness of my using the term Arab-Jew, a term that might be offensive to some Jews of North African and Middle Eastern origins. I resolved to use this term not to impose it paternalistically on a group that does not accept it, but in cooperation with part of the said group that engages in a political project to rehabilitate an Arab-Jewish identity (Shetrit, 1999; Shohat, 1992). Jews of European and American origins are referred to in this paper as either European-Jews or Ashkenazim.

2 Arab public schools, however, are required to teach Hebrew, as well as Jewish history and Hebrew literature, while Jewish public schools teach Arabic as an optional third language (English is the second mandatory language) and have no Arab culture and history in their curriculum (Gavison, 2000).

3 About 43 per cent of the Israeli Jewish population are Arab-Jews and 41 per cent are European-Jews. The remaining 16 per cent are mainly recent immigrants from the former USSR, who, at least in the short term, form a distinct ethno-cultural group.

4 The phenomenon of the lower classes voting for right-wing parties can be explained by the distorted division between 'right' and 'left' in Israel. Political parties in Israel differ less in their socio-economic philosophy than in their approach to the Israeli-Arab conflict. The Israeli right, associated with particularistic and nationalistic sentiments, takes the hawkish position that Israel should not make territorial concessions for peace with the Arabs, while the left, associated with universalistic and humanist perspectives, is willing to be more accommodating towards the Arabs on the questions of territories and peace. In terms of economic philosophy there is not much difference between the right and the left; both are inclined to support a capitalist free-market economy modeled on the American system (Peled, 1990).

5 The second Aliyah (1904–1914), the third Aliyah (1919–1923), the fourth Aliyah (1924–1931), and the fifth Aliyah (1932–1948).

6 In the time period between May 1948 and May 1959 the Israeli Jewish population increased by 1,163,000, from a population of 670,000 people to 1,833,000 (Kallus and Law-Yone, 2000). The anti-Jewish sentiments were encouraged and sometimes even provoked by Zionists who needed Jewish immigration in order to populate the recently conquered lands (Segev, 1986).

7 One example of the widespread negative image of the Arab-Jews can be found in a commentary by Arie Gelblum, a leading columnist, published in *Ha'aretz* newspaper in April 22, 1949:

> This is a race unlike any we have seen before. They say there are differences between people from Tripolitania, Morocco, Tunisia and Algeria, but I can't say I have learnt what those differences are, if they do, in fact, exist. They say, for example, that the Tripolitanians and Tunisians are 'better' than the Moroccans and Algerians, but it's the same problem with them all... The primitiveness of these people is unsurpassable. They have almost no education at all, and what is worse is their inability to comprehend anything intellectual. As a rule they are only slightly more advanced than the Arabs, Negroes and Berbers in their countries... they are entirely dominated by savage and primitive instincts... In the African corners of the camps you find filth, gambling, drunkenness and prostitution. Many of them suffer from serious eye diseases, as well as skin and venereal diseases. I have yet to mention robbery and theft...Have you given sufficient thought to the question of what will happen to this state if this should be its population?—And then, in addition [other] Oriental Jews will eventually join them, too! What will happen to the State of Israel and its standards with this type of population? (Segev, 1986, pp.159–160).

8 'Distinctive Schools' are public schools that offer distinctive curricula, such as arts and sciences, and which use strict selection mechanisms to pick their students, and thereby end up serving a select upper middle class clientele (Swirski, 1999).

9 Ha'aretz, 14 October, 1999.

10 H.C. 152/71, *Kramer v. the Municipality of Jerusalem*, 25(1) P.D. 767.

11 H.C. 608/75, *Kozlovski v. The Regional Council Eshkol*, 30(2) P.D. 449.

12 H.C. 416/77, *The Ramat Raziel Council v. Regional Public School Harey Yehuda*, 31(3) P.D. 794.

13 H.C. 434/80, *Hayun v. The Mayor of Herzliya*, 34(4) P.D. 780.

14 H.C. 715/89, *Sarig v. The Minister of Education*, 32 Dinim Elyon 544.

15 To complete the picture it should be added that since the early 1990s as the education authorities retreated from integration, the enthusiasm of the Supreme Court began to wane as well. See, for instance, H.C. 3533/90, *Shwartzboim v. Municipality of Ramat-Gan*, 16 Dinim Elyon 51, allowing parents to send their child to a school outside their school district due to 'personal problems', despite the objection of the local education authority.

16 H.C. 421/77, *Nir v. The Local Council Be'er Ya'akov*, 32(2) P.D. 253.

17 H.C. 567/77, *Abigail Afgin v. the Mayor of Netanya*, Local Education Authority, 32(1) P.D. 109.

18 The disparity between the meager number of petitions to the Supreme Court by Arab-Jews and the large number of petitions by European-Jews should not come as a surprise given the socio-economic and cultural gap between the two groups. It is by now well accepted in the sociology of law that a petitioner's ability to approach the legal system is closely related to socio-economic and cultural conditions (Felstiner et al., 1980).

19 *Hayun v. Herzliya* and H.C. 595/88, *Shulman v. Local Education Authority of Tel-Aviv*, 42(3) P.D. 594.

20 For a recent manifestation of such an attitude see H.C. 6741/99, *Yekutieli v. Minister of Interior* (decided April 4, 2001), pp.6–7.

21 See, for example, H.C. 51/68, *The Local Council Azur v. The Minister of Interior*, 22(2) P.D. 226, 228; H.C. 94/97, *The Municipality of Rishon-Lezion v. Minister of Interior*, 28(2) P.D. 711, 716; H.C. 489/94, *Municipality of Kiryat Ata v. Rabin, The Prime Minister and the Minister of Interior*, 38 Dinim Elyon, 182.

22 H.C. 5139/92, *Sa'ida v. Minister of Interior*, 32 Dinim Elyon 147.

23 Israeli local government law classifies incorporated local governments into three different types: Municipalities (local governments with population exceeding 20,000 people), Local Councils (local governments populated by less than 20,000 people), and Regional Councils (local authorities organizing a group of small, mostly rural, localities) (Peled, 1988).

24 This is not to say that that the jurisdictional boundaries of local government are not challenged—they are constantly challenged. Evidence of this is the large number of commissions established to inquire into the jurisdictional boundaries of various local governments and the 1998 Ministerial Commission that was established to inquire into a more comprehensive plan for the consolidation of local authorities in Israel (Ministry of Interior, 1998).

25 H.C. 421/77, *Nir v. Be'er Ya'akov*, 32(2) P.D. 253.

26 Moshavim are divided into two quite different types: 'pre-state Moshavim' and 'new immigrants' Moshavim' (hereinafter Moshavim). The pre-state Moshavim, which preceded the establishment of the state of Israel, were usually affluent and their ethnic composition was almost exclusively

Ashkenazi Jews. In contrast, the new immigrants' Moshavim are often poor and are comprised mainly of Arab-Jewish immigrants. We refer here to new immigrants' Moshavim (Schmelz et al., 1991).

27 It is important to emphasize that in some New Towns the demography began to change in the mid-1990s with the arrival of new-immigrants from the former Soviet Union. 'The recent addition of Soviet immigrants to the towns, despite affecting rapid growth in population, did not change the prevailing socio-economic profile of the towns, mainly because they attracted the least educated and the least well off from among the new immigrants' (Yiftachel, 1998, p.47).

28 Moshavot are the Jewish private enterprise agricultural communities established by the Zionists pioneers prior to the establishment of the state of Israel. After the establishment of the state the Moshavot became largely mid-sized cities.

29 The preference of the Israeli Jewish middle classes for inner cities can be explained by several factors. One, inner urban living was part of the residential culture in their countries of origin. The overwhelming majority of Jews constituting the middle class came from continental Europe, where the better off classes resided in the urban centers. Second, life in suburban areas prior to the establishment of the state—but also several decades into the years of statehood—was characterized by a low level of personal security, and thus most middle class Jews opted to reside in the safer inner cities. Third, poor transportation systems between the suburbs and the inner city, where most of the employment opportunities were located, was another factor encouraging inner urban residence. By the time an efficient system of transportation was developed in the late 1960s, the inner urban concentration of the urban middle class had become an established pattern in most Israeli cities. Fourth, unlike the situation in many industrial cities of Northwest Europe and North America, the inner urban areas of Israeli cities did not suffer from the environmental damage caused by industrialization. Israeli cities do not owe their development to the industrialization of the inner core, but rather to its growing commercialization. By the early 1960s, when large-scale manufacturing was introduced into Israeli cities, the cities and towns were already fully formed. The new factories were located in peripheral urban areas, leaving the urban core free of large scale manufacturing and of residential decay, common in many Western cities (Gonen, 1995).

30 European-Jewish immigrants who were settled in public housing projects usually quickly found their way out to more favorably located neighborhoods in the inner urban areas. The accelerated exit of European Jews from outlying immigrant housing estates was a widespread process during the 1950s and the early 1960s (Gonen, 1995).

31 Sara Leibovich-Dar, 'You're Not Welcome in this Club', *Ha'aretz Magazine*, 28 June, 2001.

32 115 S. Ct. 2038 (1995).

33 418 U.C. 717 (1974).

34 The United States Supreme Court held that the autonomy of the suburbs represents a basic constitutional value and therefore a remedy may only be implemented within the boundaries of the school district where segregation exists.

35 Regional councils were originally created as highly homogeneous local governments, catering for specific political-ideological sectors within the Zionist movement, and were initially set up to serve the needs of the cooperative sector within the rural settlement system. As a result, non-cooperative settlements, such as the Moshavot, were excluded from the regional municipal organizations. Moreover, in many cases attempts were made to set up 'homogeneous'

regional councils, in which all of the settlements were of the same type [i.e. cooperative settlement (Moshav), collective settlement (kibbutz)]. The situation of regional councils' homogeneity changed during the 1950s, as many new settlements—mostly immigrants' Moshavim—were founded and automatically annexed to the existing regional councils (Newman, 1995).

36 H.C. 617/75, *Keller v. Kibbutz Farod*, 30(2) P.D. 457.

37 H.C. 421/77, *Nir v. the Regional Council Be'er Ya'akov*, 32(2) P.D. 253.

38 H.C. 715/89, *Sarig v. The Minister of Education*, 32 Dinim Elyon 544.

39 See also H.C. 4383/91, *Sefekman v. The Municipality of Herzliya*, 46(1) P.D. 447 (The Court overturned a decision by the local education authority of Herzliya to shut down a distinctive program due to its negative impact on integration).

40 347 U.S. 483, 493 (1954).

41 418 U.S. 717 (1974).

42 Milliken at 783 (Marshal, J., dissenting).

43 More than five commissions addressing the reform of the structure of local governments have been established in the last three decades but none of them yielded any changes. The result is that 'except for a few small modifications, the map of local government... has remained unchanged since the 1950s' (Razin, 1994, p.13). It should be noted that an increasing number of researchers and policy makers perceive the structure of local governments as a problem. This is due not to equality issues but to the financial crisis of local governments and the enormous structural inefficiencies embedded in them, as well as the massive changes Israeli society has undergone as it became increasingly urbanized. These issues will be discussed at length in the last chapter.

Chapter 3

The Reemergence of Space: The Case of the Bedouin

The focus of this chapter is on the relationship between a community and its space. Specifically, it addresses the ongoing attempts by Israeli governments to settle the entire Bedouin population in a number of segregated planned townships. As we shall see, in contrast to the case of the Arab-Jews in which political space completely disappeared from legal analysis, in the Bedouin case space has played a conspicuous role in legal analysis. The Israeli Supreme Court unambiguously 'recognized' the existence of a Bedouin space, and, in fact, created and enforced it on the Bedouin community. This chapter explores the various mechanisms and practices used by the state to concentrate and segregate the Bedouin population within racially defined spaces, including land expropriation, land use regulation, municipal services and territorial jurisdiction, in an attempt to understand the unifying logic underlying these practices. The chapter further exposes the crucial role played by law in creating homogeneous Bedouin spaces and describes the ways in which judges, urban planners and other national and local state agents participated in producing a discourse of 'cultural difference' that enabled and justified the restriction of the Bedouin to segregated localities. Lastly, the chapter criticizes progressive scholars from the multicultural left, who, by uncritically embracing cultural difference, assisted in the production and dissemination of a 'fetishism of difference' necessary for the legitimization of the state's segregationist practices.

The Socio-Spatial History of the Negev Bedouins: From Nomadism to Urbanism

Israeli Bedouin are a national minority usually referred to as an ethnic minority, but which I will refer to as a racial minority in this chapter. It is part of the larger Palestinian-Arab minority.[1] The Bedouin population is concentrated mainly in two regions: the Galilee in the north and the Negev in the south. This chapter focuses primarily on the Bedouin of the Negev, where the majority of the Bedouin population lives. This population raises most of the issues of significance to our study.

The Negev constitutes 60 per cent of the total area of Israel, extending over 12,500 square kilometers, out of the 20,500 square kilometers total area of Israel (excluding the occupied territories and the Golan Heights). The Negev is mostly a desert, the ecological conditions of which improve as one advances northwards and westwards from the south-east, reaching its least arid part in the Beer Sheva plain near the city of Beer Sheva (Marx, 1967). Approximately 120,000 Bedouins live in the Negev area, divided into more than 48 different tribes,[2] and constitute about a quarter of the entire Negev population (Meir, 1997). Approximately half the Bedouins live in seven planned townships and the rest dwell in about 45 'unrecognized settlements'—settlements that do not appear on official maps and lack basic services such as running water, electricity, education or other services. The Bedouin population is one of the most underprivileged groups in Israeli society (Shamir & Chinski, 1998).

The Negev Bedouins—The Pre-Israel Era

The Ottoman Empire (1520–1917) Until the mid-nineteenth century the Negev Bedouins were primarily pastoral nomads, constituting an integral part of the Middle Eastern Bedouin society both socially and culturally (Meir, 1997). The origin of the Bedouins can be traced to the Arabian Peninsula from which they migrated to Palestine over the centuries (Marx, 1967).

Palestine had been under Ottoman rule since the early sixteenth century. During most of this period, the Ottoman administration ruled the Negev Bedouins in a haphazard fashion. Ottoman officials were not involved in the Bedouins' affairs, and supervision over the tribes was exercised through chiefs whose election by their tribesmen had to be confirmed by the authorities (Marx, 1967). The political situation changed during the second half of the nineteenth century. In light of the growing involvement of the European colonial powers in the Suez Canal zone, the Ottoman government sought to tighten its control over the Negev region and to stabilize it politically (Meir, 1997). They began thenceforth to pay greater attention to the Negev and to intervene more directly and in a more sustained fashion in Bedouin affairs. The promulgation in 1858 of the Ottoman Land Code, as well as the establishment of the town of Beer Sheva in 1903 as the administrative center of the Negev were both part of these efforts.

The British Mandate (1917–1948) The British administration that took over from the Ottomans in 1917 pursued only limited objectives in the Negev. It did not seek to change or improve the Bedouin way of life but only to maintain peace and security. Some aspects of Bedouin life, primarily those related to legal and political order, were subject to British regulation but, in general, the British intervened as little as possible in Bedouin affairs and left them to their own devices (Marx, 1967). Towards the end of the British rule there were approximately 65,000 Bedouins in the Negev divided into 95 tribes, 92 of which resided in the Beer Sheva area in the northern Negev. It is important to note that from the nineteenth century onward, as a result of various political and economic transformations, the Negev Bedouins had undergone a gradual process of sedentarization. By the time the British Mandate over Palestine came to an end, most of the Bedouins were sedentarized and some sought employment outside their tribes (Marx, 1967; Meir, 1997).

The Negev Bedouins—The Israeli Era (1948–Present)

The 1948 war between Israel and the Arab states and the subsequent Israeli occupation of the Negev changed dramatically the geopolitical landscape. The Egyptian army that invaded the Negev expelled many of the Bedouins suspected of having cooperated with the Jewish settlers as well as those who had refused to support the Egyptian invasion (Meir, 1997). After the Israeli army occupied the Negev at the end of 1948, it continued the work initiated by the Egyptians. Some 17,000 Bedouins were expelled by the Israeli army during and after the war, and many more fled the area in fear of the new rulers (Morris, 1993). In 1953, when the dust had finally settled, only about 11,000 Bedouins, belonging to 18 tribes or fractions thereof, remained in the Negev region (Marx, 1967; Meir, 1997). A military administration was set up over the remaining Bedouins and many were removed from their traditional territories and transferred into a closed reservation called the Enclosure Zone. The Enclosure Zone was approximately 1,000 square kilometers in size (about 10 per cent of the land previously held by the Bedouins) and was located to the east of Beer Sheva on lands that had been occupied, prior to 1948, by seven Bedouin tribes of the Tiaha Confederation (Falah, 1989; Meir, 1997). The remaining 11 tribes, estimated at about two thirds of the Bedouin population, had owned lands only in other areas of the Negev and this forced relocation left them practically landless (Marx, 1967). The process of relocation to the reservation was accompanied by a massive expropriation of lands previously owned by the Bedouin both in and outside the Enclosure Zone.

During the 1950s almost all of the Bedouin land outside the Enclosure Zone and about 55 per cent of the land within it was declared state land. Some of the expropriated land inside the Enclosure Zone was leased back to the Bedouins on an annual basis (Meir, 1997). The military administration, which was vested with considerable powers derived from the defense emergency regulations of 1945 originally issued to combat terrorist activities, imposed strict restrictions on the movement of Bedouins and regulated the details of their daily life. The Bedouins were required to obtain a permit in order to leave the Enclosure Zone and were rarely allowed to work outside it. Until 1958 movement permits were issued in limited numbers and usually for short periods of time. After 1958 the policy of issuing movement permits was slightly relaxed and permits were issued more frequently, although usually with some restrictions and limitations (Marx, 1967). The military administration was lifted in 1966 but to date the Bedouins are still concentrated within the territorial boundaries of the Enclosure Zone due to various planning practices to be described later.

In the early 1960s, several years prior to the termination of the military administration, the foundations were laid for the next phase—the resettling of the Bedouin in a small number of permanent planned townships. This process began in 1962 with the appointment of an inter-ministerial commission to advise the government on suitable places for permanent settlements for the Negev Bedouins. In 1965 a ministerial committee for economic issues approved a plan to establish three Bedouin settlements—Tel-Sheva, Rahat, and Kusifa. In addition, the committee outlined a model for these settlements, authorized financial aid for potential Bedouin settlers and determined the measures to be taken against Bedouins who build illegally, namely anywhere outside the planned settlements. This plan would become the blueprint for all subsequent plans of Bedouin settlement (Ben-David, 1993).

The ministerial committee was succeeded in the 1970s by an inter-ministerial committee—the Supreme Bedouin Committee—established to deal comprehensively with all Bedouin issues. In 1973, the Supreme Bedouin Committee resolved to establish four more settlements. The current settlement map was finalized in 1975 and included, in addition to Tel-Sheva, Rahat, and Kusifa, the settlements Segev-Shalom, Aroer, Houra, and Laqiah. The committee appointed a team of planners and entrusted them with the preparation of a master plan for the settlement of the Negev Bedouins, a plan that was completed in 1976 (Ben-David, 1993).

Since the early 1970s, successive Israeli governments have endeavored to settle the Bedouin in planned settlements with only limited success. After thirty years of settlement efforts more than 50 per cent of the Bedouins still live outside the planned townships.[3] The most recent initiative to settle the Bedouin is included in a 2003 governmental plan that proposes to establish seven additional planned townships that would absorb the growing Bedouin population of the Negev and evacuate all the unrecognized villages.[4] We shall now proceed to a detailed analysis of the different stages of the settlement process.

Expropriation of Bedouin Land: The Logic of Race

Expropriation of Bedouin land has been taking place since the early 1950s soon after the establishment of the State of Israel. Sociologist Ronen Shamir (1996) and legal historian Alexander Kedar (1998; 2001) have shown that land expropriation was carried out through a complex web of legal mechanisms that imposed insurmountable procedural and evidentiary obstacles preventing the indigenous Bedouin from effectively protecting their land. Taking advantage of the unwillingness of the Bedouin to register their land in the Ottoman official land registry, the Israeli government managed to nationalize most of the Negev land using old legal categories 'revivified' from the anachronistic Ottoman Land Code of 1858. An example that illustrates the potency of these legal mechanisms is the *Al-Hawashlla*[5] case from 1974.

In the course of the land settlement in the Negev, thirteen Bedouins of the Al-Hawashlla tribe claimed ownership of a number of tracts of land. The settlement officer rejected their claim and registered the land as state property. Following a rejection of their appeal by the District Court, the Bedouins filed an appeal with the Supreme Court. The appellants asked the Court to recognize their ownership rights despite the lack of registration by virtue of prescription, namely possession of the land for many generations. The state argued that the disputed land was vacant land classified as Mewat and therefore belonged to the state.

The Ottoman Land Code defined Mewat, literally translated as 'dead land', as land sufficiently distant from any village or town which was left uninhabited and uncultivated for a long period of time (Kedar, 2001). Mewat land was state property by operation of law. Ottoman law recognized, however, the right of a person to acquire ownership of Mewat land by 'revivifying' such land. Article 103 of the Ottoman Land Code declared the right of the first person who transformed uncultivated land into agricultural land to acquire good title to it, even if such revivification was done without official permission. The rationale underlying Article 103 was the interest of the Ottoman authorities in bringing as much land as possible under cultivation which was the Ottoman Empire's primary source of income (Goadby & Doukhan, 1935).

The British Mandatory regime did not like Article 103, which left the administration in a state of uncertainty as to the total land it had under control. As a result, one of the first amendments to the Ottoman Land Code was designed to suppress the facility with which Mewat land could be acquired. The Mewat Land Ordinance of 1921 repealed Article 103 and substituted it with a rule stipulating that: 'any person who, without obtaining the consent of the Administration, breaks up or cultivates waste land shall obtain no right to a title-deed for such land, and, further shall be liable to be prosecuted for trespass'. The legal significance of the Mewat Ordinance was immense. Instead of acquiring good title, the cultivator of Mewat land was transformed overnight into a trespasser, without any consideration for the length of time said person had cultivated the land. There was only one exception to the rule: any person who had cultivated Mewat land prior to the enactment of the Mewat Ordinance could acquire good title to it if he registered his right at the land registry within two months of the promulgation of the Ordinance in April of 1921. The British administration, however, did not apply the law strictly and it was not uncommon for Mewat land revivified prior to 1921 to be registered in the name of the cultivator long after the prescribed date (Kedar, 2001).

The Ottoman Land Code, as amended by the British, remained in effect even after the State of Israel was established and was repealed only in 1969, with the enactment of the Israeli Land Act. The new act abolished the Ottoman land categories entirely and provided that all land previously classified as Mewat would be registered as state property unless a formal legal title could be produced by the claimant (Shamir, 1996).

In the *Al-Hawashlla* case the state relied on the 1969 Israeli Land Law that transferred all Mewat lands to the state and pointed out that the last opportunity to obtain good title for Mewat land had been June 1921, a date after which only a formal title-deed could prevail. Without a title-deed the only legal remedy open to the appellants was to convince the Supreme Court that said lands were not of the Mewat category. The entire discussion was therefore focused on this issue. In order to classify land as Mewat, the state had to meet two requirements: one, the land must be barren and held by no one; second, the land must be either three kilometers away from the nearest settlement or at such a distance from a village or a town that a loud human voice could not make itself heard there. The Supreme Court found that the state met both requirements. As to the first requirement, the Court held that the land had indeed been barren and had not been possessed by anyone. It relied on a report of a nineteenth century British traveler who 'toured the area and closely studied the Negev condition'. The traveler, stressed the Court, 'found desolation, ancient ruins and nomadic Bedouins who did not particularly work the land, did not plough it and did not engage in agriculture at all'.[6] As to the distance requirement, the Supreme Court found that the nearest settlement to the disputed plots was at least 36 kilometers away. The Court dismissed the appellants' claim that an older settlement, Kurnov, existed near the disputed lands in earlier times and that a Bedouin village, Seer, existed near these lands until the middle of the nineteenth century. It held that Kurnov had been more than three kilometers from said lands and that it was not 'a village or town' in the meaning of the relevant statutory provisions since it consisted only of 'a police station and an adjacent Bedouin tent-encampment'. As to Seer, the Supreme Court found, based on a nineteenth century traveler's tour book, that 'in said area there had been no village and no agriculture and except for a visible Bedouin tent-encampment and wild vegetation the whole area was nothing but barren desert' (Shamir, 1996, p.242).

The racial motivation that underlies land expropriation is quite conspicuous. Alexandre Kedar (2001) argues that Arab land expropriation is part of a deliberate strategy of ethnic migration and settlement pursued by settler societies, aiming at altering the country's geographic and ethnic structure. Borrowing a concept coined by political geographer Oren Yiftachel (1998; 1999), Kedar asserts that Israel is an 'ethnocracy'—namely a regime in which the principle of ethnicity, instead of the principle of territorial citizenship, is the main organizing logic for the allocation of state goods and resources. Ethnocratic settler societies usually contain three major social groups: a charter group of founders, groups of immigrants and indigenous people. The distribution of land is an arena in which this social stratification is highly conspicuous:

> Settling ethnocracies attempt to extend or preserve the control of the 'founding' group over a contested multi-ethnic territory. Frequently, this charter group controls most land resources; immigrants usually receive only a small part; while indigenous and alien groups, who often serve as the main contributors of land, are generally denied a fair share (Kedar, 2001).

The legal system played a crucial role in facilitating the transfer of land from the indigenous Bedouin population to the state by simultaneously concealing the dispossession and legitimizing the new land regime (Kedar, 2001).

Ronen Shamir (1996) agrees that the dominant logic underlying land expropriation is the logic of race. But he argues that the role of the legal system in this scheme is much more complex. The law should not be treated as a mere arm of the state or as an echo of the specific historical-cultural context in which it is embedded. Court decisions involving expropriation of Bedouin land should not be explained exclusively in terms of Zionism's thirst for land or, for that matter, any other external political interests imposed on courts of law. Rather, law should be understood within its own internal logic and constitutive technology. The internal logic of Israeli law is embedded in the legacy of 'modern law' willingly inherited from former colonial powers and from England in particular. Modern law with its obsession with stability, certainty and calculability 'works by imposing a conceptual grid on space—expecting space to be divided, parceled, registered and bounded' (Shamir, 1996, p.234). The Israeli legal system, loyal to the basic tenets of modern law, performs the crucial task of asserting Zionism's identity as a modern Western project that resists the backward-looking and chaotic East (Shamir, 1996).

The claim that expropriation of Bedouin land is racially motivated is strengthened by a newly established policy of 'individual settlement'. Under this policy farms of between 800 to 2,500 acres are being leased to Jewish families and individuals who are willing to settle in the Negev. Behind these efforts lies a declared governmental policy to Judaize the Negev and to prevent the Bedouin from occupying land in the Negev. As candidly admitted by a senior official in the Ministry of Agriculture in an interview to Ha'aretz newspaper: 'It is a declared and overt war over land... if we are not here, the Bedouin will be here... and if, God forbid, we do not bring Jews to live here, within several decades we will lose the Negev.'[7] The policy has borne fruit and, as of 1997, 300 Jewish individuals and families occupy more than 30 per cent of the entire Negev lands.[8]

The Settlement of the Negev Bedouins: The Interplay of the Logics of Race and Capital

Plans to settle the Bedouin in permanent townships were unsuccessfully implemented for the first time in 1966 with the establishment of Tel-Sheva. The settlement program began, however, to gather momentum only about a decade later, in the late 1970s, with the establishment of three additional planned settlements in different parts of the Enclosure Zone and the introduction of an incentive program for the settlement of the nomadic population (Ben-David, 1993). The motivation behind the planned settlement policy is subject to dispute. One narrative portrays the state as a benevolent agent of development and modernization and the other considers the state as an agent responsible for deceleration and subordination.

The Planned Settlement Policy: Narratives of Development and Deceleration

The official story—A benevolent state The declared purpose of the Bedouin settlement policy is to advance the Bedouin population, providing them with modern economic infrastructure and public services such as roads, health care clinics, electricity, water and education (Falah, 1985a). This official narrative was restated by several Israeli geographers and urban planners who argued that 'the sole purpose of the government policy of planned settlement was to create viable settlements, in which services and infrastructure could be efficiently provided' (Kliot & Medzini, 1985, p.428). According to this narrative, which is based on notions of development, modernization and rational administration, the Bedouin settlements are classified into two categories: 'spontaneous' and 'planned' settlements. Spontaneous settlements are defined as settlements established by the Bedouin and their major characteristics are 'the lack of any order or plan and the general absence of infrastructure and community services which characterize most modern communities' (Kliot & Medzini, 1985, p.429). Planned settlements, on the other hand, are those settlements established by the state and are characterized by order, efficiency and an orderly supply of public services.

Advocates of this rationale put forward a narrative that we shall call the 'benevolent state narrative'. This narrative is historically linear: it opens with Bedouin nomadic tribes scattered chaotically throughout the Negev, living in deplorable conditions and stuck in a world without time. Then, in 1948, the State of Israel appeared on the stage setting in motion a positive process of modernization among the Bedouin (Stern & Gradus, 1979). This desirable process was, however, tainted by the Bedouin's scattered pattern of spontaneous settlements and wasteful land use patterns—such as widespread grazing of flocks and low-density habitation (Stern & Gradus, 1979; Frenkel-Horner, 1982). The inefficient land use patterns 'stood in conflict with the development program for the Negev' (Stern & Gradus, 1979, p.224). It was inimical to the present and future development of land resources and prevented the state from effectively providing the Bedouin with municipal and regional services required in a modern society (Frenkel-Horner, 1982). The need to modernize the Bedouin and prevent these inefficiencies led to recurrent attempts to settle them in planned townships. The result is praised as the triumph of order and rationality over disorder and inefficiency: 'continuous planning efforts which integrated socio-cultural considerations finally gave rise to a successful and unique type of settlement in the Israeli urban mosaic—an urban settlement populated solely by former nomads' (Stern & Gradus, 1979, p.224). The planned Bedouin townships are presented in this narrative as a successful achievement of a benevolent state.

The benevolent state narrative has two variants, strong and weak. The strong version, explored above, argues that the sole purpose of the planned settlement was to benefit the Bedouin and that 'there is certainly no policy designed to damage [the Bedouin] and lead to [their] dispossession' (Soffer & Bar-Gal, 1985, p.424). There is, however, a subtler and more sophisticated version of the same narrative. According to the weak version the state made many mistakes in dealing with the Bedouin, mistakes that stemmed from failing to understand their unique culture. The ultimate goal of the settlement policy was, however, to benefit the Bedouin population and provide them with a decent level of services (Ben-David, 1993; 1994a) and, in any case, the Bedouins in Israel were 'treated more liberally than are their brethren in other Middle Eastern countries'

(Falah, 1985a, pp.35–36; Ben-David, 1976).

It is important to note how central Bedouin culture is to the benevolent state narrative. According to this narrative, the Bedouin's nomadism presented a whole set of problems that Israel as a modern state had to deal with. The planned settlement policy is portrayed as the cure for these problems. It is worthwhile quoting the arguments against the Bedouin's nomadic culture at some length:

> First, the nomads were dispersed over large areas—a fact which has made access to them in the past very difficult. Second, the nomads' traditional way of life, based on robbery and smuggling as sources of income, conflicted with the laws of the state and with order. Third, the relationship between neighboring states was frequently affected by the activities of the nomads, who ranged across international boundaries. Fourth, the Bedouin found it difficult to recognize central authority in legal matter and taxes (Kliot & Medzini, 1985, p.429).

We will discuss Bedouin culture and the important role it played in the Bedouin's continuous subordination toward the end of this chapter.

The benevolent state narrative, in both its versions, is, however, hard to sustain. It runs into deep problems when one examines the actual services and economic infrastructure provided to the Bedouin in the planned settlements. As mentioned earlier, the declared aim of the Bedouin settlement policy was to modernize them and provide them with modern services. A crucial question to be asked, then, is whether the Bedouin who resettled in the planned townships are indeed better off economically or otherwise. In the case of the Negev Bedouin the answer is a resounding no. The Bedouin townships were built with no economic infrastructure and unemployment rates skyrocketed (Chertok, 1999). These townships repeatedly top the infamous list of the poorest settlements in the country,[9] giving rise to a new class among the Bedouin—the urban poor (Ben-David, 1993). The situation with regard to 'modern' public services is not much better. Government investment in services for the Bedouin planned settlements is minimal at best. Most of the Bedouin townships do not have central sewage systems, the streets lack sidewalks, internal roads are unpaved, and public libraries are nonexistent (Meir, 1997; Chertok, 1999). The quality of health services in the townships is quite poor with 'ridiculously small' clinics (Chertok, 1999) and a rate of only 0.5 physicians and 0.3 nurses and paramedical staff per 1,000 population (Meir, 1997). A similar situation exists in the welfare services realm, in which 'the burden of responsibility for welfare and social services borne by the municipal departments is tremendous, outweighing capabilities and resources' (Meir, 1997, pp.189–190). In Rahat, the largest Bedouin settlement, 15 government employees provide welfare and social services to a population of over 23,000 (Chertok, 1999). The Bedouin education system is substandard and understaffed. Classes are overcrowded, at least one quarter of the teachers are uncertified and high dropout rates persist. Although the number of (male) Bedouin students attending high school has increased dramatically over the years, reaching 65 per cent in 1995, their academic level remains very poor. An extremely low percentage of students reach senior class level, an even lower number take the matriculation exams and only a meager 5 per cent are granted full matriculation certificates, a prerequisite for admission to institutions of higher education (Ben-David, 1994b; Meir, 1997).

The tragedy of the Bedouin planned settlements is epitomized in a recent pamphlet issued by the Central Bureau of Statistics: 'at the top of the national unemployment chart are six of the seven Bedouin settlements and at the bottom of the chart that shows the rate of matriculated high school students are those same settlements'.[10] It is clear, therefore, that the benevolent state account is flawed and does not live up to the test of reality.

The unofficial story—A malevolent state Unofficial narratives provide very different rationales for the Bedouin planned settlement policy that echo, to a great extent, the reasons provided earlier for the land expropriation policy.

Bedouin scholar Ghazi Falah argued that the 'Israeli policy toward settling the Bedouin in the Negev has developed…with one principal objective in mind: to transfer Negev lands into the hands of the state' (Falah, 1989, p.88). The planned settlement program is, according to Falah, the second phase in a two-stage scheme to appropriate Bedouin lands. The first phase took place in the 1950s and involved transferring the Bedouin from various localities into the Enclosure Zone and registering the evacuated land as state property. The second phase involved the relocation of the Bedouins who lived in villages inside the reservation to a small number of planned townships. At the core of both these phases, however, lies a single goal: transforming all Bedouin land into state land, a goal that originates in the discriminatory Zionist ideology that seeks to 'place all of the land in Palestine under Jewish control' (Falah, 1989, p.77; Falah, 1985b).

In a like manner, geographer Avinoam Meir ties together the expropriation of Bedouin lands and the settlement policy, arguing that the forced settlement program was in fact an extension of the land expropriation efforts and was motivated by the same logic: 'relocation of the Bedouin after 1949 to the Enclosure Zone took place not only for security reasons but also in order to prevent their settlement on those Mewat lands that now became state land administered by the Israel Land Administration' (Meir, 1997, p.196). And also 'in order to protect state land from further Bedouin encroachment, a policy of planned urbanization was launched, ...calling for the establishment of towns into which all Bedouins were eventually suppose to relocate' (Meir, 1997, p.196).

These arguments are only partly true. It is undeniably correct that a Zionist 'greed for land', motivated by the impetus to Judaize the Negev, provides a good rationale for the first half of the process—namely the vast land expropriation. Greed for land, however, although definitely part of the story, cannot fully account for the second phase—the forced settlement of the Bedouin in planned townships. Something is missing from the picture. The 1976 Master Plan for the Settlement of the Negev Bedouin provided that 'land disputes [between the Bedouin and the state] are unrelated to the need to settle the Bedouin in permanent settlements' (Ben-David, 1993, p.40). Such official statements should not, of course, be taken at face value. Nor would I go so far as to claim that the two processes are unrelated. This statement, however, does carry some truth and is supported by external evidence. It is a fact that the overwhelming majority of the Bedouins who agreed to resettle in the planned townships, were landless—namely, either Bedouins of peasant descent who never owned any property or Bedouins who owned property outside the Enclosure Zone which was expropriated already in the early 1950s (Meir, 1997). Almost all the Bedouins who consider themselves landowners have persistently refused to move into the planned townships and tie their willingness to resettle to a satisfactory resolution of the land dispute (Ben-David, 1993). Still, the state was eager to settle not only the landowners but also the landless Bedouins and in fact resolved to settle the latter hoping that they would convince the landowners to join them. We must therefore assume that it was not only greed for land that induced the Israeli government to initiate and implement the settlement policy. There was also another reason. Moreover, even if we were to agree that greed for land is the sole purpose behind the Bedouin settlement policy, the specific way in which the settlement policy was designed and carried out indicates there was another goal that it aimed to achieve.

Racial Ethic and the Spirit of Capitalism: The Settlement of the Negev Bedouins Revisited

Analytic framework—class, race and the city In his seminal work *Land, Labor and the Origins of the Arab-Israeli Conflict*, historian Gershon Shafir (1989) pointed out that the Palestinian-Israeli conflict has been thought of as primarily a conflict over land and, as a result, its resolution as fundamentally political in nature. This understanding, he argued, has generally led historians to underestimate or ignore altogether the importance of economic aspects of Palestinian-Israeli relations in understanding the dynamics of the conflict.

This insight is also applicable to the Bedouin settlement policy. A rereading of the planned settlement policy and the various institutional practices involved in its implementation reveals that economic motives have played a crucial role in its genesis and perpetuation. Tracing the 'impact of economic interests and the structure of production as phenomena in their own right' (Shafir, 1989, p.4) indicates that the forced settlement program functioned not only to appropriate Bedouin land but also to incorporate the Bedouin into the capitalist system of the rapidly evolving Beer Sheva metropolis as an urban underclass. In other words, I would like to introduce into the matrix a factor that has been hitherto either marginal or completely missing—the class factor. This new understanding is important not only because it sheds light on the origins of and motivation for the planned settlement policy, but also because it suggests a solution to the conflict different from the ones envisioned so far.

The introduction of the logic of capital into the analysis of the Bedouin settlement policy does not undermine, in any way, the importance of the racial factor. On the contrary, race and class, although belonging to 'separate spheres of experience with different epistemological and ontological valences' (Gilroy, 1987, p.15), are interdependent and must be understood in relational terms. The creation of underclass communities in segregated townships, reservations or inner cities cannot be analyzed in terms of either class or race alone, but should be understood as an interplay of the two. Such an analysis, in turn, is bound to leave its imprint on the very concepts of race and class. As argued by Paul Gilroy (1987), the concept of class cannot be banished from the inquiries into racial politics but, at the same time, race can no longer be reduced, as in traditional Marxism, to the effects of economic antagonisms arising from production. Instead, class analysis must be opened up so that it can be supplemented by additional categories that reflect different histories of subordination.

Preliminary thoughts about the relationship between ethnicity (referred to in this chapter as 'race') and class in the Israeli context can be found in Oren Yiftachel's discussion of ethnocratic regimes. According to Yiftachel (1999) labor markets and development in ethnocratic regimes are ethnically segmented, thereby creating an ethno-class structure:

> Typically, the founding charter group occupies privileged niches within labor, while migrants are marginalized, at least initially, from the centers of economic power, and thus occupy the working and petit bourgeois classes. Indigenous people are typically excluded from access to capital or mobility within the labor market, and are thus virtually 'trapped' as an underclass (Yiftachel, 1999, p.367).

This analysis raises fundamental doubts as to the homogeneity of the so-called 'Israeli working class'. The Israeli working class is divided first and foremost along racial lines. The Jewish working class is currently unable to represent a class 'that is outside of the categories in which capital structures and reproduces it by means of race' (Gilroy, 1987, p.29). In other words, in contemporary Israel, just like in Gilroy's Britain, 'race is the modality in which class is lived, the medium in which it is appropriated and fought through' (Gilroy, 1987, p.30).

We have discussed the interrelation between race and class, but we have yet to find an analytical framework suitable for the 'process', namely the settlement of the Bedouin in permanent urban localities. Manuel Castells (1983) offered a framework for understanding processes of urbanization and social change. 'Cities', he argued, 'like all social reality are historical products not only in their physical materiality but in their cultural meaning, in the role they play in the social organization and in people's lives... Urban is the social meaning assigned to a particular spatial form by a historically defined society' (Castells, 1983, p.302). Therefore, in order to understand urban social change of the kind we deal with here, we must determine the mechanisms through which spatial structures are transformed and urban meaning redefined. Defining an urban meaning is a conflictive process. Due to the fundamental role of space in the organization of social life, the conflict over the assignment of certain goals to certain spatial forms is one of the most basic mechanisms of domination and resistance in the social structure. 'Urban meaning', emphasized Castells, is not a spatialized copy of a culture. Rather it is one of the fundamental processes through which historical actors (such as social classes and racial and ethnic groups) have structured society according to their interests and values. Moreover, the definition of urban meaning is a social process in its material sense. In other words, it is not a mental representation of a spatial form, but the assignment of a structural task to this form in accordance with the conflictive social dynamics of history. Thus, 'the definition of urban meaning might vary both with different modes of production and with different outcomes of history within the same mode of production' (Castells, 1983, p.303). Historical processes of defining urban meaning determine the characteristics of 'urban functions'. If, for example, a city is defined as a colonial center, the use of military force and territorial control will be its basic function. If, on the other hand, the city is defined as a capitalist center, its function will be subdivided between extraction of surplus value in the factories, the reproduction of labor power, the organization and circulation of capital in financial institutions, the exchange of commodities in the commercial system and the management of all other operations in the directional centers of capitalist business. Urban social change is produced as a result of the assignment of new meaning to the urban realm, namely the redefinition of urban meaning (which does not necessarily imply improvement). Urban planning is the negotiated adaptation of urban functions to the shared urban meaning, and since defining urban meaning is a conflictive process so is urban planning (Castells, 1983).

This simplified version of Castells' analytic framework should suffice to get us started. In what follows I revisit the Bedouin settlement policy in light of the analytic framework laid out above.

The Birth of the Bedouin Urban Underclass—Rereading the Bedouin Settlement Policy

1. Background

   The forced relocation of the Bedouin into the Enclosure Zone in the early 1950s dramatically changed the structure of their economy. Land, which served as the major source of livelihood for the Bedouin, became extremely scarce. As a result, livestock production in the Bedouin economy declined further. Dry farming agriculture, which was the Bedouin's other major economic activity, alone could not provide sufficient subsistence for the entire Bedouin community. Given this major ecological and political change in the structure of their economy, the Bedouin became almost totally dependent upon the state for their survival (Meir, 1997).

   At the time, the Israeli economy was in a depression that continued until the early 1960s. Jewish immigrants from North Africa and the Middle East were pouring into the country and the labor market was suffering from a chronic oversupply of labor. The Bedouins were subjected to military rule and were not permitted to leave the Enclosure Zone or work outside it without written permission from the military administration. The few employment opportunities available (mostly non-professional in intensive agriculture) were reserved for the new Jewish immigrants and the Bedouins were permitted to work only if employers were unable to hire non-Bedouin workers (Falah, 1985a). Anthropologist Emanuel Marx described the Bedouins' poor labor situation:

> The military administration strictly delimited the number of movement permits issued to Bedouin, and acceded to requests for such permits only for purposes it considered reasonable. Thus when a man applied for a permit to work outside the reservation, the officers knew how scarce jobs were and would refuse unless he could produce a written offer of employment. ...No labor statistics are available, but it is estimated that in a male working population of approximately 2,850, the average number of Bedouin employed outside the reservation was, up to 1958, well under 100, or about 3.5 per cent (Marx, 1967, pp.46–47).

The economy and the labor-market gradually improved and by the late 1950s the balance had tipped the other way. In 1959 there was a pressing shortage of seasonal agricultural workers. The military administration reacted accordingly and the distribution of permits for work outside the Enclosure Zone was significantly increased (Marx, 1967). Economic conditions continued to improve and by the mid-1960s, with the growing need for manual labor in agriculture and manufacturing, confinement of the Bedouins to the Enclosure Zone no longer made sense. In 1966, the military administration was abolished and with it the restrictions on Bedouin movement and employment. At about the same time, the government started to work on a comprehensive plan for the resettlement of the Bedouin in permanent townships.

As discussed above, urban social change occurs when a new urban meaning is produced through conflictive processes that stand in opposition to one or more social agents. One such process, arguably the most suitable for the Bedouin case, is when the dominant group in a society, which has the institutional power to restructure social meaning according to its interests and values, transforms the existing urban meaning. This process is called 'urban renewal' (in the case of cities) and 'regional restructuring' (for an entire region) (Castells, 1983). Such urban social change has been taking place in the Negev since the late 1960s when state authorities, dominated by the Ashkenazi Jewish elite, imposed new urban meaning on the Bedouin. In 1966, with the revival of the economy, the planning division in the Ministry of Interior (1966) proposed a master plan for the development of the northern Negev. It was the first time serious planning considerations were given to Israel's southern region. The self-proclaimed purpose of the Master Plan was to serve as a guide for the economic development of the region. Consistent with the desire to 'utilize state land optimally for productive purposes', the 1966 Master Plan outlined a number of objectives and principles. Among them were: (i) the economic utilization of natural resources, (ii) the expansion of cultivated areas wherever possible, (iii) the development of transportation infrastructure (highways, airports etc.), (iv) the development of maximum Jewish population density in the northern Negev, and (v) the establishment of planned Bedouin settlements (Frenkel-Horner, 1982).

A decade later, in 1976, a more comprehensive master plan was propagated outlining with greater specificity land use proposals for the northern Negev (Ministry of Interior, 1976). The 1976 Master Plan proposed a 'national industrial area' for enterprises requiring large operating areas and isolation from the more heavily populated areas. These industries, mainly science-based and petrochemical, were intended to draw workers from the Jewish New Towns in the Negev (i.e. Arad, Beer Sheva, Yerucham, and Dimona) and from the planned Bedouin townships. The master plan also proposed to build an airport for the southern region. The suggested location for the airport was the area of the former Enclosure Zone, which was heavily populated by Bedouin tribes. Lastly, 100 new Jewish settlements based on intensive agriculture were planned in the northern Negev (Frenkel-Horner, 1982; Falah, 1989). As in the case of heavy industry, these settlements were intended to draw their cheap labor from the planned Bedouin settlements.

The 1976 Master Plan was in essence the culmination of a conceptual revolution in planning for the Negev region, the seeds of which were sown in the 1966 Master Plan. The original development scheme, influenced by the Zionist population dispersal policy, envisioned the Negev as a decentralized region with various towns serving as residential and service centers for mining industries and factories in their immediate area. Over time it became clear that the natural resources of the Negev would not be able to form an economic base for the southern region, since the quality of the minerals in the area was inferior and prices on the world market were depressed at the time (Gradus & Stern, 1980). That, in addition to the 1970s ideological shift from socialism towards a more capitalistic free enterprise system, resulted in a change in conceptual planning. Instead of decentralized development, the new planning policy advocated the creation of a 'regiopolis'—'an integrated system of cities, towns, villages and industrial complexes, serving as a single regional growth center' (Gradus & Stern, 1980, p.414). Within this new planning scheme, the Beer Sheva metropolis emerged as the primary regional service center transmitting socio-economic impulses of development to its periphery.

2. Planning the Bedouin Settlements

Research into the theory and practice of urban and regional planning has concentrated on its capacity to contribute to the attainment of well-established social goals, such as residential amenity, economic efficiency, social equity, or environmental sustainability (Yiftachel, 1995). Far less attention has been devoted to the ability of planning to promote goals of an opposite nature, such as political subordination, social segregation, or economic deceleration. 'In particular, the links between planning policy, the problem of ethnic minorities and the political impact of modernist concepts in developing societies, are yet to be fully explored' (Yiftachel, 1995, p.121). The planning of the Bedouin settlements is a good example of the adverse impact of urban and regional planning.

The planning of the Bedouin settlements was done in accordance with the 1976 Master Plan's goal of regional economic development, but neglected to include the Bedouin in the development scheme. The Bedouin were indeed incorporated into the Negev regiopolis, but the role that was assigned to them was that of a source of cheap labor for the surrounding Jewish settlements and factories and, as a result, they were doomed to economic deceleration. In 1976, the Master Plan for the Bedouin Settlement in the Negev was submitted to the Supreme Bedouin Committee. The Master Plan discussed several types of settlements as planning options for the settlement of the Bedouin. The first option was the establishment of one big settlement that would serve the Bedouin population as a whole. This option was the most efficient from the state's point of view, if we assume its primary interest was the appropriation of Bedouin land. The Master Plan rejected this option arguing that: first, the Bedouin were not interested in this type of settlement because it contradicted their conception of tribal based settlements; second, a large urban locality of over 100,000 inhabitants would attract Bedouins and possibly other Palestinians from other parts of the country, thus shifting the demographic balance between Jews and non-Jews in the southern district (Ben-David, 1993). The second option, the one preferred by the Bedouin, was the establishment of many small agricultural villages, each accommodating between 1,000 to 5,000 inhabitants. This option was rejected due to the water shortage in the Negev and the limited agricultural land. At the same time, however, large tracts of land were leased to Jewish agricultural settlements and later also to Jewish individuals. The last option, the one recommended by the planners, was the establishment of several medium-size urban settlements of between 15,000 and 25,000 inhabitants. The reasons provided for this decision were: (1) it was predicted (a self-fulfilling prophecy) that only 10 per cent of the Bedouin would engage in agriculture in the future while the majority would be employed in industry, construction and services. Medium-size urban settlements would provide the residents with varied employment opportunities both inside and outside the townships; (2) medium-size settlements would encourage inter-tribal integration among the Bedouin; (3) the concentration of the Bedouin in a small number of localities would permit a decent level of services with a minimum investment by the state (Ben-David, 1993).

The Master Plan was clearly moving in the direction of incorporating the Bedouin into the evolving regional economy. The Bedouin were denied both the option of small agricultural settlements and that of a big metropolis that might have been capable of generating its own economic growth. As a result, the Bedouin were forced to undertake employment as wage laborers in the neighboring Jewish cities and agricultural settlements.[11] The Bedouin townships were located within the Enclosure Zone at a distance close enough (between five and 50 kilometers) to Beer Sheva and other Jewish localities. They were conveniently connected to the Jewish settlements by an efficient system of highways that provided easy and fast access to work places in these localities yet were residentially segregated from them. The Bedouin townships Rahat, Tel-Sheva, Laqiah and Houra cater primarily to the city of Beer Sheva and the rural Jewish settlements surrounding it. Kusifa also serves, in addition to Beer Sheva, the city of Arad, and Aroer also serves the city of Dimona (Map 1).

The use of urban or regional planning as a means of reform or control can be assessed by examining several interrelated dimensions of planning policy (Yiftachel, 1995). In what follows, I briefly explore two such dimensions—the territorial and the socio-economic—and examine the ways in which the Bedouin settlement policy guaranteed the segregation of the Bedouin in impoverished townships and their incorporation into the regional economy as an urban underclass.

Economic infrastructure One of the rationales provided in the Master Plan for choosing medium-size urban localities for the Bedouin settlements was that such settlements could, with an appropriate infrastructure, sustain their own economic growth and provide employment within the towns to at least some of their residents. In reality this never happened. The areas zoned for industry in the Bedouin settlements' outline plans were never built (Ben-David, 1993). Nor did the government ever intend to invest in the economic growth of the Bedouin settlements. The state refused to designate the Bedouin settlements as 'development towns', which would have enabled them to entice potential industrial investors with tax incentives and without which they could not compete with the neighboring Jewish New Towns (Chertok, 1999). Denied both the options of industry and of agriculture, the Bedouin townships turned into impoverished dormitory settlements (Soffer & Ben-Gal, 1985) and their dwellers 'were drawn toward Jewish settlements, first as seasonal farm laborers, and later as tenured blue-collar job holders in construction, transportation, and industry' (Meir, 1997, p.93).

Bedouin employment figures are striking. As of 1991, about 70 per cent of all Bedouin adults of working age were employed in the Jewish labor market in construction, low-tech industry, and the service sector.[12] If we limit our survey to young employees only, the percentage of Bedouin employed in the Jewish labor market increases to 91 per cent (Ben-David, 1993; Meir, 1997). Unemployment rates in the Bedouin townships were and still are the highest in the country. Official reports estimate unemployment rates at more than 20 per cent in most of the planned settlements and unofficial figures exceed 50 per cent.[13] Such structural unemployment can be interpreted, in the spirit of classic Marxism, as a means of keeping wages down to subsistence level by maintaining a 'reserve army of the unemployed'. Or, using a more up-to-date theoretical apparatus, a reflection of the existence of a dual labor market, with the Bedouins relegated to the secondary market which is characterized by lower wages and suffers from chronic unemployment (Beck et al., 1978).

'We should transform the Bedouins into an urban proletariat—in industry, services, construction, and agriculture', stressed Moshe Dayan, the Minister of Agriculture, during the period in which the government initiated the Bedouin settlement project;

> 88 per cent of the Israeli population are not farmers, let the Bedouins be like them. Indeed, this will be a radical move which means that the Bedouin would not live on his land with his herds, but would become an urban person who comes home in the afternoon and puts his slippers on. His children would be accustomed to a father who wears trousers, does not carry Shabaria [the traditional Bedouin sword] and does not search for vermin in public. The children would go to school with their hair properly combed. This would be a revolution, but it may be fixed within two generations. Without coercion but with governmental direction ... this phenomenon of the Bedouin will disappear.[14]

Jurisdictional boundaries The territorial jurisdiction of the Bedouin townships was demarcated pursuant to the master plan in a way that left them with virtually no land reserve, thus preventing the Bedouin localities from using their inherent zoning and land use powers to spur economic and social progress. The uneven division of space is conspicuous. Jewish municipalities control 98.5 per cent of the northern Negev area while Bedouin local governments control only 1.5 per cent of the region, despite the fact that the Bedouin constitute approximately 25 per cent of the Negev's population (Yiftachel, 1998).[15] The material attributes of jurisdiction, although very important to the understanding of its operation, tell only part of the story. Jurisdiction is much more than a material technology that determines the spatial boundaries of local control; it is 'simultaneously a material technology, a built environment and a discursive intervention' (Ford, 1999, p.855). As a discursive practice, jurisdiction is a way of understanding the social world and one's own place in this world. Territorial jurisdictions do more than separate territory; they also separate types of people. They produce political and social identities by defining the identity of the people that occupy them. In other words, jurisdictions are not a geographical representation of preexisting social reality, but a set of social practices that can be represented graphically on a map (Ford, 1999). Ideally, jurisdictional boundaries could have fostered integration among different ethnic and racial groups. Unfortunately, more often than not they reinforce segregation. An illustration of the way jurisdiction work as a social practice can be found in the following 'tale of two jurisdictions'.

Only slightly more than one kilometer separates the local governments of Tel-Sheva and Omer; a kilometer that separates two entirely different worlds. Tel-Sheva is a Bedouin township with a population of more than 8,500 people that has jurisdiction over 1,250 acres of wasteland. It has no economic infrastructure and substandard municipal services (Ben-David, 1993). The local council of Tel-Sheva has no industrial zone under its jurisdiction and thus the Bedouin residents commute every day to Beer Sheva, located about five kilometers away, or to nearby Omer to seek employment as wage laborers in construction, low-tech industries and services.

Unemployment rates in Tel-Sheva exceed 20 per cent and the number of high school graduates is less than five per cent (Gan-Mor & Prois, 1998). Omer, on the other hand, is a Jewish town with a population of 7,300 that has jurisdiction over 3,500 acres of oasis. The official book of Israeli local governments describes Omer as 'a picturesque residential community which boasts one of the highest standards of living in Israel. ...Many of Omer's residents hold senior positions in the university, hospital, industry, and commerce. Omer has a high technology industrial park. ...The magnificent country club with swimming pools, a heated pool, dry and wet sauna and a Jacuzzi is open year round' (Gan-Mor & Prois, 1998, p.447). The number of high school graduates who pass the matriculation exam each year exceeds 90 per cent. Despite the conspicuous inequality of the two neighboring local governments, the jurisdictional boundaries that separate Tel-Sheva and Omer are absolutely compelling not only for the affluent residents of Omer but also for the underprivileged residents of Tel-Sheva. Jurisdiction as a social practice is what enables and legitimizes the uneven treatment by the government of what would otherwise be apparent for what it is—sheer discrimination. It presents social and political relations as impersonal. As Richard Ford argued 'a primary reason for multiple and distinct territorial jurisdictions is inescapably to separate distinctive groups of people with distinctive views and desires' (Ford, 1999, p.848). The two jurisdictions are thought to contain two organic communities with distinct cultural particularity and political subjectivity that make not only segregation but also differential treatment a taken for granted reality, a fact of nature. The success of the jurisdictional discourse lies in convincing not only the Jewish residents of Omer but also the Bedouin residents of Tel-Sheva of the inevitability, indeed the desirability, of 'territorial autonomy' thus making them accomplices in their own segregation and subordination.

The result of these territorial policies and the discursive practices they engender is the transformation of a large part of Bedouin society into an urban underclass that resides in segregated impoverished townships and serves the growing Jewish regional economy, while deriving no benefit from the economic surplus created, in part, by their labor.

Creating Homogeneous Spaces: The Role of the Legal System

So far we have established the logic of race and capital underlying governmental efforts to resettle the Bedouin in planned townships and the territorial and discursive practices used in this process. This part discusses the role of the legal system. Law played a crucial role in the various stages of the Bedouin settlement program that included resettling the Bedouin in segregated townships and forcing them into the wage labor market. But above all, law was imperative in legitimizing the resettlement policy as either a necessary and beneficial act of progress and modernization or, what seems like the opposite, recognition of the cultural particularity of the Bedouin community. As we will see, these two justifications are not mutually exclusive but in fact complement each other.

From the outset, the implementation of the Bedouin settlement policy encountered severe problems. The Bedouin, who were not blind to the serious deficiencies of the planned townships, did not respond well to government efforts to resettle them. Particularly stubborn were those Bedouins who considered themselves landowners and suspected that by agreeing to move into the townships they would be waiving their rights to their lands (Shamir & Chinski, 1998). As a result, after two decades of settlement efforts, more than half of the Bedouin population was still scattered throughout the Negev in a large number of 'unrecognized' or 'spontaneous' settlements. In order to convince the Bedouin to settle in the planned townships, the state introduced practices aimed to make the lives of recalcitrant Bedouins as unbearable as possible. Among those practices, which are known by the euphemism 'incentive program for settlement of nomadic population' (Stern & Gradus, 1979), were the systematic demolition of houses outside the planned townships, the deprivation of services and the obstruction of attempts by Bedouins to engage in traditional occupations such as agriculture and grazing. As we shall see, the courts, loyal to their own autonomous normative discourse, were not equally responsive to all these practices and, while supporting almost unequivocally the state's efforts to concentrate the Bedouin within racially defined spatial boundaries, were hostile to state attempts to deprive the Bedouin of municipal services.

Spatial Cleansing: Demolition of Bedouin Houses

In 1986, alarmed by the ineffectiveness of the Bedouin settlement policy, the government accepted the recommendation of an intergovernmental committee—the Markovitz Committee—and began to rely aggressively on the Planning and Construction Act of 1965 to prevent the Bedouin from improving their life conditions outside the planned townships. The Markovitz Committee recommended the demolition of some 6,600 'illegal constructions' in the Negev and explicitly stated that 'the enforcement of the Planning and Construction Act in the Bedouin sector is tightly connected to the policy of settlement in urban existing and planned towns' (Ministry of Interior, 1986, p.59). The Planning and Construction Act requires permits for the construction of houses and for making changes to existing houses. It furthers provides punishments for violations of its regulatory provisions which include administrative and judicial demolition orders as well as heavy fines and incarceration for not obeying a demolition order. The territorial jurisdiction of the existing townships as well as the areas designated for future townships, were recognized as the only areas in which the Bedouin could legally construct houses. All other areas, not being regulated under the state's planning scheme, became forbidden zones in which no construction was allowed. Consequently, new constructions were illegal and thousands of existing constructions became potential targets for demolition. And indeed, a massive number of demolition orders were issued concerning

Bedouin constructions all across the Negev (Shamir, 1996; Shamir & Chinski, 1998). The only option left for a Bedouin who wished to obtain a construction permit was to resettle in one of the planned townships or, otherwise, to become a delinquent.

The Planning and Construction Act is a particularly powerful tool since, from a legal standpoint, ownership claims to land do not exempt the Bedouin from the legal requirement to obtain a building permit for any construction. 'Thus, from possible claimants in land ownership disputes between them and the government, the Bedouins are transformed into criminal defendants. ... In other words, a central characteristic of the Bedouin encounter with the law is that the original collective conflict over land is diffused and fragmented into an endless series of minute and meticulous practices in which the Bedouins are targeted as individual law-breakers' (Shamir & Chinski, 1998, p.229).

Demolition orders are a primary source of litigation between the state and the Bedouin. Lower tier courts in the southern district are flooded with hundreds of petitions filed by Bedouins challenging demolition orders issued by the state. These petitions, which are almost always rejected by the courts, usually look for some reason to argue that their case is exceptional. They do not attempt to convince the courts that the law unjustly ignores and thus perpetuates historical injustice (Shamir, 1996). Instead, lawyers for the Bedouins search for technical irregularities or special circumstances that might exonerate their client. Court decisions tend, therefore, to be formalistic, hyper-technical and emphasize the prime and overriding importance of the rule of law. Two cases with strikingly similar facts illustrate this point. The first is the 1987 case *State of Israel v. Abu Ayash.*[16] Jamia Abu Ayash, a woman from the El-Azazmeh tribe, was criminally indicted for an illegal construction of a shack in an area unregulated under the Planning and Construction Act. Her defense was based on a plea for special treatment. She suffered from kidney failure and needed dialysis treatment. The construction, which was built in order to store the dialysis machine, was the one targeted for demolition. Under the circumstances, the defense asked the court to use its discretionary power and nullify the demolition order since its execution would cause irreversible damage to the defendant's health. The district court acknowledged in its decision the severe health problems of the defendant, as well as the fact that inappropriate living conditions might worsen her condition. Nonetheless, the court upheld the demolition order. However severe her health condition may be, the court stressed, it still did not justify breaching the law. The defendant should have sought residence in a regulated area and obtained a construction permit like every other citizen.

Salem v. the Planning and Construction Committee[17] from 1996 had identical facts. Once again a shack containing a dialysis machine was targeted for demolition and an order was issued to that effect. This time, however, in addition to the plea for special treatment, the lawyer for the defendant included, five technical legal claims that, if proved, invalidated the demolition order. The district court spent most of its decision discussing the technical arguments in detail, rejecting them one by one. Only in the last paragraph, after having already denied the appeal, did the court address the issue of the defendant's severe illness:

> At the margins of the decision, I see fit to address the appellant's claim that the construction was built in order to enable medical treatment for the appellant, who needs dialysis treatment. This is undoubtedly an important need. The trial court determined, however, as a matter of fact, that the shack was not suitable for this purpose... Nonetheless, since the purpose is so important, and in light of the fact that the demolition order was not executed for a very long time, if the appellant's lawyer asks for an additional extension of time in order to build a new construction with a permit or obtain a permit for the existing construction, such a request would be considered approvingly.

The court ignored, however, the fact that obtaining a permit for the construction, either ex-post or ex-ante, was not feasible since the construction was outside the planned Bedouin settlements, the only areas where such permits were granted.

As Ronen Shamir has argued, these rulings reaffirm the image of the Bedouin as lawless nomads who must be regulated and settled, though individual Bedouins may be singled out for more lenient treatment. Such decisions 'allow the court to appear as a benevolent keeper of both justice and the rule of law' (Shamir, 1996, p.248).

Cases that reach the Supreme Court are usually of a different nature. They are either criminal appeals that raise complicated issues for which reason certiorari is granted, or petitions to the High Court of Justice.[18] We shall discuss three cases—one criminal appeal and two High Court petitions.

El-Saria v. State of Israel[19] requires some background. In the late 1970s, following the signing of the peace treaty between Israel and Egypt and the subsequent Israeli withdrawal from the Sinai Peninsula, the Israeli government announced its plan to build an airport in the northern Negev. The area chosen for the airport was located at the heart of the Bedouin reservation in an area called Tel-Malhata. The 6,000 Bedouins who lived in Tel-Malhata and claimed ownership of its land resisted the expropriation. They were, however, forced into an agreement with the state, according to which they would receive some compensation for the land expropriated and be relocated into two townships that had been planned but had not yet been built—Aroer and Kusifa. In 1980, the agreement was legislated into law—the Negev Land Acquisition (Peace Treaty with Egypt) Act—and a new entity, the Execution Administration, was entrusted with its implementation (Ben-David, 1993).

The appellant, Subikh El-Saria, from the El-Suria tribe, lived with his family in Tel Malhata. On September of 1982, the family was evacuated from Tel-Malhata in accordance with the Negev Land Acquisition (Peace Treaty with Egypt) Act of 1980. Due to the housing shortage in the newly built Bedouin settlements, the Execution Administration granted El-Saria permission to settle temporarily on unregulated land adjacent to Aroer. The El-Saria family settled on the unregulated land and built eleven shacks for themselves and their livestock. In 1989 the state issued a demolition order against the constructions, claiming that they were illegally built on unregulated land.

El-Saria's plea to the court was rejected by both the magistrate court and the district court. The Supreme Court granted certiorari. El-Saria's main argument was that the constructions should not be considered 'illegal' since they were built with explicit permission from the Execution Administration. The Execution Administration, claimed El-Saria, was authorized by law to resettle the Bedouins and therefore it also had the power to authorize these constructions and no further permit under the Planning and Construction Act was required. The appellant conceded that the permission to settle on unregulated lands was temporary. Nonetheless, he argued, it had not yet expired, since neither the Execution Administration nor any other state official had approached him and offered to resettle his family in a planned township.

In a short decision the Supreme Court rejected El-Saria's argument. The Execution Administration, the Court stressed, was not authorized under the Planning and Construction Act to grant building permits. Therefore, the authorization by the Execution Administration did not exempt the appellant from the requirement to obtain building permits for his constructions. (The fact that such permits could not have been obtained on unregulated lands did not bother the Court). Nonetheless, continued the Court, although the administrative promise that led El-Saria to believe no legal action would be taken against him did not revoke the demolition order, it did entitle him to a one year postponement of its execution. In this time, concluded the Court, El-Saria should obtain a suitable dwelling within the planned townships. Once again the Bedouin were presented as law-breakers who threatened state owned land, while the Court—the oracle of modern law—was portrayed as tough and uncompromising in applying the rule of law, yet fair and compassionate toward individual Bedouins.

The first time the Court was directly confronted with the Bedouin claim of historical injustice was in *El-Sanaa v. Attorney General.*[20] The *El-Sanaa* case was an attempt by lawyers for the Bedouin to go beyond the particular grievance and develop a general claim on behalf of the Bedouin population as a whole. The particular case involved demolition orders issued by the local planning and construction committee of Omer against 14 constructions built 'illegally' by members of the Tarabin El-Sanaa tribe on an unregulated area north of Omer. Instead of attempting to differentiate the case on a technical legal basis or to plead for special circumstances, the petitioners decided to make it a test case for the Bedouin cause. The petition detailed the history of the Bedouins under Israeli rule and argued that the Bedouins in the Enclosure Zone were promised, implicitly if not explicitly, by the government that they would be able to construct their houses in that area in exchange for the land expropriated from them outside the Enclosure Zone. The petitioners further argued that the state did not come up with a suitable planning solution for the Bedouin and that they were being systematically discriminated against with regard to demolition of illegal constructions under the Planning and Construction Act. The relief sought by the petitioners was a Court order instructing the state to abrogate the policy of targeting Bedouin constructions for demolition.

The Supreme Court rejected these arguments. The Court provided a counternarrative of the Bedouins' plight echoing the benevolent state narrative, which was fundamentally at odds with the Bedouins' version. According to the Court, prior to the establishment of the State of Israel the Bedouins of the Negev were nomads who dwelled on state lands in temporary dwellings without appropriate infrastructure. The state decided, for the Bedouin's own good, to concentrate them within the Enclosure Zone, provide them with permanent dwellings and lease agricultural lands to them. In the 1960s, the state authorities began to search for a permanent solution to the Bedouins' severe dwelling problem. During that entire period, the state did not take any action against the Bedouin for illegal construction, since no planning alternatives were available to them. Only after the state had provided the Bedouin with convenient dwellings in modern planned settlements did it start to take action against Bedouins who build illegally in unregulated areas. Never, concluded the Court, had the state's planning authorities given permission to the Negev Bedouin to build illegally. Instead, the authorities employed and are still employing many measures in order to ease the Bedouins' predicament and to facilitate their transition from nomadic life to convenient permanent settlements.

> The Bedouins' claims of injustice are answered with a completely different framework in mind. The version that the court articulates sees virtue where the former speaks of evil, salvation and good intentions where the former emphasizes oppression, and progress, order and modernization where the former complains of silencing and denial (Shamir, 1996, p.251).

The Supreme Court sided with the Bedouins only when they requested to be assigned housing in the planned townships and the state was not responsive to their request. In these cases the Court stepped in and forced the state to live up to its agreement to settle the Bedouins in permanent settlements. The 1999 case of *Salim Abu Ratyush v. Israel Land Authority*[21] is a good example of such cases. Salim Abu-Ratyush, together with fifty other members of the El-Sanaa tribe, appealed to the High Court of Justice, arguing that the Israel Land Authority had not kept its 25 year-old promise to provide them with housing in a planned township. Prior to the establishment of Israel, the El-Sanaa tribe inhabited the area on which Laqiah was later built. In the early 1950s, they were expelled to Jordan but following negotiations between tribal chiefs and state officials they were allowed to return to the Laqiah area. This agreement, however, was never put into effect and the tribe had to settle instead in the Tel-Arad region. In the early 1970s, as part of the broader effort to relocate the Bedouin to planned settlements, the government instructed the El-Sanaa tribe to evacuate Tel-Arad in exchange for permanent housing in Laqiah. The tribe left Tel-Arad and moved to the outskirts of Laqiah waiting for the state to provide them the agreed housing. When the petition was filed, they had already been waiting for over 25 years for the state to fulfil its part of the agreement. They were living in decrepit conditions, lacking basic infrastructure like running water, electricity or sewage and, of course, unable to build permanent dwellings. The state, however, was unresponsive to their grievances.

The Supreme Court ordered the state to expedite the process of allocating housing to El-Sanaa tribe members in Laqiah, stressing that 'the time has come for a solution to be found'.[22] In a follow-up hearing, which took place six months later, the Court took judicial notice of the fact that 'construction works are being carried out to prepare an infrastructure in the temporary site', and added that it hoped that this construction work would soon be completed.

In this case it was the state's failure to act, rather than the Bedouins' action, that was impeding order and modernization. The Court's message was that whoever stands in the way of progress, whether the Bedouin or the state, will be held accountable.

Turning Shepherds into Wage Laborers: Grazing Land for the Bedouin

The story of the Bedouin is, however, not only a story of dispossession but also of economic exploitation. The state's policy has always been to limit the Bedouin agro-pastoral economy, forcing them to give up their traditional occupations and become wage laborers in the service of the Jewish economy. A practice widely used by the state toward this end was to strictly regulate dry farming and to impose severe restrictions on grazing territories and livestock herd sizes (Meir, 1997). This practice resulted, as expected, in a considerable reduction in these occupations. It is worth noting that here we are not dealing with claims to ownership of land or with 'illegal' activities of any kind, but simply with Bedouins who wish to engage in land cultivation and livestock production.

Bedouins who lease state land for either agriculture or livestock production are required to obtain in addition to a land lease agreement, a grazing permit and license for livestock production, all renewable on an annual basis (Abu-Rabia, 1994). State authorities place bureaucratic obstacles in the path of Bedouins interested in leasing agricultural land and good personal relationships with state officials is often the only way to obtain the necessary contracts, permits and licenses (Abu-Rabia, 1994). Even for those few Bedouins fortunate enough to obtain permits, these permits do not render them eligible for state compensation for natural disasters. In the case of dry farming, for instance, the 'drought line'—south of which no compensation is paid—was demarcated by the Ministry of Agriculture north of the Enclosure Zone in order to deprive the Bedouin of any compensation when drought ruins their crops (Meir, 1997). Water resources, which are also state property, are allocated to the Bedouin only sparingly, thus making grazing and agriculture even harder to sustain. Lastly, a special unit—the Green Patrol—was established in 1976 under the auspices of the Ministry of Agriculture to supervise the usage of state lands. The activities of the Green Patrol, that include the corruption of crops and poisoning of livestock, are notorious among the Bedouin.[23]

Unlike land expropriation and house demolition cases that often reach the courts, not many cases involving Bedouin requests for grazing permits and leases for agricultural lands are litigated. The many yet minute bureaucratic obstacles the Bedouins confront with every application for a grazing permit or a lease agreement are not easily translated into coherent legal claims, and the chaotic and arbitrary flow of events does not easily lend itself to the law's demand for clear and fixed categories. Many potential claimants, although undoubtedly feeling injured by state practices, do not perceive these actions as 'injurious experiences' that give rise to legal claims; they cannot 'name' their experience of being wronged and thus cannot translate it into a legal action (Felstiner et al., 1980). Of the Bedouin who are able to name their injurious experience—as discrimination for instance—the large majority do not believe they have any remedy and therefore do not advance from 'naming' to 'blaming' (Felstiner et al., 1980). An even smaller number are able to move from 'blaming' to 'claiming' by voicing their grievances and if their claim is rejected file a suit with the court. One Bedouin who did manage to overcome these significant barriers was the petitioner in *Abu-Kaf v. Ministry of Agriculture*.[24]

In 1993, Ibrahim Abdulla Abu-Kaf and nine other Bedouins from the Abu-Kaf tribe filed a petition with the High Court of Justice following the refusal by the Ministry of Agriculture and the Israel Land Administration (ILA) to lease them grazing land in the northern Negev. Following the filing of the petition, a compromise agreement was reached between Abdulla Abu-Kaf and the authorities which entitled him to grazing land sufficient for a herd of approximately 110 sheep and 30 head of cattle. In addition, the Ministry of Agriculture promised to recommend that Abu-Kaf be allocated land for 'individual settlement', provided he applies appropriately and meets the criteria set by the ILA and the grazing authority at the Ministry of Agriculture.

Relying on this agreement, Abu-Kaf applied for 'individual settlement' and, after being delayed for a long time, his application was eventually rejected. Abdulla Abu-Kaf renewed his petition with the High Court of Justice, asking the Court to order the state to lease him 750 acres of grazing land in the Adorayim area or 1,000 acres in the Adolam-Lakhish region, both located in the northern Negev. At the heart of the petition was an anti-discrimination argument. Abu-Kaf claimed that he was being discriminated against as a Bedouin. The applications of Jewish people, he argued, to lease larger areas of grazing land (more than 2,500 acres) were being regularly approved, while his application, as well as those of other Bedouins were being repeatedly rejected. The petition also raised a contractual claim, arguing that the Ministry of Agriculture breached its administrative obligation to approve Abu-Kaf's application for 'individual settlement'.

At the outset of the decision Justice Heshin, delivering the opinion of the Court, dismissed the petition as frivolous:

> Our Rabbis said: 'the handful does not satiate the lion' and for the present we shall add: 'and the grass of the Negev is not enough for all the cattle, for it is large'. This is the beginning of things and this is also their ending, and if between beginning and ending we shall also add a middle, it is solely out of respect for the petitioner's lawyer, who bothered and toiled trying to convince us that his client deserves that his request be fulfilled. Bothered and toiled—but for no avail.

The Supreme Court rejected both of Abu-Kaf's arguments. Relating to the discrimination argument, the Court stressed that Abu-Kaf had raised a very serious claim of discrimination without providing any factual evidence to support it. The Court insisted that Abu-Kaf should bear the burden of proof although it was clear that he did not, indeed could not, have access to such evidence, while state authorities who possessed a complete list of people approved for grazing land in the Negev were in a much better position to provide such evidence.[25]

As for the administrative promise argument, the Court pointed out that the Ministry of Agriculture took upon itself to 'recommend' the approval of Abu-Kaf's application, not to approve it and thus did not breach its obligation. The Court failed to acknowledge, however, the fact that the Ministry of Agriculture was not acting in good faith when it promised to recommend Abu-Kaf for individual settlement. 'Individual settlement' is a Zionist project designed to Judaize the Negev and reduce the living space of the Bedouin to a minimum.[26] Therefore, allowing a Bedouin to participate in this project is an oxymoron.

Even more interesting is the way the Court framed the dispute. The opening remark made clear that underlying the decision was the assumption that grazing land in the Negev was a very scarce resource. The grazing land requested by Abu-Kaf, stressed the Court, was in fact a military training area controlled by the Israeli army. The army allows the area to be used for grazing only several months each year (February through May) and many Bedouins were interested in grazing this land. Is it just, asked the Court rhetorically, to favor Abu-Kaf over all the other Bedouins?

The origins of the conflict between the state and the Bedouin were set aside. For the Court the effective history began at the present, with most of the Negev grazing land held either by the army or by Jewish settlements. Everything that happened before was irrelevant. The generations-old history of the Negev as the habitat of pastoral Bedouins was ignored. The scarcity of grazing land in the Negev was presented as a fact of nature, not as a product of the deliberate action of the state that nationalized most of the Negev land to prevent the Bedouin from engaging in their traditional agro-pastoral economy. Within the Court's conceptual framework, the conflict between the Bedouins and the state disappeared, and was replaced by an internal conflict among the Bedouins over the scarce resources of the Negev. Abu-Kaf is presented, in this new account, as an immoral individual attempting to dispossess his 'Bedouin brothers' from their fair share of grazing land. No less than three times in a short three-page decision the Court questioned Abu-Kaf's sense of morality: 'We did not hear from the petitioner a good reason', stressed the Court, 'or put more accurately, any reason, why he [Abu-Kaf] should be preferred over his Bedouin friends and why we should grant him exclusive [grazing] rights, while depriving his brothers of their own right.'

The ending of the opinion relocates the conflict from the realm of the historical and situates it in the horizon of Jewish mythology, thus imparting a trans-historical perspective to the decision and bestowing on the Court an almost prophetic status.

'We have opened by saying that the handful does not satiate the lion. We shall end likewise and add: and the grass of the Negev and Adolam and Lakhish is not enough for all the cattle, for the cattle are too many.' The Court went on to remind the reader that this was not the first time a dispute over grazing land in the Negev had arisen. It had happened before:

> It was when our father Abraham went up out of Egypt 'he, and his wife, and all that he had, and Lot with him...' (Genesis 13:1). 'And Abram was very rich in cattle... And Lot also, who went with Abram, had flocks and herds and tents' (Id. at 2–5). Abram had plenty of cattle and Lot also had sheep and cattle. 'And the land was not able to bear them, that they might dwell together; for their substance was great, so that they could not dwell together' (id. at 6). According to Rashi's exegesis: 'was not able to bear them'—was not sufficient to graze both their herds ...and the expected [result] did not take long to happen (id. at 7–9): 'And there was strife between the herdsmen of Abram's cattle and the herdsmen of Lot's cattle. And the Canaanite and the Perizzite dwelt then in the land. And Abram said unto Lot: 'Let there be no strife, I pray thee, between me and thee, and between my herdsmen and thy herdsmen; for we are brethren. Is not the whole land before thee? Separate thyself, I pray thee, from me; if thou wilt take the left hand, then I will go to the right; or if thou take the right hand, then I will go to the left.'

Indeed, concluded the Court, by referring to the Book of Ecclesiastes, 'as the wisest-of-men said: "The wind turns around continually as it goes, and the wind returns again to its courses... That which has been is that which shall be; and that which has been done is that which shall be done: and there is no new thing under the sun" (Ecclesiastes 1: 6, 9).'

A possible reading of this enigmatic paragraph is that the Court provided a historical example of a dispute arising out of the scarcity of grazing land in the Negev. The subtext, however, should not be ignored. It is not a coincidence that Abu-Kaf is associated with Lot, the brother of Abraham—the mythic Father of Israel. Lot settled in Sodom and was influenced by the immoral behavior of Sodom. Sodom was notorious for its distorted sense of morality and deformed interpersonal relationships, and Abu-Kaf is described in similar terms. The fate of Lot is not mentioned in the decision, but is well known. Lot got drunk, slept with both his daughters and gave birth to Amon and Moav, the two nations that became worst enemies of the people of Israel and were forbidden, by divine decree, to mingle with the people of Israel for eternity.[27]

Abraham's pleading to Lot: 'Separate thyself, I pray thee, from me', which would have been redundant had the story been used as an example of the scarcity of grazing land in the Negev, resonates and sends an unambiguous message to contemporary Bedouins.

The Betrayal of the Court?: Public Services for Unrecognized Bedouin Villages

The management of urban services has long been one of the most powerful and subtle mechanisms of social control and institutional power over everyday life (Castells, 1983).

The use of public services as a mechanism to impose compliance with 'planning programs' is a well-known tactic, used by both central and local governments.[28]

Public services were used by the state to manipulate the Bedouin into relocating to the planned townships. The state identified the increasing need among the Bedouin for basic services, such as water, roads, electricity and telecommunication, and made their supply conditional upon moving into the planned townships (Falah, 1985a). Electricity and running water, for instance, were supplied only to the planned settlements, while requests of the peripheral unrecognized villages, which host more than 50 per cent of the Bedouin population, to be connected to electricity and water networks were constantly denied (Meir, 1997). At the same time the state prohibited the Bedouin from drilling for water thus subjecting them to impossible conditions.

The same is true for other public services such as education, healthcare and welfare. Due to practices such as those described above, the Bedouin community began to abandon its traditional economic and social structures. This led, in turn, to the decline of internal support systems and a growing dependence on the state to provide public services (Meir, 1997). This dependency was exploited by the state. The quality and location of educational facilities have been used by the state to manipulate the Bedouin and to relocate them in permanent settlements. The vast majority of schools were located in the planned townships, posing severe problems of accessibility for Bedouins living in the unrecognized villages. Moreover, the state avoided investing in schools located outside the planned townships and, as a result, the few peripheral schools usually lack any fixed permanent structures and learning conditions there are very poor (Meir, 1997). Similar patterns are evident in the areas of health and welfare services. It is a state policy that the development of health care and welfare services should follow the growth of the planned townships, with the exclusion of the peripheral population. A study on the accessibility of primary health clinics in the Bedouin sector, conducted in 1985, revealed that health clinics are accessible for only 30 per cent of the Bedouin population. Although health clinics in the planned townships also serve the peripheral population, accessibility is very constrained (Meir, 1997).

The reaction of the legal system to state practices concerning public services is, at first glance, quite surprising. Unlike house demolition and land use in which the conceptual model of the courts coincided with state policies, the courts were generally quite hostile to state attempts to deny public services to the Bedouin. In recent years, several cases concerning public services have been brought before the Supreme Court. The Court was very sympathetic to the Bedouins' plight, and state officials, sensing the attitude of the Court, did not wait for a court order but supplied, on a case by case basis, the public services requested by the petitioners.

In the 1998 case of *Abu-Fraikh v. Bedouin Education Authority*[29] the petitioners sought an order mandating the state to connect several schools located outside the planned townships to the electricity network. At the first hearing, the Supreme Court made the following unambiguous statement: 'The current situation in which Bedouin schools...

are not connected to electricity 50 years after the establishment of the state is unacceptable and speaks badly of the State of Israel.' 'This situation cannot continue' stressed the Court and ordered that the Bedouin schools be connected immediately to the electricity network.

This has also been the position of the Supreme Court with regard to other public services. The Court instructed the Minister of Health to establish primary care and mother-and-child clinics in unrecognized villages of the Bedouin in the Negev.[30] It ordered the Ministry of Labor and Welfare to assign eleven additional welfare positions for the unrecognized Bedouin villages.[31] And it took judicial notice of the Ministry of Education's promise to review the planning aspects of establishing more schools and kindergartens in the unrecognized villages and to pave roads that would facilitate access by Bedouin students living in the periphery to schools in the planned townships.[32]

The pro-Bedouin attitude of the Supreme Court is surprising only to the extent that we understand law as a mere arm of the state, as a superstructure reflecting the relationship to some imagined base. Law, however, should be understood in terms of its mode of operation and be treated as culture in its own right, rather than solely as a mirror of culture. The culture characterizing Israeli law is deeply embedded in the colonial legacy it inherited from the colonial powers, and particularly the British Empire (Shamir, 1996). Colonialism is not only a legacy of a long-gone regime, but, for the Bedouin, also a living reality. 'In its broader meanings colonialism has been expanded to include any situation in which a distinctive cultural group exists within a larger society or state which controls it. This situation has been labeled internal colonialism' (Merry, 1991, p.895). The role law plays in the colonial project is an illustration of its capacity to reshape culture and consciousness, but this has always been done so in a way that is curiously ambiguous. It served to extract land from pre-colonial users and to create a wage labor force out of peasants and subsistence producers. Yet, at the same time, law provided a way for these groups to mobilize the ideology of the colonizers to resist some of the more excessive demands of the settlers. In so doing, however, it also served to justify and legitimate expropriation and control (Merry, 1991).

Central to the colonial order is the 'civilizing mission', the notion that Western institutions represent a higher form of civilization that should be imparted on the backward indigenous population. The civilizing mission is premised on the idea that 'advanced peoples had an obligation to help those less advanced, to provide guidance and instruction and even to rule them' (Merry, 1991, p.896). In order to establish such a 'universality of reason', the colonial power has to legitimate itself through its colonial double, through a distinction between civilized nations and barbarians. Law, with its unparalleled capacity to transform conceptions of time, space, property and the state, and its claims of justice and universality served a crucial role in the civilizing mission (Merry, 1991).

Loyal to its civilizing mission, the Supreme Court did not cooperate with the state in its attempt to deny public services, the hallmark of Western modern societies, to the Bedouin. On the contrary, within the Court's conceptual model the role of the state was to 'civilize' the Bedouin, help them overcome their backward nomadic culture and incorporate them into modern society. Therefore, denying the Bedouin public services such as education, health, welfare or electricity contradicted everything the courts stood for.

The source of legitimate authority in the modern bureaucratic state is a formal legal order which justifies and rationalizes relations of domination and promotes the voluntary consent of the ruled (Shamir, 1990). For the judiciary to legitimize domination, however, it must first secure its own legitimacy. Legitimacy is derived from the ability to distinguish oneself from other social forces in general and from those holding state power in particular. The refusal by the Court to uphold state actions paradoxically helped the state to sustain its legitimacy. By occasionally overruling governmental policies the judiciary asserted its independence from the polity. 'Thus, the court can cast a cloak of legitimacy over the state as a whole by vindicating other decisions that uphold governmental actions as rightful and reasonable' (Shamir, 1990, pp.782–783). This is the role the courts played in the public services cases. By refusing to vindicate state policies designed to deny public services to Bedouins who lived outside the planned townships, the courts were able to maintain their own legitimacy as autonomous from state power. In turn, this legitimacy bestowed an aura of inevitability and justification on other state practices concerning the Bedouin that were being upheld by the courts such as land expropriation, enforced settlement and mandatory segregation.

Living with Bedouins: Court Mandated Segregation

We have seen so far that the courts were very sympathetic to state policies aimed at concentrating the Bedouins within defined spatial boundaries and integrating them into the labor market of the Beer Sheva metropolis. Integration, however, even if intended to be limited to the labor sphere, carries with it the danger of seeping into other realms. Such seepage threatens the project of producing and maintaining homogeneous Bedouin spaces. The Supreme Court had an opportunity to address this threat in *Avitan v. Israel Land Authority*,[33] an important ruling involving an attempt to transgress the boundary lines between Jewish and Arab spaces.

Eliezer Avitan, a high-ranking officer in the Beer Sheva district police department, was involved in Bedouin affairs in the course of his duty and befriended many of them. In the late 1980s, when one of his Bedouin friends—Awda Mansur Abu-Muamar, the Chief of the El-Azazmeh tribe—settled in the planned settlement of Segev-Shalom, Avitan decided to also move into the Bedouin township. His primary motive was admittedly economic. In order to convince the Bedouin to relocate to the planned townships, the state subsidized the land which was quite cheap in the first place. 'Half a dunam in the Jewish settlement of Omer', said Avitan in an interview he gave to Ha'aretz newspaper, 'cost $100,000, while a whole dunam, not far away, in Segev-Shalom cost $2,000, so I wanted to buy the cheap land.' The economic reason was not, however, the only reason that induced Avitan to seek housing in Segev Shalom. In order to live with his Bedouin friends, Avitan was willing to give up all the economic benefits and buy the land at its market value. 'It was also an ideological issue', Avitan declared, 'I would like to raise my kids to coexist with others. [I would like them to] go to school with the Bedouin kids. It would turn them into better citizens.' According to Avitan, several of his Jewish friends from the Beer Sheva police department announced they would consider following his footsteps and settle in Segev-Shalom. The Israel Land Administration (ILA)—the owner of the land—loyal to its segregationist Zionist ideology, refused to lease him land in Segev-Shalom arguing that the land in the Bedouin settlements was to be leased solely to Bedouins. Avitan, represented by the Association for Civil Rights in Israel, appealed to the High Court of Justice arguing that the ILA's refusal to lease land in Segev-Shalom to Jews constituted unlawful discrimination. Even if we accept the need to resettle the Bedouin in permanent urban settlements, argued Avitan, there is no justification for segregating them. Segregation does not benefit the Bedouin community, and at least some of the Bedouins oppose segregation. To substantiate his claim, Avitan enclosed the affidavits of Bedouins who lived in Segev-Shalom to his appeal announcing their willingness to accept Eliezer Avitan, as well as other Jews, as their neighbors.

The Supreme Court upheld the Israel Land Authority's decision, refusing to allow Avitan, or any other non-Bedouin, to lease land in the Bedouin settlements. The Court's decision was divided into two parts: the first part dealt with the argument that non-Bedouin should be able to lease subsidized land in the Bedouin settlements. The second part responded to the argument that non-Bedouin should be entitled to lease land in the Bedouin settlement at its market value. For the purpose of this study, the Court's response to the second argument is more relevant and will therefore be examined in detail. Before we discuss the Court's decision a brief theoretical introduction is in order.

Organic and synthetic jurisdictions 'Jurisdictions are described through a dialogical opposition: they are either organic/authentic or synthetic/convenient' (Ford, 1999, p.858). Synthetic jurisdictions are created by institutions in order to serve their purposes and are imposed on groups of people from the 'outside'. They exist for the convenience of the institutions that they serve. There is no independent reason for the existence of synthetic jurisdictions, nor can one object to them on the basis of rights. They are created in order to provide local services, to facilitate enforcing the law, or to collect taxes. Synthetic jurisdictions are a product of a 'liberal' conception of space, since they assume 'that the individual is the primary agent in political life and that territory serves strictly instrumental purposes… The group defined by the synthetic jurisdiction has no moral relevance; it is a lonely crowd' (Ford, 1999, p.861).

Organic jurisdictions, on the other hand, are defined socially rather than metrically and are legitimated by their pedigree—an organic community that occupies its spatial boundaries. Organic jurisdictions are perceived as the 'natural growth of circumstances, conditions and principles that, morally, preexist the state' (Ford, 1999, p.859), and thus are imbued with an air of the inevitable. 'Organic jurisdictions appear as a matter of right and are defended against attack in terms of autonomy, self determination and cultural preservation' (Ford, 1999, p.860). They are associated with the 'communitarian' conception of space, since they assume the primacy of social groups on the individual, and therefore the jurisdictions that 'house' such social groups are also believed to have moral weight independent of their citizens (Ford, 1999).

According to the synthetic/organic dichotomy, synthetic jurisdictions are state creations that are imposed on local communities, while organic jurisdictions pre-exist the state and are only recognized and respected by the state. 'This conceptual split between creation and recognition', Ford stressed, 'is a subset of a familiar split between subjectivity and objectivity in decision-making. According to this conception, creation is a subjective decision to bring into existence that which was previously not there, whereas recognition is an unavoidable decision to recognize an objective fact that would exist regardless of state action' (Ford, 1997, p.1368). In reality, however, conceptual boundaries are blurred. Organic jurisdictions that are thought to preexist the state can be as much a product of centralized power as synthetic jurisdictions are. 'Organic jurisdiction divides society into groups that need no further justification. The explanation for the character of the group may be nature, culture or voluntarism, but the effect is to justify the uneven treatment of individuals by the state' (Ford, 1999, p. 914). The case of the Bedouin settlements nicely illustrates state creation and imposition of an 'organic' jurisdiction.

Permanent Settlements for Nomadic People: The Unsettling Paradox of the Bedouin Settlements

Restrictions on the freedom to choose membership in a jurisdiction are usually defended as a necessary measure to maintain 'community character' (Ford, 1999). It is not surprising, therefore, that the Court justified its decision to enforce segregation on the Bedouin townships by appealing to the organic nature of the Bedouin community and its cultural particularity. The assumption of the petitioner, stressed the Court in *Avitan*, that he was discriminated against on the basis of nationality is fundamentally wrong. According to the Court, the real rationale that justified precluding non-Bedouins from living in the Bedouin townships has nothing to do with their Arab nationality but with their particular nomadic culture and tribal history.

The Bedouin in Israel, continued the Court, are an ethnic minority with a unique culture and distinct customs and tradition: 'Originally, the Bedouins were nomadic tribes subsisting on grazing of camels and sheep. They retain an ancient culture and tradition with origins in the Arabian tribes that precede the emergence of Islam. Since their appearance and until the mid-twentieth century few changes have taken place in their customs and way of life.' In the last several decades, attempts have been made by the government to transform the nomadic Bedouin into urban dwellers, attempts that, according to the Court, should be encouraged and supported. Their nomadic culture and way of life, rather than their Arab nationality, stressed the Court, is what makes the Bedouin a 'particular group' requiring a homogeneous space.

Using the Bedouin's nomadic culture as a justification for their spatial segregation introduces an internal tension into the Court's logic. When explaining why non-Bedouins should not be allowed to lease subsidized land in the Bedouin settlements the Court argued that the permanent settlements were designed, among other things, to 'change the values, traditions and way of life the Bedouin have been practicing for many generations'. Therefore, subsidizing land for the Bedouins while denying subsidy from non-Bedouins is justified. Yet, when explaining why non-Bedouins should not be allowed to live in Bedouin settlements, the Court appealed once again to the values, traditions and ways of life of the Bedouin, only this time in order to emphasize their cultural particularity that justifies the concentration of the Bedouin in distinct homogeneous jurisdictions constructed to suit their unique ways of life. In the Court's own words: 'due to the distinct character and unique customs of the Bedouin community it was necessary to learn and examine separately its needs and plan settlements for this society in a way suitable for the Bedouin way of life'.

Nomadism plays a double and contradictory role. On the one hand, the nomadic culture is what the state is trying to eradicate by settling the Bedouin in planned townships. Yet, at the same time, nomadism is also what makes the Bedouin an organic cultural group, which justifies, indeed requires, a separate territorial jurisdiction. Nomadism turns, in fact, into an essentialist and a-historical attribute of the Bedouin, replacing, but at the same time serving as a referent for, immutable characteristics such as race and nationality.[34] Changing the Bedouin culture is a Sysiphian project, since nomadism is part of what defines the Bedouin in essence and therefore cannot be changed. Without nomadism there are no Bedouins. The puzzle of nomadism illustrates a phenomenon Richard Ford called 'the Janus faced nature of contemporary racial ideology', which advances colorblind assimilative ideology while reinforcing the idea of distinctive and inassimilable, if not opaque, racial cultures (Ford, 2002).

This contradictory logic led the Court to the paradoxical conclusion that the Bedouins' segregation serves, in fact, as a tool for their future integration. 'The state's policy of leasing land in Bedouin settlements to Bedouins only', stressed the Court, 'is a temporary policy until the integration of the Bedouins in Israeli society.'

The jurisdiction of apartheid Israeli-style As explained above, organic jurisdictions divide society into groups that need no further justification. Although organic jurisdictions appear to 'recognize' the uniqueness of various social groups, in fact they are often imposed on them. This is done through the 'discursive production of localism'. Localism is produced through a meticulous collection of information about the social groups that make up the nation-state, their history, character, tradition and culture (Goldberg, 1993). This information is collected by 'experts' on behalf of the government in order to catalogue and map the different social groups, and is used, in turn, to construct separate jurisdictional spaces that appear to be their own construction (Ford, 1999). The most notorious example of the oppressive production of localism and difference is the apartheid of mid to late twentieth century South Africa, which marked, in both its material and ideological effects, 'a conspicuous expansion of jurisdictional strategies' (Ford, 1999, p.914).

Production of localism, apartheid-style, takes place in contemporary Israel and is illustrated in the *Avitan* case:

> Due to the distinct character and unique customs of Bedouin society it was necessary to separately learn and examine its needs and plan settlements for this society in a way suitable for the Bedouin way of life. For this purpose a special team of planners was set up, comprising experts on the Bedouin's life and heritage who prepared a master plan for permanent settlements for the Bedouin. The establishment of permanent settlements for the Bedouin involved special planning of these settlements so they would be appropriate for the Bedouin's needs, customs and traditions.
>
> In this framework, the experts concluded that the planned townships must be designated for particular Bedouin tribes and factions due to the extraordinary sensitivity of the Bedouin to their tribal, factional and familial belonging. According to the respondent's [the Israel Land Authority] experts it is undesirable to 'open' the Bedouin settlement to others, since it might undermine completely the purpose of establishing these townships.[35]

Segregationist practices were rhetorically transformed into respect for 'cultural difference' and racism was translated into the language of 'recognition'. Similar to late apartheid South Africa, each Bedouin tribe is recognized and celebrated for its unique culture, which is spatially expressed in a separate organic jurisdiction.

In order to 'respect' the Bedouin's cultural difference, the Court had to be disrespectful of Bedouin individuals. The Court gave no weight to affidavits by Bedouins who announced their interest in desegregation. 'It is impossible to know', stressed the Court, 'what lies behind the consent of the Bedouin, and whether it was not an act of politeness or the inconvenience of voicing an objection to the residency of Jews in their settlement, particularly since they knew that the petitioner is a police officer from Beer Sheva.'

The Court refused to acknowledge the agency and full subjectivity of the Bedouin. The speculations of state-appointed (Jewish) experts, who argued that it was in the best interest of the Bedouin to live in segregated townships, were preferred to the manifested will of individual Bedouins. In a remarkable departure from established procedural rules regarding written testimony, the Court looked for 'hidden motives' behind the affidavits, and even hinted that the sworn testimonies were coercively obtained. The Court treated the Bedouins as defenseless creatures that needed the Court's guardianship. They were portrayed as less than full subjects, like the insane or the juvenile, who require the paternalistic protection of the law.[36]

The conclusion that the Court's politics of recognition functioned to justify racial difference and segregation becomes evident when considering: (1) the Court's attitude toward tribal culture in other cases, and (2) the origins of contemporary Bedouin tribes.

The Contradictory Politics of Recognition

The Supreme Court justified the concentration of the Bedouin in segregated jurisdictions by appealing to a rhetoric of respect for Bedouin culture and tribal particularity. 'In light of the great sensitivity of the Bedouins to their tribal, factional and even familial belonging', stated the Court in *Avitan*, 'the Bedouin settlements are planned in advance for particular Bedouin tribes.' The cultural unit requiring organic jurisdiction is not even the entire Bedouin community, but particular Bedouin tribes.

When the matter at hand, however, was not an attempt to transgress racial boundaries but internal rivalries among the Bedouin, tribal particularities attained much less significance. In *Sa'ida v. Ministry of the Interior*,[37] two Bedouin villages—Shibly and Um-El-Ganem—challenged a decision by the Minister of Interior to unify them under a single local government, arguing that a long history of rivalry and antagonism between the two tribes residing in those villages did not enable the annexation. The Supreme Court rejected their argument. The decision to unify the two villages was reasonable, explained the Court, because 'Um-El-Ganem is a Bedouin village with a population of 900 and Shibly is also a Bedouin village with a population of 2,500. The cultural and social background of both villages is identical. The geographical and demographic proximity enables consolidating the two villages in the future'. The historical rivalry and hatred between the two tribes did not convince the Supreme Court to intervene. The Court stressed that according to state officials past experience teaches us that after a primary resistance, the objection of the Bedouin residents to annexation disappears when they realize the advantages that accompany such annexation.

When not threatened by the transgression of racial boundaries, respect for the Bedouins' tribal particularity evaporated, giving way to a disdain of internal divisions and pragmatic considerations of efficiency and administrative convenience.

Colonial Recognition and Cultural Racism

Another factor to consider when examining the Supreme Court's apparent respect for the Bedouins' tribal culture is the way these tribes were formed. The current tribal structure is, in fact, a product of recent political oppression rather than a natural cultural outgrowth with its origins in traditions from time immemorial, as the Court would have us believe.

A major problem for the Israeli government in the early 1950s was how to exert control over the remaining Bedouin in the Negev, who were relocated to the Enclosure Zone. Several political and administrative measures were employed by the government in order to control the Bedouin, arguably the most important and effective of which was reorganizing the Bedouin tribal structure by establishing new tribes, appointing new chiefs (Sheikhs) for existing tribes and deposing others (Meir, 1997). By awarding tribal status to extended families that were loyal to the government, the number of formally recognized tribes increased from about 18 in 1960 to 48 by the early 1990s, and internal rivalries among the tribes grew accordingly (Marx, 1967; Meir, 1997). The government encouraged, if not inflamed, these internal rivalries and exploited them to enhance its control over the Bedouin population and gain its cooperation. Therefore, in addition to the general authority and responsibility allotted to tribal chiefs, they were selectively granted control over water outlets, permits for farming, grazing, labor, travel and other economic ventures. Loyal tribes were also given priority in the allocation of state land within the Enclosure Zone (Meir, 1997). Tribal affiliation was not a matter of choice for the Bedouin but was mandated by the military administration. Every Bedouin had to have a tribal affiliation. Tribal affiliation could have been altered only by consent of the military administration, which in the early years was rarely forthcoming (Marx, 1967). The Israeli policy of reconstructing the Bedouin social structure in accordance with administrative convenience 'was no new departure, for previous administrations had ruled in the same manner for many years' (Marx, 1967, p.40).

With this historical background in mind, state deference to the 'cultural sensitivity of the Bedouins to their tribal belonging' appears much less liberating. In a powerful speech delivered in 1956 before the First Congress of Negro Writers and Artists, Franz Fanon (1967) analyzed cultural racism in colonial settings. The old fashioned biological racism, argued Fanon, tends to disappear and is transformed into cultural racism. The object of cultural racism is no longer the individual person but a certain 'form of existing'. We must look for the consequences of this racism on the cultural level. Colonial systems, Fanon observed, do not of themselves bring about the death of native cultures. History reveals, on the contrary, that the aim sought is rather a continued agony than a total disappearance of the pre-existing culture. 'This culture, once living and open to the future, becomes closed, fixed in the colonial status, caught in the yoke of oppression. Both present and mummified, it testifies against its members' (Fanon, 1967, p.34). We witness, continued Fanon, the setting up of archaic, idle institutions, functioning under the oppressor's gaze and patterned like a caricature of formerly fertile institutions. These institutions appear to embody respect for the tradition, the cultural particularity and personality of the subjugated people. But in fact this pseudo-respect is tantamount to utter contempt, to the most elaborate sadism (Fanon, 1967).

In what follows I argue that the commitment of critical scholars of the multicultural left to the value of cultural difference played an instrumental role in justifying the forced segregation of the Bedouin townships and the ensuing economic exploitation and political subordination. In other words, the racial-class based conflict disguised as ethnic-cultural conflict led even progressive scholars to emphasize cultural difference over status hierarchy. The result is that the cultural identity of the Bedouin was foregrounded at the expense of the reality of discrimination and economic exploitation.

The Dark Side of Multiculturalism: The Cultural Politics of Race and Nation

The politics of difference, and its spatial expression—jurisdictional autonomy—which emerged in the early 1980s as the dominant approach of the multicultural left, is a double-edged sword. Depending on the nature of the group involved, it can be either liberating or subordinating. The multicultural left does not acknowledge this duality. For them the ultimate evil is assimilation—the destruction of cultural difference; they remain completely oblivious to the harmful aspects of the politics of difference—'the incessant production of difference, the creation of categories, the exploitation of particularities, the making of the Other' (Ford, 1999, p.921). The culturally based division of society into distinctive local units that are imposed on social groups is often, as exemplified in *Avitan*, a critical part of nationalist hegemony (Ford, 1999).

The Court's ruling in *Avitan* was indeed hailed as a progressive decision by both lawyers and academics. Dina Zilber, a lawyer in the State Attorney's office, saw the importance of the decision in legitimizing differential treatment of different groups as a tool for accomplishing social justice. 'Such an approach', argued Zilber, 'offers an alternative to affirmative action. Affirmative action is based on the assumption that some individuals in society are considered inferior and their condition should be improved. The Avitan decision suggests that instead of ascribing inferiority to these individuals, it is possible to present differential treatment as a social need, or public interest.'[38] Apart from the distorted justification for affirmative action manifested in this argument, it is clear that the 'differential treatment' Zilber is referring to is based on 'cultural difference'.

Ronen Shamir (1996), a progressive sociologist committed to the tenets of multiculturalism, although critical of the ruling, was not bothered by the segregationist ideology underlying the Supreme Court's decision or its harmful economic and political outcome. Instead, what bothered Shamir was the detrimental effects of the Court's decision on Bedouin culture. 'Even cases in which Bedouin culture seems to be protected', he argued, 'rest on a foundation that robs them of their own history and culture' (Shamir, 1996, pp.248–249). Shamir pointed to the fact that the fundamental rational underlying the Court's decision was not a genuine concern for the well-being of Bedouin culture, as the Court argued, but 'compelling state interest' to prevent the Bedouins from taking over state land. Shamir accepted, however, the basic premise that acknowledging the 'historic particularity of the Bedouin collectivity' and their 'particular tribal culture and history' is indeed the ultimate goal (Shamir, 1996, p.249). So strong is Shamir's commitment to the politics of difference that, even though he rightfully pointed to the essentialization of the Bedouin culture by the Court, he still clung to cultural preservation as the right path to save the Bedouin. In other words, the problem, according to Shamir, is not the evocation of culture but its misrepresentation. If we could only get the Bedouin culture right everything else would fall in place.

The exclusive focus of the multiculturalist discourse on culture, its exaggeration of cultural difference and denial of commonality has had unfortunate consequences for legal and political analysis, including, among other things, inattention to economic inequality, rehabilitation of segregation and political subordination (Ford, 2002). As a result of the uncritical embrace of cultural difference by the multicultural left, the narratives of the nationalist-right and the multicultural-left paradoxically converge. Both see the Bedouin as an 'organic community' with a 'distinct culture' and, although their motivations are diametrically opposed, the result is the same—production of a fetishized cultural difference that justifies the persistence of segregation and discrimination against the Bedouin. It enabled the assimilation of the Bedouin into the capitalist system as an underclass and their rejection from the body politic as 'Others', which justified their confinement to segregated localities.

Illustrative of the claim that the advantages of cultural difference have been overemphasized at the price of economic inequality and political oppression is a new governmental plan to support peripheral communities. The Ofek program, sponsored by the Prime Minister's office with a prospective state expenditure of $300 million, was designed to promote the socio-economic development of eleven towns located in the country's geographic and social periphery. The settlements that were chosen for the program are all plagued with high unemployment, high rates of crime and various other socio-economic problems. It was the first time that the government included a Bedouin settlement—Tel-Sheva—in such a program. The program sets separate development goals for each town:

> Investment in Ofakim, for example, will be aimed at developing the community as a southern-region suburb, with solid access to services and employment possibilities offered by Beer Sheva. In contrast, the focus in Beit She'an will be tourist-related investment—the development plan aims to capitalize on Beit She'an's archeological assets and its location at a crossroads between the southern and northern regions of the country, and between Israel and Jordan. ...Efforts will be made to develop educational, tourist and health spheres in Yerucham. Investments in Tel-Sheva will go toward strengthening aspects of the Bedouin culture.[39]

While in all the Jewish towns the governmental investment was to go toward improvement of the economic infrastructure, in the Bedouin case it was culture that was prioritized as the most crucial area for improvement. Tel-Sheva has no sewer system, decent schools or paved roads. Unemployment rates in the Bedouin township are the highest in the country. Nevertheless, what the Bedouin residents of Tel-Sheva need, according to state officials, is a boost to their culture. Not only was the Bedouin culture accentuated at the price of their economic marginalization, the logic of capitalism also dictated the exploitation of the Bedouin's cultural particularity, turning them into an exotic 'exhibition' which was to be part of the Negev's attractions. This is reflected in a governmental plan for the development of the Negev: 'The Negev offers a variety of tourist attractions ... wild desert view, special geological and geopological phenomena, desert wildlife, desert flora, impressive historical and archeological sites, important religious sites, exotic Bedouin population, as well as bathing, fishing, diving and healing sites' (Ministry of Interior, 1977, pp.8–9).

Cultural Difference: How Other Really is the Other?

Traditionally, it has been assumed by leftist scholars that cultural survival is an important goal to be pursued, and its opposite—cultural assimilation—is an evil to be avoided. It is therefore assumed that policies meant to preserve cultural structures are good, while those designed to eliminate them are bad and should be avoided at all cost. At the heart of this philosophical stance lies a fetishized one-dimensional conception of culture. 'It is so taken for granted that each country embodies its own distinctive culture and society that the terms "society" and "culture" are routinely simply appended to the names of the nation-states' (Gupta & Ferguson, 1997, p.34), as in 'American culture' or 'Indian culture'. The notion of pure and homogeneous cultures that are congruent with the borders of essentially homogeneous nation-states was, and still is, a crucial component of nationalist and racist thought. The tragic popularity of the idea of the integrity and purity of cultures both among the right and the left is what makes possible discriminatory conceptions of national identity. Against such hegemonic notions of 'exclusive cultural communities', Paul Gilroy (1993) offered an alternative—the idea that racial, ethnic and national communities have forged a compound culture from disparate resources. In opposition to both of these nationalist or ethnically absolute approaches, Gilroy celebrates the hybridity, interstitiality and complexity of cultures.

Such a perspective would reveal that cultural difference is not exclusively a feature of the alien, the foreigner or the other—it exists within each of us (Ford, 2002). We should problematize the unity of the 'us' as well as the otherness of the 'other'. Cultures are, by definition, hybrid, complex and multi-dimensional bodies that change over time due to both internal pressures and external influences. Cultural difference divides racial and national groups internally and can often create alliances across racial, ethnic or national boundaries. This understanding has political implications. Racially mixed institutions and cultural hybrids should not be rejected as dangerous assimilation, but should be accepted and even encouraged as enriching our lives by enlarging the cultural 'scripts' available to us. Such institutions are likely to produce more intercultural people like Avitan, who defined himself as 'Jewish in my religion, Israeli in my nationality and Bedouin in my worldview'.[40]

The transformation of the conception of territoriality among the Bedouin The Bedouin culture is, as all cultures are, much more complex and heterogeneous than as portrayed by both the left and the right. In fact, the Bedouin culture has been influenced by Western notions of territoriality and the Bedouin had been undergoing an urbanization process since the first half of the nineteenth century (Meir, 1997). The important point for our discussion is that by the late 1960s, the time the Israeli government began to implement the settlement program, the Bedouin were already fully sedentary. This section describes the process of sedentarization the Bedouin underwent in the nineteenth and early twentieth century in order to illustrate that essentialist arguments which use cultural difference to justify segregation are untenable.

Until the mid-nineteenth century the Bedouin conception of territory was both tribal (i.e. non-individualistic) and flexible. The Bedouin were nomadic tribes scattered throughout the Middle Eastern deserts, subsisting mostly on a pastoral economy. They did not regard their habitat (Dira) as a fixed geographical location. Rather, it was a 'moving territory' with permeable boundaries which were defined socially rather than spatially (Meir, 1997). The development of spatial flexibility can be explained from an economic-ecological perspective. The patchy rainfall patterns in the semiarid and arid environments in which the Bedouin lived created erratic and random distribution of pasture areas. Under such conditions it was not beneficial to rely on fixed territory and thus a strategy of open grazing territories was adopted (Perevolotsky, 1987). Farming land did not provide a fixed or solid basis for Bedouin subsistence and, therefore, did not have market value so competition for its possession was almost nonexistent (Meir, 1997). Land was not exclusively owned, sellable or economically valuable (Lancaster & Lancaster, 1986). In other words, land was not a 'commodity'.

This situation continued uninterrupted until the first half of the nineteenth century. In the first half of the century, a combination of political and ecological processes generated a transformation from pastoral nomadic subsistence to a semi-nomadic system of more balanced pastoral and farming modes of production. Consequently, the Bedouin habitat changed from the flexible traditional type and assumed greater rigidity. The inclusion of cultivated areas by definition transformed the Bedouin habitat into a spatially fixed entity (Meir, 1997).

The promulgation of the Ottoman Land Law in 1858, defining any uncultivated land in the Negev as dead land (Mewat) and therefore state property, functioned as a major catalyst to the transition in land use patterns among the Bedouin. The demand for and competition over farming land in the Negev intensified considerably and land began to assume 'exchange value', rather than the 'use value' it previously had (Meir, 1997). As a result, tribal territories with fixed boundaries began to take shape and the communal use of grazing resources—customary in the past—was no longer possible. 'This process culminated in the fixation of tribal territories by the Ottoman government in 1890 and their formalization in a tribal territory map in 1906' (Meir, 1997, p.80).

These processes at the macro tribal level inevitably infiltrated the micro level of the Bedouin family and individuals. 'The significance of these processes is that they implied the beginning of ideological change among individual Bedouin with regard to territory and territoriality' (Meir, 1997, p.81). Indeed, after 1858, tribal grazing lands were gradually transformed into arable land by undergoing parcellation into small family units, which were then privatized. The changes in the nature of land and habitat further affected the already diminishing status of the tribe as an economic and political unit and increased existing tendencies of individualism among the Bedouin (Kressel et al., 1991).

The growing political stability that characterized the region near the turn of the century and the increasing demand for Middle Eastern agricultural products in European markets encouraged an increasing number of Bedouin to invest in agriculture instead of, or in addition to, livestock production (Meir, 1997). The emerging agricultural nature of the Negev, coupled with better economic prospects began, in turn, to attract landless peasants (fellaheen) from other areas, particularly the Egyptian Nile valley (Meir, 1997). As a result, at the turn of the century competition for land resources in the Negev grew fiercer and took place not only among the Bedouin, but also between the Bedouin and the peasants who came into the region en masse. These peasants were often adjunct to the Bedouin economy as tenants on Bedouin lands. In some cases a division of labor evolved—the Bedouin engaged in livestock production while their land was leased and cultivated by the peasant-tenants as share-croppers (Grossman, 1994).

The next important milestone in the sedentarization process was the establishment of the town of Beer Sheva by the Ottoman government in 1903 as the administrative center for the Negev. Beer Sheva evolved into a market town for the Bedouin, especially for the surplus agricultural crops that began to accumulate (Ben-David & Kressel, 1995). Consequently, the Bedouin began to integrate into the local, regional and in some ways also the international market economy and their standard of living rose dramatically as a result (Ben-David, 1989). The most significant phenomenon was that land transactions became a common phenomenon. The first to take part in such transactions were those Bedouin who engaged in farming and used land as collateral. This practice, however, legitimized land transactions by Bedouin who did not engage in farming but were anxious to keep pace with the rising regional standard of living (Meir, 1997). Consequently, by the early twentieth century, Bedouin land was completely commodified.

The occupation of Palestine by the British in 1917, following World War I, and the ensuing declaration of the British Mandate over Palestine, accelerated the tendencies of land commodification and sedentarization among the Bedouin. The British conquest brought the entire region into Western economy's sphere of influence. The economy of the region gradually opened up and the Bedouin economy was boosted by a massive inflow of capital (Meir, 1997). This development entailed old as well as new sources of pressure on Bedouin farming and grazing lands. Migration of peasants into the northern Negev continued. Merchants and other capitalists from Beer Sheva and the area increasingly purchased or otherwise gained control over Bedouin lands. In addition a new player appeared in the region—the Jewish Zionist movement began to demonstrate an increasing interest in purchasing land in the Negev (Meir, 1997). The growing pressure on Bedouin land resulted in further 'intensification of agriculture at the expense of pastoral activities, further parcellation and privatization of tribal lands into household ownership, and further legalization of land issues' (Meir, 1997, p.84). The opportunities for profit from farming induced increasing numbers of Bedouin to abandon livestock production and become directly involved in dry farming, rather than assigning cultivation to their peasants tenant. The increased capital inflow enabled them to purchase new types of seedlings, tools and machinery, stimulated the gradual technological progress of dry farming, and improved its economic prospects (Meir, 1997). During the mandate period, these activities were integrated into the previous pastoral nomadic economy to such an extent that the notion of a locality became a state of mind among the Bedouin, and permanent dwellings began to appear (Meir, 1997). Already in the 1930s, the Negev—and particularly the northern Negev—was described, by the traveler Aref El-Aref, as primarily agricultural. Parcellation and privatization of tribal lands further intensified during the British Mandate as a result of British hostility toward collective land ownership, and the establishment of the Land Court in Beer Sheva in 1921 entailed the formalization of the holding and selling of lands (Meir, 1997). These accumulated changes mark the transition of the Bedouin society from a social definition of territory to a territorial definition of social relations.

These processes, and the ensuing transformation in the conception of spatiality, naturally intensified considerably after 1948, with the establishment of the State of Israel and the spatial practices it imposed on the Bedouin. However, this historical account of the development of Bedouin spatiality supports the claim of Ghazi Falah that the Negev Bedouin were already 'fully sedentarized when the Israeli government began to implement its settlement program' (Falah, 1989, p.72).

Fetishism of difference and cultural survival From this reconstructed historical narrative it is clear that the Zionist image of the Bedouin as nomads with no attachment to the land (or in its multiculturalist version—with a distinct conception of territoriality illegible to the Western mind),[41] which justified practices of dispossession and segregation, is not anchored in historical reality. In fact, the Bedouin had engaged in a dialogue with modernity long before the State of Israel was established. The State of Israel has indeed been a significant agent of change for Bedouin society in many respects (mostly detrimental ones), 'in some crucial respects, however—primarily territorialization and sedentarization—change in fact began earlier' (Meir, 1997, p.73). The conflict between the Bedouin and the state should be conceptualized, then, not so much in terms of culture, as argued by both state agents and the multicultural left, but mostly in political and economic terms. The production of cultural difference occurs in a continuous, connected space, traversed by economic and political relations of inequality (Gupta & Ferguson, 1997). The multicultural spin given to the conflict plays into the hands of the nationalist right by hiding the economic exploitation and political oppression of the Bedouin behind an ethnic/cultural disguise.

Contrary to arguments made by scholars from both the right and the left, who, with very different political motives, stress an essentialist and fetishized form of cultural difference, I have attempted to show that in many important respects, especially territorial and economic ones, the Bedouin culture is not different from that of modern Israel. Economic and political global powers forced nomadic pastoral groups all over the world to change their way of life. Modern states, which are based on the logic of order and rational administration, are usually hostile to nomadic groups,[42] and late capitalism made nomadic life harder to maintain even under favorable political conditions. The Bedouin culture was not immune to those political and economic transitions and changed dramatically over the past two centuries. The flexible notion of territoriality that characterized the nomadic Bedouin tribes in the early nineteenth century was replaced by a notion of fixed territoriality and institutionalized private ownership of land modeled after the Western land regime even before the imposing power of Israel. With the aid of the Israeli State, this 'cultural' revolution was accelerated and, as of 1999, only 1,470 of the 120,000 Bedouin who live in the Negev are registered as livestock owners.[43] This is an inevitable, if also lamentable, process characterizing the modern world.

It should be emphasized that my argument is not that the Bedouin have no culture, or that they should all assimilate into Jewish Israeli society. Rather my argument is that cultures in general, and the Bedouin culture in particular, are much more hybrid and complex entities than what both popular imagination and official portrayals would have us believe. Nor do I deny that the state participated in destroying the Bedouin culture. At the same time, however, it was also crucial for the government to uphold a fetishized form of cultural difference in order to justify the dispossession of the Bedouin, and maintain the policy of residential segregation. Without cultural difference, state actions would have been relegated to the realm of unlawful discrimination. Thus, the multiculturalist attempt to 'preserve' the indigenous Bedouin culture is, as is any case of trying to artificially restore indigenous cultures and freeze them in time, hopelessly romantic and inevitably ends up helping those trying to subordinate and oppress the indigenous population.

The imminent problem Bedouin society faces is not cultural extinction, but economic exploitation and political subordination which turned the Bedouin into one of the most underprivileged groups in Israeli society. What the Bedouin urgently need is a conscious policy designed to rectify the long history of oppression and exploitation. If these wrongs are undone, culture will take care of itself. Ultimately, as Richard Ford argued, a race conscious policy that focused on the need to undo the legacy of racial subordination, would have made a greater number of racial 'scripts' available and would encourage a richer and more nuanced understanding of racial culture and identity (Ford, 2002).

Toward a Regional Integration

Where do we go from here? While new urban and rural developments changed the Bedouin economy and culture dramatically, traditional economic pursuits within the old frameworks have persisted despite the vast economic changes (Marx, 1984). A minority of the Bedouin still retains the traditional way of life, live in tents and engage in dry farming and livestock production.[44] Those Bedouin should be allowed to maintain their way of life. The vast majority of the Bedouin, however, especially those of younger generations, are not likely to give up modern life, move back into tents and engage in livestock production or dry farming. The solution for them should be found in the framework of regional economic development. The current settlement scheme, presented as an attempt to modernize the Bedouin, is rejected by the majority of them. It would be a great mistake, however, to conclude that the Bedouin reject modern services because they prefer to live in a 'world without time'. As rightly observed by Ghazi Falah, 'when such services are offered as a recompense for the appropriation of Bedouin lands, one should not wonder why Bedouin reject government settlement schemes' (Falah, 1985a, p.50).

Residential integration of Jews and Bedouins in the Negev is not likely to happen in the near future, even if the legally mandated segregation was lifted from the Bedouin settlements. Conceptions of racially based cultural difference abound, making integration a policy repudiated by the majority on both sides of the racial line. Although the current segregation enforced on the Bedouin settlements must be abolished, the sad fact is that people like Avitan are very rare. Even if the Bedouin townships had been opened for Jewish settlement, very few Jews would have taken up the opportunity, if not due to racism than for economic reasons. After all, who wants to live in a town with substandard municipal services and poverty levels that are the highest in the country.

It is also unlikely that Bedouins will settle in Jewish localities. Jewish cities and towns of the Negev are not hospitable to Arab residents. Even localities in which segregation is not mandated, such as the city of Beer Sheva, do not welcome Bedouins. There is absolutely no infrastructure for an Arab-Muslim community in the 'capital of the Negev'.[45] The city that serves as a regional center for more than 120,000 Bedouins, and employs tens of thousands of them has not built even one Arab school or one Muslim mosque. When asked to reopen an ancient mosque that had served the Muslim community of Beer Sheva prior to1948, former mayor David Bonfeld replied: 'Beer Sheva is a Jewish city. There are 27 mosques in the Beer Sheva surroundings', and vowed to turn the mosque into a museum.[46] As a result, only about 3,000–5,000 Arabs (some of whom are Bedouins) reside in Beer Sheva, a city with a population exceeding 180,000. Given this background, it is clear that integration of Jews and Bedouins, on the local level, will not occur without mandated residential desegregation, which is neither feasible nor desirable.

Politico-geographical policies should advance, instead, the integration of the Bedouin into the regional economy of the Beer Sheva metropolis and the Negev regiopolis. As discussed above, the Negev regiopolis, with the Beer Sheva metropolis at its center, is already a reality. The place of the Bedouin localities in the planning scheme should, however, be altered so as to foster their economic development. This idea is not new. It has been advocated by Bedouin grassroot movements since the mid-1990s. In 1996, the Steering Committee for Strategic Planning for the Bedouin-Arab Settlements in the Negev, an entrepreneurial Bedouin entity, published 'A Plan for the Bedouin-Arabs in the Negev 2020'. The plan proposed to solve the Bedouin problem by fully integrating them into the planning and development schemes on both the regional and national levels. It was presented as a practical alternative to the government policies in the areas of planning and development. The Plan assumed that by 2020 the Bedouin population in the Negev would increase to 230,000 and advocated the development of a bi-national metropolis.[47]

In 1999, the embryonic Regional Council of the Unrecognized Bedouin Arab Villages of the Negev, in cooperation with the Center for Jewish-Arab Economic Development, drafted and filed a master plan calling for the approval and recognition of the 45 largest Bedouin villages in the Negev.[48] The plan was presented as an alternative to the current district and national plans that insist on concentrating the entire Bedouin population in seven permanent urban settlements, which have already been proved economic and social failures.[49] The advantage of regional integration is that it can be achieved without integrating the Bedouins on the local level, integration which is currently opposed by large segments in both the Bedouin and Jewish communities.

Planning practices, as political geographer Oren Yiftachel reminded us, are not inherently a tool of oppression. Urban and regional planning emerged, in fact, 'out of the unacceptable and inhumane living conditions prevalent in the rapidly expanding industrial cities of the eighteenth and nineteenth centuries' (Yiftachel, 1995, p.123), and were designed, first and foremost, to improve people's living conditions. It is time we reinstated planning as a tool of reform.

Conclusion: The Fallacy of Opaque Spaces

This chapter has recounted the sad story of political oppression and economic exploitation of the Bedouin-Arab minority in Israel and the role the Israeli legal system played in this process. On a theoretical level, this chapter analyzed the spatial implication of cultural difference. It demonstrated that both nationalist and multicultural ideologies can be easily translated into a racially-based division of space, creating homogeneous territories that house what are imagined and constructed as organic political communities. It also supported the argument that the production of difference within the nation-state does not necessarily undermine the integrity of the body politic but is sometimes a critical part of the nationalist hegemony. The chapter concluded by presenting an alternative to both the idea of total segregation and to that of complete integration in the local government level—the regional integration of the Bedouin into the Beer Sheva metropolitan region. Regional integration is a necessary step in the direction of eliminating political subordination and advancing economic improvement in an environment hostile to local integration.

Notes

1 An important terminological clarification is in order. The Bedouin, as well as the Palestinian citizens of Israel, are commonly defined as an ethnic or national minority but never as a racial minority since both Jews and Arabs are Semite. Defining the Arabs in Israel as an ethnic minority is, however, somewhat misleading. The term ethnicity 'refers to aspects of relationships between groups which consider themselves, and are regarded by others, as being culturally

different' (Eriksen, 1993). As Richard Ford argues, the ethnicity model by its very nature emphasizes cultural difference over status hierarchy. In the ethnicity model the position of Palestinian Arabs is analogous to that of Arab-Jews: both have a distinctive cultural background which is different from that of European-Jews. What is excluded from and silenced by this model is the ongoing state-sponsored subordination of non-Jews which makes the status hierarchy of the two groups very different. The price that we pay for using the ethnicity model is therefore very high. The cultural identity of the so-called 'ethnic' minority is emphasized at the expense of the reality of political and economic subordination (Ford, 2002).

Another source of confusion is the complex relationship between race/ethnicity and nationality. The Bedouin, as part of the Arab minority, are also referred to as a 'national minority', being Israeli citizens of Arab nationality. The politics of race in Israel, as will be discussed later, is inspired by conceptions of national belonging and homogeneity that not only blur the distinction between 'race' and 'nation', but also rely on that very ambiguity for their effect. The nation is represented in terms that are simultaneously biological and cultural. The legal concept of nationality, introduced in the Law of Return of 1950, codified this cultural biology of race into statute law as part of a strategy for the exclusion of Arabs. This notion of 'race' can be equated to what Paul Gilroy (1987) has called the 'new racism', whose novelty lies in the capacity to link discourses of patriotism, nationalism, xenophobia, Israeliness and militarism into a complex system which gives 'race' its contemporary meaning. These themes combine to provide a definition of 'race' in terms of culture and identity.

I use the notion of race, as conceptualized above, and not that of ethnicity or nationality since I believe it conveys a clearer message of status hierarchy which is, in my opinion, the most important component of contemporary Jewish-Arab relations, and is missing in both the ethnic and the nationality models. However, this terminological choice comes not without a price. In some ways, the notion of nationality is more apt than that of race. Arabs, unlike blacks in the United States, are feared and disdained more as a collective than as individuals. Jews who might be tolerant toward an individual Arab would be hostile toward an Arab presence as a 'phenomenon' (Rabinowitz, 1992). The individual/collective distinction is, however, very much blurred and completely collapses at times of crisis such as that of the Palestinian Intifada since the individual Arab is perceived as representing the collective.

The reader should interpret the term 'race' in light of the novel understanding presented above. And since the terms ethnicity and nationality are engrained in the literature on the Arab minority in Israel these terms will keep popping up throughout this book.

Moreover, unlike most of the Arab population, the Bedouin community is considered (or at least was considered until recently) loyal to the state. The Bedouins serve in the Israeli army and are not considered a threat to national security. Therefore, the Bedouins represent a 'pure' case of the way the state deals with a national-racial minority through the mechanisms of space and does not raise questions involving national security that would have complicated the analysis.

2 Tribes served historically as territorial and administrative units led by elected chiefs whom the authorities recognized as official representatives of the tribes. Tribes combined into Confederations, which were mainly larger territorial divisions whose contiguity was expressed in terms of common descent (Marx, 1967).

3 Yosef Algazi, 'The Biggest Discrimination', *Ha'aretz*, 27 November, 2000.

4 Rotem Zahar, 'A Plan: 1.175 Billion Shekels will be Invested in the Negev Bedouin', *Ha'aretz*, 7 January, 2003.

5 C.A. 218/74, *Salim El-Hawashlla v. State of Israel*, 38(3) P.D. 141.

6 Al-Hawashlla, p.150.

7 Daniel Ben-Simon, 'Buky and Guly in Bedouinland', *Ha'aretz*, 4 March, 1998.

8 Ammar Alhozeil, 'This Land is also Mine', *Ha'aretz*, 18 September, 1997, at B2.

9 Daniel Ben-Simon, 'Endless Poverty', *Ha'aretz*, 10 December, 1999; Baruch Kra, 'Unemployment as Lifestyle', *Ha'aretz*, 16 January, 2000.

10 Daniel Ben-Simon, 'Common Fate', *Ha'aretz*, 24 January, 2000.

11 Although it is impossible to dismiss the possibility that this planning disaster was an innocent mistake, this is very doubtful given the experience Israeli planners had had since the 1950s with the New Towns in which the planning concept of medium size urban localities in under-developed areas had proven to be a complete failure (Lissak, 1999).

12 The Bedouin as well as other Palestinians replaced the Arab-Jews as a main source of non-professional labor. This is apparent from comparing the number of non-professional laborers among the Arab-Jews in 1954 and in 1999. In 1954, over 50 per cent of the Arab-Jewish work force was employed as non-professional wage earners. In 1999 the number dropped to 22 per cent. Data for the year 1954 was taken from Lissak, 1999. Data for the year 1999 was taken from The Israeli Central Bureau of Statistics, Vol.50.

13 Yossef Algazi, 'Good Local People are Needed', *Ha'aretz*, 14 January, 1997; Yossef Algazi, 'First Place in Disrepair, Poverty and Unemployment', *Ha'aretz*, 30 January, 2003.

14 Moshe Dayan, 'On Land Policy and the Bedouin Problem in Israel', *Ha'aretz*, 31 July, 1963.

15 This calculation does not include the large tract of land in the center of the Northern Negev that lacks municipal status.

16 Cr.A. (B.S.) 4578/87, *State of Israel v. Jamia Salah Abu Ayash* (12.15.87).

17 Cr.A. (B.S.) 566/96, *Jamia Salem v. the District Planning and Construction Committee* (11.5.97).

18 In its capacity as the High Court of Justice, the Israeli Supreme Court exercises equitable jurisdiction. As the High Court of Justice, the Supreme Court rules as a court of first instance, primarily in matters regarding the legality of governmental decisions, both state and local, and the legality of actions by other bodies and persons performing public functions under the law.

19 Cr.A. 5766/93, *Subikh El-Saria v. State of Israel*, 94(2) Takdin-Elyon 240.

20 H.C. 2678/91, *El-Sanaa v. The Attorney General*, 46(3) P.D. 709.

21 H.C. 6459/99, *Salim Abu-Ratyush v. Israel Land Authority* (18 October, 1999).

22 Moshe Reinfeld and Aliza Arbeli, 'Court Orders Government to Fulfill Land Promise to Bedouin', *Ha'aretz*, 19 April, 2000.

23 See for instance Yizhak Baily, 'The Bedouin were convinced', *Ha'aretz*, 15 March, 1994.

24 H.C. 6532/94, *Ibrahim Abdulla Abu-Kaf v. Ministry of Agriculture* (10 November, 1996).

25 The same (il)logic was applied by the Court in another case. In the *Salem Harsh* case the state ordered the Jahalin Bedouin tribe to evacuate the land they resided on near the village of Abu-Dis in the occupied territories, which was declared state land in 1982. Members of the Jahalin tribe filed a petition with the High Court of Justice seeking an invalidation of the order. The dispute between the Bedouin and the state came down to a factual question: when did the Jahalin tribe first settle in the area? The state claimed that the Jahalin occupied the land only around 1988, while the Bedouin argued that they settled there already in the 1950s.

The Court dismissed the petition arguing that the petitioners were unable to prove that they indeed settled the land in the 1950s and therefore the evacuation order should not be invalidated. In a dissent, Justice Dorner argued that in cases such as this in which the state is in possession of 'objective evidence' that can easily prove or disprove the petitioners' claim (in this case aerial photos of the area from different points in time), the burden of proof on the petitioners should be minimal, and the principal burden should be shifted to the state to disprove the claim with the objective evidence it possesses. H.C. 2966/95, *Salem Harsh v. Minister of Defense*, 50(2) P.D. 9.

26 Daniel Ben-Simon, 'Buky and Guly in Bedouinland', *Ha'aretz*, 4 March, 1998, at B2.

27 Genesis 19: 30–38.

28 In the early twentieth century, for instance, the city of Los Angeles, which controlled the water of the Los Angeles river, used water as the key weapon in its program of expansion. In 1913 the city adopted the recommendation of the Municipal Annexation Commission that Los Angeles provide water only to those adjoining communities that agreed to be annexed (if unincorporated) or consolidated (if incorporated). This tactic proved very successful, and by 1930 the city of Los Angeles covered 442 square miles, more than ten times its area at the turn of the century (Miller, 1981).

29 H.C. 4671/98, *Awad Abu-Fraikh v. the Education Authority for the Bedouin in the Negev* (23 August, 1998).

30 H.C. 4540/00, *Abu-Afash v. Minister of Health* (June 27, 2000); H.C. 7115/97, *Adalah v. Ministry of Health* (27 October, 1998).

31 H.C. 5838/99, *Regional Council for the Unrecognized Villages in the Negev v. Minister of Labor and Welfare* (14 February, 2000).

32 H.C. 5221/00, *Abu-Gardud v. Regional Council Ramat Ha-Negev* (4 September, 2000).

33 H.C. 528/88, *Eliezer Avitan v. Israel Land Authority*, 43(4) P.D. 297.

34 Ronen Shamir has already observed the fact that the Court transformed nomadism into an essentialist category 'that provides rational foundations for appropriating land on the one hand and for concentrating the Bedouins in designated planned townships on the other hand' (Shamir, 1996, p.236).

35 *Avitan v. Israel Land Authority*, p.303.

36 Treating the Bedouins as less than full subjects is apparent in other realms as well. The state, with the court's blessings, deprived the Bedouin of access to their internal political resources by appointing Jewish officials to govern the Bedouin local governments. It took more than two decades before municipal elections were held in the first two Bedouin townships, Rahat and Tel-Sheva, and local power was transferred from the state to the Bedouin in terms of self-management (Meir, 1997).

37 H.C. 5139/92, *Sa'ida v. Minister of Interior*, 32 Dinim-Elyon 147.

38 Iris Milner, 'The Courageous', *Ha'aretz Magazine*, 12 April, 1996.

39 Government Endorses Plan to Support Periphery Communities, *Ha'aretz*, 6 November, 2000.

40 Milner, 'The Courageous', *Ha'aretz Magazine*, 12 April, 1996.

41 An important source of comparison for the Israeli multicultural scholars, in this respect, is the attitude of American scholars from the left toward the Native American. Carol Rose in a famous article—Possession as the Origin of Property—argued that Native American tribes have

a conception of property different from that of the Western society and illegible to it. Rose claimed that 'possession-as-text' is premised on the existence of an interpretive community that produces and reads symbols of possession in a shared manner and argued that it explains why the claims of indigenous people—who lack such a priori agreed-on symbols of control over land—cannot be recognized in modern Western societies (Rose, 1985). Ronen Shamir, for instance, argued the following about the connection of the Bedouin to their land: 'the land is said to contain the personality of its owner and as such cannot be taken away even with changed circumstances or long periods of absence' (Shamir, 1996, p.235). As we have illustrated, however, the Bedouin are well versed in the Western texts of possession and property.

42 Nomadism is being discouraged, not only in Israel, but all over the Middle East. Over the past 50 years conscious attempts have been made by governments throughout the Middle East to settle nomadic and semi-nomadic Bedouin populations and bring them into the context of sedentary society. 'This has been manifested in planned settlements schemes initiated in, for example, Abu-Dhabi, Egypt, Jordan, Kuwait, Iraq, Israel, and Saudi-Arabia' (Frenkel-Horner, 1982, p.175).

43 Yosef Algazi, 'The Whole Area Was Blackened of Escapees', *Ha'aretz*, 5 March, 1999, at B6.

44 These phenomena may result from state practices rather than 'cultural difference'. The prevalent usage of tents is likely to result from the prohibition on erecting permanent constructions outside the planned townships. This is used, in turn, by state officials in order to prove that the Bedouin are still nomads with no attachment to the land. Some scholars also downplay the importance of 'culture' in the persistence of traditional economy and tribal social ties, and argue that traditional affiliation and economic pursuits are maintained for reasons of economic security. 'Economic and political conditions are insecure, and people are aware that they are likely to lose their urban jobs at any time. The dependence on external sources of employment over which no control can be exerted, entails serious risks… They safeguard the tribe, their territory, and the indigenous economy, so that they can resume a pastoral way of life at short notice' (Marx, 1984, p.2). Bedouins who manage to achieve a large measure of economic security oftentimes break away from the tribe. Others belong to the two worlds. Unable to achieve a permanent foothold in the world of wage labor, they make every effort to insure against an unexpected loss of employment (Marx, 1984).

45 Ori Nir, 'A Mosque by Any Other Name is Still… A Museum', *Ha'aretz*, 29 March, 2001).

46 Ori Nir, 'A Mosque by Any Other Name is Still… A Museum', *Ha'aretz*, 29 March, 2001).

47 Yossef Algazi, 'Good Local People are Needed', *Ha'aretz*, 14 January, 1997, at B3.

48 Center for Jewish-Arab Economic Development, Negev Bedouin Projects <http://www.cjaed.org.il>.

49 Yossef Algazy, 'Bedouin Settlements Get a Blueprint at Last Plan's Advocates Label Unrecognized Villages Economic and Social Failures', *Ha'aretz*, 2 December, 1999.

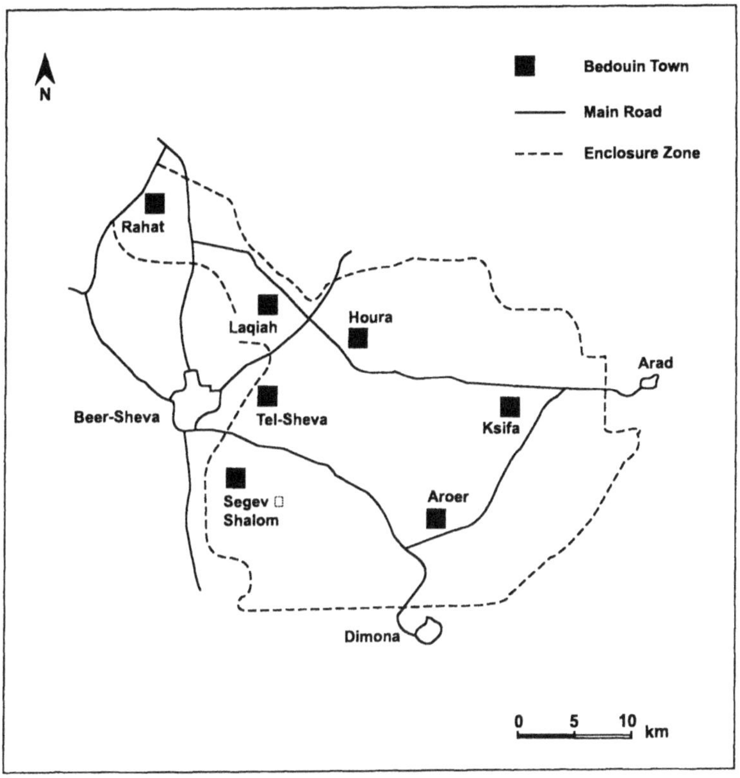

Map 1 The Bedouin Townships in the Negev

Chapter 4

Spaces of Ambivalence: The Case of the Ultra-Orthodox

This chapter continues to examine the relationship between a community and the space it occupies and the way such a relationship is imagined and constructed through legal discourse. More specifically, this chapter addresses the struggle of the ultra-Orthodox community in Jerusalem to draw the boundaries of what they perceive as their territory. One instance in this ongoing struggle was the successful legal battle of the ultra-Orthodox to close a major highway in Jerusalem that crosses their neighborhoods on the Sabbath. The Supreme Court's decision reveals internal disagreements among the Justices with regard to the nature of an ultra-Orthodox community and its space, and illustrates different attitudes toward geographical separatism.

The first part of this chapter provides a historical and sociological background on the ultra-Orthodox, shedding light on their aspiration for geographic separatism that resulted in the formation of the ultra-Orthodox 'ghetto'. The second part addresses the 'Sabbath Struggles'—struggles between the ultra-Orthodox community and secular society over the closing of streets and roads on the Sabbath. These struggles, it is argued, should be interpreted as continuous efforts on part of the ultra-Orthodox to define their own autonomous communal sphere. The third part of this chapter focuses on the single most important case involving the Sabbath Struggles—the *Bar-Ilan Road* case. The doctrinal arguments of both the majority and the dissent in the *Bar-Ilan Road* case are examined in an effort to trace their philosophical premises and the different conceptions of space underlying them. The fourth part of this chapter identifies the implicit political philosophy guiding ultra-Orthodox ideology, an ideology based on communal solidarity and an inter-subjective notion of self.

The Ultra-Orthodox Community in Israel

A Society within a Society

The ultra-Orthodox community in Israel or as it is commonly called *Haredi*[1] society is a peculiar group even within Israel's complex social structure. The term ultra-Orthodox refers to various Jewish groups that share a fervent and meticulous practice of Orthodox

Judaism, an anti-Zionist world-view and an obligation to sustain the study of the Torah. For them, the traditional Jewish communal way of life as developed in eastern Europe up to the mid-nineteenth century, before modernization and secularization took place, expresses the authentic Jewish life (Friedman, 1991).

Contemporary ultra-Orthodox society was largely shaped by two historical events: one was the secular revolution of the nineteenth-century with the social consequences it brought upon the traditional eastern European Jewish communities, and the other was the Holocaust with its tragic aftermath. Nineteenth century eastern Europe 'was rife with social, economic, and political crises, migration and displacement, that almost completely undermined the traditional social structure and led to increasing drift away from religion and tradition' (Friedman, 1991, p.ii). In this hostile world the foundations for the future ultra-Orthodox society were laid, ideological principles were set forth, hero images shaped, and cardinal myths coalesced. The traditional community was replaced by the Yeshiva—an institution that took young men, sheltered them from the outside world and transformed them into Jewish scholars, wholly devoted to the ideals of Torah study and religious perfection. These Yeshivas were the embryonic cells of the future ultra-Orthodox society, based not on the family as the agent of socialization, but on all-inclusive institutions detached from the surrounding society both socially and economically (Friedman, 1991).

Prior to World War II, traditional-religious society in eastern Europe managed to maintain its way of life, shielding itself from the secular world through the Yeshivas as well as through traditional Hasidic courts. Many Yeshivas were established throughout central and eastern Europe accommodating tens of thousands of students and enabling the traditional-religious Jewish life to flourish. The Holocaust brought an abrupt and cruel end to this flourishing society. Most ultra-Orthodox Jews died in the gas chambers; only a few survived. After the war ended, most survivors immigrated either to Israel or to the United States. As a result, east European traditional-religious Jewry vanished almost entirely and was replaced by ultra-Orthodox communities in Israel and America, the two contemporary centers of ultra-Orthodox Judaism, with smaller communities in such European cities as London, Paris and Brussels (Friedman, 1991).

The immigration to the West dramatically changed the social setting in which the ultra-Orthodox community operated. Ultra-Orthodox society became a 'small, well defined, discrete minority, organized in contiguous voluntary communities, set within a modern, open society with competition, confrontation, dependency and interrelations with this surrounding society' (Friedman, 1991, p.i). The response of the ultra-Orthodox to these new conditions is very significant.

Until the early 1950s, the ultra-Orthodox rabbinical leadership espoused an attitude of absolute separatism from the Zionist state and its society. This separatism included a refusal to recognize the legitimacy of the Zionist state or to participate in its political system and social life. It also included a complete prohibition on accepting funds or services from the state. After several years, however, as the 'society of scholars' grew beyond expectation and the revived ultra-Orthodox culture began to flourish, it became clear that this society could not sustain itself without significant financial support from the state (Friedman, 1991). The principle of absolute separatism was therefore abandoned and was replaced by partial separatism. The principle of partial separatism dictated the acceptance of instrumental benefits from the state, such as financial support and public services which require participation in the political system, while at the same time rejecting Israeli society at social and cultural levels (Shihav & Friedman, 1985).

The strategy of partial separation achieved its goals. The ultra-Orthodox community successfully separated itself, both socially and culturally, from the rest of Israeli society (Friedman, 1991). One of the most crucial components of their successful separatist strategy is their ability to maintain spatial segregation, not allowing the 'bad' influences of the outside to penetrate their community. The following section will provide a brief historical and anthropological introduction to the spatial dimension of the ultra-Orthodox community.

The Ultra-Orthodox Community: The Spatial Dimension

'Sacred community' within a 'Sacred Space' The desire of the ultra-Orthodox community to segregate itself territorially has both internal and external rationales. From an internal perspective spatial self-segregation is necessary to ensure the perpetuation of their traditional-religious way of life. The practice of Judaism is based not only on an intimate relationship between the individual and his or her God but also on a community of co-believers (Shilhav & Friedman, 1985). As described in Louis Wirth's classic study *The Ghetto*:

> To the Jews the geographically separated and socially isolated community seemed to offer the best opportunity for following their religious precepts, of preparing their food according to the established religious ritual, of following their dietary laws, of attending the synagogue for prayers three times a day, and of participating in the numerous functions of communal life which religious duty imposes upon every member of the community (Louis Wirth, 1998, p.19).

The spatial dimension of ultra-Orthodox Jewish life is most clearly manifested in the laws of the Sabbath that prohibit Jews from driving a car and delimit the range they can walk to about one kilometer in diameter ('Sabbath Domain'). Observant Jews are also prohibited from carrying objects outside the home. These spatial constraints require Sabbath observers to live in geographical proximity to each other as well as to their synagogue, which is the center of Jewish life both socially and religiously (Wirth, 1998).

This internal rationale is related to the familiar tendency of people with similar religious, racial or ethnic background to concentrate in geographically defined spaces in order to facilitate socialization processes and permit cultural dominance within those spaces (Timms, 1971; Davies & Herbert, 1993). It is strengthened by what is perceived by the ultra-Orthodox community as external threats to its existence. The ideological origins of the ultra-Orthodox territorial self-segregation lie in the fear that interaction with secular society would entice the ultra-Orthodox youth away from the traditional-religious way of life. This is reflected in the reason provided by Rabbi Haim Meir Hagger for the establishment of a segregated neighborhood for his Hasidic group. 'We are not willing' he stressed, 'to live together with secular people, thus assisting in exposing our children to the bad influence of their behavior' (Friedman, 1991, p.116).

Ultra-Orthodox Judaism is expressed at the individual level by meticulous observance of religious practices. On the communal level it is expressed through nurturing a consciousness of integration between the community and its space by creating a 'sacred space'. The sanctity of the territory stems not from the quality of the space itself (as is the case with 'holy sites') but from the nature of the people inhabiting it (Shilhav & Friedman, 1985). As asserted in an ultra-Orthodox newspaper article:

> in our times, when darkness covers the earth, no man is allowed to live in a city that is not surrounded by a wall of holiness protecting the handful of ultra-Orthodox Jews that remain faithful to God and the Torah... We have no desire to go outside [the wall of holiness] or letting inside it people who hold ideas contrary to everything we were taught by our Rabbis.[2]

According to this separatist ideology, ultra-Orthodox Judaism can fully express itself only within a segregated territory—an ultra-Orthodox ghetto (Shilhav & Friedman, 1985). In the ghetto both the private and the public domains are dominated by a 'sacred culture', which is an inverted image of what they consider to be the hedonist and permissive secular culture. The sacred space governed by a sacred culture is the basis for the creation of the 'sacred community'. The sanctity of the public sphere is achieved through an aggregation of social practices—such as the presence of a large number of Yeshivas and synagogues, the Eruv,[3] and a strict dress code enforced by 'modesty commandos'[4]—in a restricted geographical area. The single most significant socio-spatial practice, however, is the closing of streets and roads to traffic on the Sabbath, which circumscribes the boundary lines of the ultra-Orthodox ghetto (Shilhav & Friedman, 1985). Roads and streets that are closed to traffic on the Sabbath are considered, for all practical purposes, by both the ultra-Orthodox and the secular as part of the ultra-Orthodox ghetto. As a result, the struggles over closing roads on the Sabbath are in fact struggles over drawing the boundary lines of the ultra-Orthodox territory and are taken very seriously by all parties involved in these struggles.[5]

The Ghettoization process The majority of the ultra-Orthodox in Israel live in two urban localities—Jerusalem and Bnei-Brak. This study focuses on the ultra-Orthodox community in Jerusalem, although similar spatial patterns can be found in Bnei-Brak as well as in other smaller ultra-Orthodox localities.

The ultra-Orthodox community in Jerusalem emphasizes its distinctiveness through social, cultural and geographical separatism (Shilhav & Friedman, 1985). Jerusalem's ultra-Orthodox ghetto grew out of a small neighborhood in the northern part of Jerusalem called Me'a She'arim that had been inhabited by a small group of ultra-Orthodox Jews since the early twentieth century. Following the Second World War, with the massive migration of Holocaust survivors to Israel, Me'a She'arim attracted many of the ultra-Orthodox immigrants and was the point of departure for the expansion of the ultra-Orthodox ghetto. New ultra-Orthodox families continued to flow into the neighborhood even once it was filled. After there was no more housing in the neighborhood, they began to settle on its periphery driving out the secular and modern-Orthodox inhabitants. New housing projects and the large supply of Arab houses, whose owners were forced to flee during the 1948 war, offered more housing opportunities for the non-ultra-Orthodox residents who moved to more attractive neighborhoods and left Me'a She'arim to the ultra-Orthodox (Shilhav & Friedman, 1985).

Through a long process of 'invasion and succession' (Park, 1936), which was violent at times, the ultra-Orthodox ghetto continued to expand. From the core area of the Me'a She'arim neighborhood, the ghetto was expanded to the northwest to include neighborhoods such as Geula, Beith-Israel, Kerem-Abraham, Zikhron-Moshe, and later also Kiryas Tsanz, Tel-Arza and Romema, accommodating the fast growing ultra-Orthodox population.[6] By 1985, several years before the battle over the Bar-Ilan road began, the ultra-Orthodox ghetto encompassed more than 20 neighborhoods accommodating over 60,000 people, with the Bar-Ilan road intersecting it in the middle. Before we turn to a discussion of the Sabbath battles, and particularly the struggle over the Bar-Ilan road, an important terminological clarification is in order.

The Ultra-Orthodox Community: Diversity within Unity

By choosing the term 'community' to describe the ultra-Orthodox, I have already expressed a viewpoint as to the nature of this social group. The term community is commonly used to refer to a group of people who share a common sense of identity, history and values and who seek to foster the bonds they share (Frug, 1999). The use of the term community in the case of the ultra-Orthodox, as is the case for most social groups, is not unproblematic. A close look at the ultra-Orthodox reveals not one social group but many groups that share certain common characteristics but at the same time are also divided along numerous axes.

There are four major divisions that split ultra-Orthodox society. One is the rift between Lithuanians and Hasidim; another is between Ashkenazim and Sepharadim, a third is between the various Hasidic courts, and a fourth is between the adherents of cooperation with the Zionist state and their opponents. The Lithuanians, also called the Misnagdim, the Hebrew word for 'opponents', are historically the avowed enemies of the Hasidim. The rivalry stems from their different conceptions of Judaism and the relationship between the individual believer and God. With respect to the Hasidic courts themselves the situation is not much better. Long and bitter rivalries among the various Hasidic courts run very deep and deteriorate, every once in a while, into violent clashes. The ethnic rift between Ashkenazim and Sepharadim which divides Israeli society, also divides the ultra-Orthodox society. Finally, the level of cooperation with the Zionist state is a constant source of struggle among the various ultra-Orthodox subgroups—while some ultra-Orthodox groups, such as the Lithuanians, take the position that the ultra-Orthodox should maintain and even strengthen their cooperation with the Zionist state for instrumental-financial reasons, other groups, such as the Satmar Hasidim and Neturey Karta, are firmly opposed to any cooperation with the Zionist state (Friedman, 1991).

How, then, can we speak of the ultra-Orthodox as a community? The answer to this question lies in their common struggle against secular society for territory and identity. A sense of community was developed within the various ultra-Orthodox groups in the course of their common struggle to distinguish themselves from secular society and to carve out an autonomous communal sphere. The ability of political struggles to help shape the collective identity of the groups taking part in them is commonplace in socio-legal studies (Espeland, 1994). This is all the more true when what is at stake is a territorial jurisdiction, which has in itself the power to construct political subjects 'who understand themselves as—and in a sense in fact are—intimately connected in groups that are defended by territorial autonomy' (Ford, 1999, p.899). According to this account, the ultra-Orthodox as a community did not precede the struggle over their territory and identity but was constituted by it.

This argument is further strengthened by examining the ultra-Orthodox newspapers.[7] The newspapers of the various ultra-Orthodox groups that covered the struggle over the Bar-Ilan road never mentioned the internal divisions within the ultra-Orthodox groups. The newspapers referred to the ultra-Orthodox as a 'community', 'community of Sabbath observers', and 'sacred community', but never as Lithuanians or Hasidim, Ashkenazim or Sephardim. As against the secular society that threatens their territory and identity they are all, self-consciously, one community. To paraphrase a famous distinction, the ultra-Orthodox are, in this context, not only a community in itself but also a community for itself.[8] The term 'community' used to describe the ultra-Orthodox hroughout this study has to be understood in the specific context of the struggle against the secular society over territory and identity and not as a false romanticizing of an anthropological Other.

The Sabbath Battles

Historical Background

A central focus of the struggle to define a territory for the 'sacred community' was and still is the attempt to close streets and roads for traffic on the Sabbath. In this context the *Bar-Ilan Road* case is but one battle in a long war over the public sphere of the ultra-Orthodox neighborhoods.[9]

The first stone in this war was thrown in 1949, only one year after the establishment of the State of Israel. In 1949 the road to the Mandelbaum Gate—the passage connecting Israeli west Jerusalem and Jordanian east Jerusalem—crossed the ultra-Orthodox neighborhood Me'a She'arim, and traffic passed through this neighborhood on the Sabbath. The residents of the neighborhood considered traffic on the Sabbath an intolerable provocation directly interfering with their way of life and began to demonstrate against it (Segev, 1986). These demonstrations quickly deteriorated into violent clashes between the ultra-Orthodox and the police. Bechor Shalom Shitrit, the Minister of Police, complained in the parliament that 'those people [the ultra-Orthodox] hit everybody, Jews and Gentile... They attacked them in ways which are not to be tolerated by civilized people—spitting in faces, throwing rocks, scattering glass on the road. They went so far as to attack foreign diplomats and the staff of the United Nations'. These complaints provoked MP Rabbi Levin from the ultra-Orthodox Agudat-Israel party to exclaim: 'why will you not understand our anxiety ... When Jews, men and children, go out into the street and see the Sabbath publicly violated they cry out, Sabbath! with the tradition of Israel speaking from their throats – and then the soldiers of Israel see fit to beat them until they draw blood'. 'They were not content to cry Sabbath!,' replied the Minister of Police, 'They went up on their balconies and threw rocks, they entered houses and smashed glasses and scattered them on the road... Five policemen were injured. We have medical certificates to prove it. Some were bitten on their hands and ears, some had their clothes torn. What were the policemen to do?' 'For us', replied Rabbi Levin conclusively, 'it is a matter of life and death.'[10]

Not long afterwards the road leading to the Mandelbaum Gate was closed and Me'a She'arim effectively became an off limits area for the non-ultra-Orthodox. The Me'a She'arim riots were the first shot in a long campaign to close streets and roads in neighborhoods that had a majority of ultra-Orthodox residents. This campaign came to be known to the public as the 'Sabbath Battles'. Through a combination of political lobbying and street violence the ultra-Orthodox managed to close the streets and roads in practically every neighborhood in which they became the majority. Over time a pattern developed: when the ultra-Orthodox achieved a majority in a certain neighborhood they started to advocate the closing of roads on the Sabbath through both political lobbying and violent demonstrations. The demonstrations accelerated the flight of non-ultra-Orthodox from the area, a flight that occurred anyway once the demographic balance began to shift in favor of the ultra-Orthodox. The vacant apartments were soon filled with new ultra-Orthodox families. Once the streets and roads were closed, a set of behavioral requirements would be imposed, such as a strict dress code and a prohibition on 'inappropriate' street-signs, which signified the completion of the annexation of another neighborhood to the ultra-Orthodox ghetto (Shilhav & Friedman, 1985).

The Sabbath Battles Go to Court: The First Two Rounds

The first time the issue of road closure was brought before the Supreme Court was in a 1962 case *The League for the Prevention of Religious Coercion v. City Council of Jerusalem.*[11] The city council of Jerusalem, in its capacity as the Local Traffic Authority, issued a resolution asserting that during Sabbath morning prayers the roads bordering the Yeshurun synagogue would be closed. The rationale for the resolution was that the traffic in those streets grossly interfered with the ability of the people praying in the synagogue to concentrate on their prayers. The League for the Prevention of Religious Coercion, an organization founded in Jerusalem in 1951 for the purpose of fighting the perceived attempts of religious organizations to take over the public sphere, filed a petition with the Supreme Court requesting that the city council resolution be overruled. The Supreme Court refused to grant the requested relief. The Yeshurun synagogue, the Supreme Court asserted, is a central synagogue in Jerusalem serving a large number of people on Sabbaths and holidays. The streets bordering the synagogue, on the other hand, served a small number of vehicles. Moreover, the inconvenience experienced by drivers as a result of the closing of the roads was minimal because of the existence of alternative roads. Therefore, the Supreme Court concluded that when balancing the right of the worshippers to pray without interference against the right of the drivers to drive through these streets during the time of morning prayers, the right of the worshippers prevailed.

The second time the issue came before the Supreme Court occurred 15 years later in *Barukh v. Traffic Inspector of the Tel-Aviv and Central Districts.*[12] The *Barukh* case involved the closing of streets in the city of Bnei-Brak. The city council of Bnei-Brak, in its capacity as Local Traffic Authority, with the approval of the Ministry of Transportation, resolved to close a 1000 feet long section of a street crossing an ultra-Orthodox neighborhood in Bnei-Brak on the Sabbath. The petitioners, residents of two neighborhoods bordering the closed street, argued that the closing of the street infringed their constitutional right to freedom of movement and asked the Supreme Court to overrule the resolution. The Supreme Court rejected the petitioners' argument. It found that the number of vehicles driving through the street on the Sabbath averaged about 50 vehicles, while the number of ultra-Orthodox suffering from the vehicles crossing their neighborhood on the Sabbath was very large. Therefore, the Supreme Court concluded once again that the balance of interests favored the ultra-Orthodox.

As argued, the struggles over closing streets signify a claim to the territory involved. The boundary lines of the ultra-Orthodox ghetto are drawn and redrawn according to the territory that is closed to traffic on the Sabbath (Shilhav & Friedman, 1985). The uniqueness of *Horev v. Minister of Transportation,*[13] or as it is better known—the *Bar-Ilan Road* case, lies, then, not in the attempt to claim a territory through closing roads for traffic on the Sabbath, a strategy employed many times before, but in the type of territory claimed. Whereas prior to the *Bar-Ilan Road* case the ultra-Orthodox community had laid claims only to side streets which served its members almost exclusively, in the *Bar-Ilan Road* case they attempted for the first time to appropriate a major highway that, although crossing the ultra-Orthodox neighborhoods, was serving many people outside their community.

The Bar-Ilan Road Case

The Bar-Ilan road is a major highway connecting the northern entrance to Jerusalem with its northern neighborhoods. The volume of traffic on the road on weekdays is very high. On weekends the volume of traffic is reduced to about 21–28 per cent of the weekday volume. Until the 1967 war, Bar-Ilan was a peripheral road passing by the ultra-Orthodox neighborhoods to their east. Following the 1967 war and the ensuing occupation of east Jerusalem by Israel, two processes occurred simultaneously: one, the ultra-Orthodox neighborhoods expanded to the west of the Bar-Ilan road and consequently Bar-Ilan turned into a central road crossing the ultra-Orthodox neighborhoods. Second, new neighborhoods were built in the northern part of Jerusalem, transforming the Bar-Ilan road into an important highway connecting both the city center and the northern entrance to the city with its northern neighborhoods.

The first demonstrations by the ultra-Orthodox over the closure of the Bar-Ilan road took place in 1988, but the issue only gathered momentum following a visit to Jerusalem of the Satmar Rabbi in June 1994, which involved a one-time closing of the road on the Sabbath. This event, in addition to the substantial increase in ultra-Orthodox power at the municipal level following the 1993 municipal elections, raised the expectations of the ultra-Orthodox that the road would be closed on the Sabbath. Demonstrations over the Bar-Ilan road became a frequent event. Secular activists who fiercely opposed the closing of the road organized counter-demonstrations and the road turned into a battlefield, with violent clashes between the demonstrators. As a result of these violent clashes, at the end of 1994 the mayor of Jerusalem appointed a municipal commission, chaired by Elazar Shtrum (the 'Shtrum Commission'), to look into the issue of closing the Bar-Ilan road, as well as other roads in the ultra-Orthodox neighborhoods, on the Sabbath. In its report, the Shtrum Commission recommended that the Bar-Ilan road be closed three times during the Sabbath, once on Friday and twice on Saturday, each time for several hours during prayer times. The recommendation was perceived as a compromise between the desire of the ultra-Orthodox to create a public sphere that fit their way of life on the one hand, and the transportation needs of the secular residents of Jerusalem on the other hand.[14] The Shtrum Commission's recommendations were not adopted by the city of Jerusalem due to the objection of the Chief Inspector of the Traffic Bureau, who asserted that under no circumstances can central highways, such as the Bar-Ilan road, be closed to traffic for any period of time.

In 1996, following elections to the Parliament, the Minister of Transportation from the secular Labor party stepped down and was replaced by a religious member of parliament from the National Religious party. The new Minister supported the closing of the Bar-Ilan road and instructed the Chief Inspector to reconsider his decision, taking into account the depth of offense to feelings suffered by the ultra-Orthodox residents of the neighborhoods bordering on the Bar-Ilan road. After reconsideration, the Chief Inspector reversed his decision and approved the closing of the Bar-Ilan road on the Sabbath during the time of prayers, as recommended by the Shtrum Commission.

Following the new decision of the Chief Inspector, four petitions were filed with the Supreme Court. Three of the petitions requested that the Court overrule the ministerial direction and order that the road remain open at all times. The fourth petition, filed by the Association for the Protection of the Rights of Orthodox and Ultra-Orthodox People, requested the Court to order the closing of the road during the entire Sabbath.

The Supreme Court, hoping that a compromise could be reached, asked the Minister of Transportation to appoint yet another commission to study the matter of traffic arrangements in Jerusalem in general and the Bar-Ilan road in particular. In the letter of appointment, the Supreme Court instructed the commission that its recommendations should reflect the social agreement among different segments of the population and be based on tolerance and long term understanding of the demographic reality of Jerusalem. The ministerial commission, chaired by Zvi Tzameret (the 'Tzameret Commission'), was appointed in August 1996 and after nine weeks of deliberations it recommended adoption of the Shtrum Commission's report on the vague condition that mobility arrangements for the secular public would be guaranteed under the existing status quo. These recommendations did not satisfy any of the parties and the Supreme Court was forced to render its decision.

The Legal Framework

The legal basis for the *Bar-Ilan Road* case is Section 70 of the Traffic Ordinance,[15] authorizing the Minister of Transportation to regulate the vehicular use of roads. Under this authority the Minister issued Traffic Regulations[16] which established two legal entities and delegated to them the power to regulate traffic both locally and nationally. The Central Traffic Authority, chaired by the Chief Inspector of the Traffic Bureau in the Ministry of Transportation, is responsible for regulating traffic nationwide. Local Traffic Authorities are defined as individuals or entities authorized by the Chief Inspector of the Traffic Bureau to regulate traffic in a certain jurisdiction assigned to them by the Chief Inspector. In an official proclamation of 1970 concerning the appointment of Local Traffic Authorities,[17] the Chief Inspector designated local governments as Local Traffic Authorities within their jurisdictions. The Local Traffic Authority in the *Bar-Ilan Road* case was the city of Jerusalem.

The Traffic Regulations authorize the Central Traffic Authority to amend, abridge or overrule any decision concerning traffic arrangements made by a Local Traffic Authority, or to retract the power to regulate traffic delegated to the Local Traffic Authority altogether. The Minister of Transportation exercised its authority and seized the power to regulate traffic in the Bar-Ilan road. The authority of the Minister of Transportation to seize powers delegated to local authorities, like any other administrative authority, must be reasonably exercised. The reasonableness of the ministerial decision to assert its powers and close the Bar-Ilan road was challenged by the petitioners.

Formally, the Supreme Court ruled in favor of the three petitions seeking to overrule the ministerial direction, vacated the decision to close the Bar-Ilan road during Sabbath prayers and remanded the issue to the Minister of Transportation. The majority of the Supreme Court did not, however, find the core of the ministerial decision to close the road during Sabbath prayers unreasonable. The Justices were divided on this issue four to three. The majority ruled that the ministerial decision was, in principle, reasonable thus approving of the closing of the Bar-Ilan road on the condition that accommodation be provided for the secular minority living within the ultra-Orthodox neighborhoods. The dissent was of the opinion that the ministerial order to close the road was inherently unreasonable and that the road should remain open at all times.

Doctrinal Analysis

The majority's opinion The majority relied on constitutional law and the balancing of rights to resolve the case. Chief Justice Aharon Barak, delivering the opinion of the Court, described two sets of constitutional rights competing for priority. One was the right of ultra-Orthodox individuals not to be offended by cars driving through their neighborhoods on the Sabbath, and the other was the drivers' right to freedom of movement on public roads. After stating, in passing, that as a matter of administrative law religious considerations are relevant and can be taken into account by governmental authorities in regulating traffic, the Chief Justice turned to the issue of how to balance the competing rights.

The Chief Justice stated that neither religious feelings nor freedom of movement are absolute values. Both are relative rights that must be weighed and balanced against each other. The right of individuals not to have their religious feelings offended is derived from the democratic nature of Israeli society founded on pluralism and consideration of the feelings of every individual. 'A democratic society that protects the life, body and property of its individuals should protect also their feelings and soul.'[18] Israel, as a Jewish state, continued the Chief Justice, should be very sensitive to the religious feelings of its citizens, all the more so when these religious feelings are connected to the Sabbath, which is a fundamental value of Judaism. On the other hand, freedom of movement is also a fundamental right. In a democratic society individuals have the right to move freely and with minimal constraints. Thus, concluded the Chief Justice, the Supreme Court could only condone the abridgment of the freedom of movement when the offense to religious feelings was very severe and the freedom of movement was only minimally impaired.

After setting forth the constitutional framework, the Chief Justice identified three groups of right holders that had interests at stake in the closing of the Bar-Ilan road: one, individual drivers whose freedom of movement would be impaired since the closing of the Bar-Ilan road would require them to take longer alternative roads. Second, secular individuals who lived in the ultra-Orthodox neighborhoods whose freedom of movement would be impaired because the closing of the road would prevent them from getting to their homes. Third, ultra-Orthodox individuals who lived in the neighborhoods bordering the Bar-Ilan road whose religious feelings would be offended by the traffic on the Sabbath.

With respect to the balancing of the rights of the drivers and the ultra-Orthodox, the Chief Justice concluded that the right of the ultra-Orthodox prevailed. The Court found the offense to the feelings of ultra-Orthodox individuals who live in the neighborhoods bordering the Bar-Ilan road to be very serious. The Chief Justice explained that for observant Jews the Sabbath is very sacred, and therefore the nature of the offense was severe and the number of people whose feelings were offended was very high. On the other hand, the drivers' freedom of movement was minimally impaired because the closing of the street was limited to the time of the prayers, which lasted only a few hours, and there were alternative roads that extended the driving time by only a couple of minutes.

The Chief Justice reached a different result when balancing the right to freedom of movement of the secular inhabitants of the ultra-Orthodox neighborhoods against the right of the ultra-Orthodox not to have their feelings offended. The Court found that the harm to the freedom of movement of the secular inhabitants was very serious. They could not get to or from their homes by car when the Bar-Ilan road was closed, and, unlike the drivers, they did not have alternative routes. While admitting that he did not know how many secular individuals resided in the ultra-Orthodox neighborhoods, the Chief Justice insisted that this had no relevance, since even if their number was very few their freedom of movement could not be so significantly abridged.

Therefore, the Court vacated the Minister's decision and remanded it to the Minister of Transportation for reconsideration, with an instruction to take into account the freedom of movement of the secular inhabitants of the ultra-Orthodox neighborhoods. The Supreme Court left the Minister of Transportation the option of reissuing the order to close the Bar-Ilan road once accommodation for the secular inhabitants was provided. And indeed this was the course of action the Minister pursued. The Minister issued new regulations and the Bar-Ilan road was eventually closed to traffic on the Sabbath.

The dissent In contrast to the majority, the dissenting Justices did not believe that the Minister of Transportation was allowed to take into account the religious feelings of the ultra-Orthodox when making the decision to close the Bar-Ilan road, and therefore his decision was void. The dissenting Justices asserted, as a principle of both administrative and constitutional law, that governmental authorities can exercise their discretion only within the framework of the governing law. Religious principles are not legally binding unless explicitly enacted as law. Therefore, religious considerations cannot be taken into account by administrative authorities without explicit legislative authorization and the Traffic Ordinance contained no such authorization. The Traffic Ordinance was designed to regulate traffic not to advance religion or protect religious feelings. The role of the Minister of Transportation, as the public's trustee, was to regulate traffic for the benefit of all Israeli citizens. In certain cases, the dissent conceded, when regulating traffic on secondary roads, central and local authorities are allowed to take into consideration the well being of the local community even without explicit legislative authorization. Major highways, however, are part of the 'public sphere' and as such they are the property of the public. Only explicit legislation can take away from the public that which belongs to it by law. Absent such legislative authorization, the Minister of Transportation was not allowed to take into account the religious feelings of the ultra-Orthodox in its decision to restrict the public's use of the Bar-Ilan road. Therefore, concluded the dissent, the Minister's decision was null and void.

Ideological Analysis: Competing Conceptions of Space

An analysis of the opinions reveals not only a doctrinal disagreement between the majority and the dissent, but also an ideological one. This section examines the philosophical premises underlying the majority and dissenting opinions and the different conceptions of political space implicit in them.

The majority: A liberal conception of space The majority's opinion was premised on a strong liberal ideology. Liberalism as a structure of ideas 'posits a sharp distinction between the institutions of the state and those of civil society and argues that the state is obliged to remain impartial toward the institutions of civil society, treating each citizen solely as an individual' (Ford, 1997, p.1419). Liberal ideology lacks an independent normative conception of social groups as intermediate entities between the individual and the state, reducing all social groups to mere aggregations of individuals (Young, 1990). On this account, community is a product of individual acts of voluntary associations, an outcome of individuals who have consented to join in a group (Schragger, 2001). Group autonomy is perceived as an instrument of individual autonomy. Intermediate entities such as communities get recognition only to the extent that they conform to the individual/state dualism (Calhoun, 1995).

Informed by a strong liberal conviction, the majority did not recognize the ultra-Orthodox community as an independent entity, but saw only an aggregate of ultra-Orthodox individuals. The whole (the ultra-Orthodox community) is the sum of its parts (the ultra-Orthodox individuals). This is evident from the way the majority framed the legal question as a conflict between the drivers' right to freedom of movement and the right of the ultra-Orthodox not to have their religious feelings offended. Offense to feelings is, by definition, a psychological phenomenon: 'the creation of unwanted feelings such as sadness, frustration, insult and anger in the individual' (Statman, 1998, p.136). As such, offense to feelings, indeed feelings in general, pertains to the realm of the individual, even if suffered by a large number of individuals. 'A democratic society', the Chief Justice asserted, 'is a society that takes into account the feelings of each and every individual. Democratic values give expression to the personal-emotional feelings of the individual and his dignity as a human being.'[19]

The majority made an analogy between the ultra-Orthodox and the drivers. Both are aggregates of abstract individuals. The fact that the ultra-Orthodox are part of a socially and geographically defined community, while the drivers are indeed an aggregate of random individuals who happen to take a common route, escaped the majority. The majority's frame of reference—liberal ideology—with its hostility toward intermediate entities between the state and the individual (Frug, 1980) prevented the majority from recognizing the ultra-Orthodox as a community. For the majority, the only identity deserving of recognition was that of the individual citizen (Ford, 1997).

This is the reason that the secular inhabitants of the ultra-Orthodox neighborhoods were given such a prominent position in the majority's opinion, ultimately tipping the scales against the Minister's decision to close the road. As reflected in the concurring opinion of Justice Matza:

> Indeed, no data as to the size of this population [the secular inhabitants of the ultra-Orthodox neighborhoods] was provided. However, in my eyes it has no importance. For the purpose of this decision I am willing to assume that the overwhelming majority of the residents of these neighborhoods are ultra-Orthodox who desire that the Bar-Ilan road be closed on the Sabbath, and that the secular inhabitants (including Sabbath observers whose secular relatives and friends come to visit them on the Sabbath) make up only a small minority. The balance of interests still requires that a reasonable solution for the secular inhabitants be found before a decision to close the road is made.[20]

Inherent to liberal ideology is the principle that 'each individual is free to choose her own life plan consistently with the equal liberty of all other individuals to do the same' (Trakman & Gatien, 1999, p.5). If the life plan of some individuals conflict with those of others, the life plans are weighed one against the other stripped of any larger social or geographical settings. In other words, if the only significant social unit is the individual, there is no legal or moral basis to prefer the life plan of one individual to that of another based on communal-territorial belonging.

This philosophical standpoint is characterized also by an inability to recognize intermediate local spaces between the state's 'public sphere' and the individual's 'private sphere'. Hostility towards intermediate entities also includes hostility toward the local spaces in which such social groups are clustered. This 'deficiency' was observed by Boaventura de Sousa Santos who claimed that 'the nation-state has been the most central time-space of law for the last two hundred years... However, its centrality only became possible because the other two time-spaces, the local and the transnational, were formally declared non-existent by the hegemonic liberal political theory' (Santos, 1995, p.111).

The dissent: A multicultural conception of space The dissent is informed by an ideology that, for lack of a better term, I will call weak multiculturalism. It is, in this case, a more sophisticated version of liberalism that adopts some elements of communitarianism. Multiculturalism is a political theory that recognizes the importance of affiliation, both chosen and hereditary, of individuals to social groups, while at the same time attempting to avoid the fallacies of communitarianism. According to the communitarian account, describing a community as a voluntary association of individuals is too thin a characterization of human experience. Communitarianism challenges the liberal conception of the individual by arguing that it does not give sufficient attention to communities as constitutive of the identity of individuals. Instead it argues that the self is defined, to a large extent, by the social context. The individual is always operating 'within the discursive forms of a community that engages its members in an integrated view of their place in the cosmos, their history, their culture, and the meaning of personal experiences' (Mandelbaum, 1996, p.86). We are, at least partly, defined by our communities, their history, traditions, their goals and interests (Handler, 1994). Therefore, much more emphasis should be put on community and strong group solidarity. According to Michael Sandel, a prominent communitarian scholar, '"community" and "participation" may describe a form of life in which the members find themselves commonly situated "to begin with", their commonality consisting less in the relationship they have entered than in the attachment they have found' (Sandel, 1982, pp.151–152).

Communitarianism, however, is often criticized for serving as 'little more than foil to liberal individualism' (Ford, 1997, p.1421). The notion of community is left, for the most part, undefined. Communitarians provide only a general account of that which constitutes a community (Trakman & Gatien, 1999). As a result, it runs into trouble whenever the definition of community is itself in dispute (Ford, 1997). Communitarianism also lacks a meaningful response to the problem of unequal power relations. It conflates the issues of power and the quality of participation by arguing that, since the self is defined by the social context, the process of dialogue itself is empowering (Handler, 1994). As a result, communitarianism is often accused of being utopian and unattainable (Ford, 1997).

Multiculturalism is an attempt to remedy the shortcomings of both liberalism and communitarianism by combining elements of both:

> Multiculturalism asserts that society consists of a plurality of social groups, each of which deserves equal recognition from the state. Because the various social groups may have incommensurable norms, the state must remain neutral toward these groups. But the groups should be free to act on their particular norms within the boundaries of the group institution and without interference from the outside or the state. This articulation of multiculturalism is liberal in the sense that it requires a value-neutral state. When a liberal speaks of 'individual' freedom and autonomy, the multiculturalist substitutes 'groups'. But it is communitarian in

> the sense that, within the subgroup, the multiculturalist asserts strong solidarity and common values that take precedence over individualism (Ford, 1997, p.1423).

Multiculturalism comes in two versions—weak and strong. The strong version of multiculturalism calls for a fundamental shift in the understanding of citizenship. Cultural communities are to be granted strong, formal, legal standing that would permit them to govern their members according to their views and customs. The weak version of multiculturalism offers a more complex vision of differentiated citizenship. According to the weak version, the challenge of multiculturalism is to find a balance between the needs and interests of three entities: the group, the state and the individual. Proponents of weak multiculturalism, such as Will Kymlicka, Iris Young and Charles Taylor, seek to preserve the values and primacy of the individual while also recognizing the legitimacy of a group-based demand for accommodation (Shachar, 2000).

Informed by a weak multicultural ideology, the dissent in the *Bar-Ilan Road* case recognized the existence of an ultra-Orthodox community, defined both culturally and territorially, without abandoning the rights of the individual. Under the misleading title *The Private Sphere—for the Individual, The Public Sphere—for the Public*, Justice Heshin sketched a complex structure of political geography that undermined the liberal spatial dichotomy between the public and the private spheres. It is a fundamental principle, Heshin argued, that the private sphere belongs to the individual and the public sphere belongs to the public. In both the private and the public spheres the state would protect the freedom of religion and the freedom from religion of both the individual and the public. Thus far Heshin sounded very much like a classic liberal. The differences between Heshin's weak multiculturalism and traditional liberal ideology were revealed when Heshin defined the term 'private sphere'.

> An individual's house is undoubtedly his private sphere. A man's home is his castle. However, it seems that it is possible—indeed desirable—to extend the private sphere, for certain purposes, beyond the four walls and the yard. And so we do, with extra-caution. Here is an ultra-Orthodox neighborhood, and between the houses [there are] alleys, lanes and narrow side streets. Strangers do not use them. They serve the local residents. It would not be far-reaching to argue that, on the issue of desecrating the Sabbath in public, the space between the houses and their surroundings are also private sphere—the private sphere of the ultra-Orthodox.[21]

In the same vein, Heshin argued, it is desirable to expand the notion of the 'private sphere' of the community to include a whole village for the purpose of preventing the opening of a bar in a Muslim village. The Muslim village and the Orthodox neighborhood are both the 'extended private sphere' of the communities inhabiting them. Therefore, these communities have a right to shape them according to their view of the good, even if these views conflict with the views of the majority of the citizens in the country.

Notwithstanding this novel analytical framework, Justice Heshin concluded that the Bar-Ilan road must remain open to the public throughout the week, including on the

Sabbath. The Bar-Ilan road, Heshin argued, cannot be deemed part of the extended private sphere of the ultra-Orthodox community. It is a major highway serving many thousands of people every day and as such it belongs to the public and must remain open to the public at all times:

> The Bar-Ilan road is part of the public sphere not only in the formal sense—indeed the alleys between the houses are, formally, part of the public sphere as well—but also in the substantive sense of the concept... If the Bar-Ilan road is not public sphere—in the broader sense possible—I have no idea what a public sphere is ... The Bar-Ilan road does not belong to those living in its surroundings. The Bar-Ilan road is not a side street within an ultra-Orthodox neighborhood. The Bar-Ilan road is not a private sphere. The Bar-Ilan road is public sphere—in the true sense of the concept public sphere—and each individual has an equal stake in it; those who live by the road as well as those who do not.[22]

A similar theoretical framework also guided the other two dissenting opinions. Instead of the liberal dichotomy, conceptually classifying every political space as either part of the private or the public spheres, Justice Dorner suggested a continuum with the individual's house (the paradigmatic private sphere) at one pole, and a major highway (the prototypical public sphere) at the other. Within this framework, any claim of a community to a territory should be evaluated according to the specific type of territory involved and its place on the continuum. The closer the claimed territory is to the actual or metaphorical 'home', the stronger the community's claim to it and vice-versa. Indeed, wrote Justice Dorner:

> in both the individual and the family realms, every individual has a right to determine his or her own way of life... The Court acknowledged in its rulings similar rights in an extended realm—the realm of the community. Thus, for instance, administrative authorities are permitted to take into account in their decisions, even without legislative authorization, considerations designed to protect a community's way of life... On the other hand, in the extended realm, the public-societal one, the Court insisted on the principle that religious considerations can be considered only subject to an explicit authorization by the legislature.[23]

Dorner and Or concurred with Heshin's conclusion that, as a major highway, the Bar-Ilan road should be categorized as a 'public sphere' and thus should not be controlled by the local community. 'As much as we stretch the definition of the extended "private sphere"', concluded Justice Or:

> I do not believe that it is possible to include within this definition a major highway of the kind we deal with in our case. The road in the matter at hand is neither an alley in one of the neighborhoods, nor a side street connecting other streets within a neighborhood. It is a major highway serving a large population and many vehicles, even on weekends. Such a road is not the 'private' sphere of the local community, and the local community cannot dictate its use. It is the property of the entire public. It was designed for, and indeed should serve, the public at large. It is impossible to expropriate such a road, in whole or in part, from the public.[24]

Local governments, Justice Or argued, are the agents of local communities. While the regulation of traffic in the community's extended private sphere was delegated to local governments (Local Traffic Authorities) as agents of local communities, the regulation of traffic in the public sphere remained in the hands of the central government (Central Traffic Authority). In a somewhat tautological manner, Justice Or used this argument to prove his claim that the Bar-Ilan road was indeed part of the public sphere. The fact that the regulation of traffic in the Bar-Ilan road was taken away from the city of Jerusalem by the Minister of Transportation is, according to Justice Or, additional proof that the road was part of the public sphere and not the extended private sphere of the community.

To sum up, the dissent used a complex spatial model sensitive to the connection between social groups and the space they inhabit. A tabular form of the dissent's spatial model, applied to the matter at hand, might read as follows:

	Individual	**Community**
Home	Private Sphere	—
Secondary Road	Public Sphere	Extended Private Sphere
Major Road	Public Sphere	Public Sphere

The analytical framework constructed by the dissenting Justices provides an alternative justification for the outcome of the *Barukh* and the *Yeshurun Synagogue* cases discussed above. The decision in both cases to close roads on the Sabbath at the request of a local community was justified by the nature of the roads involved. In contrast to the Bar-Ilan highway, the roads in those cases were secondary roads, serving only a small number of vehicles, and therefore they could be classified as part of the extended private sphere of the local communities. As a result, the local communities were given the right to regulate the traffic on those roads consistent with their values.[25]

The paradox of the Bar-Ilan Road case Analysis of the ideological positions implicit in the opinions of the majority and the dissent reveals a striking paradox. The majority provided the ultra-Orthodox with the outcome they sought (namely the closing of the Bar-Ilan road during the Sabbath prayers), but refused to recognize them as a community. In other words, the majority converged with the ultra-Orthodox on the result, but its strong liberal conviction led the majority to hold an individualistic stance that is qualitatively different from the self-perception of the ultra-Orthodox as a distinct community with an autonomous jurisdiction. The dissent, on the other hand, although unwilling to furnish the ultra-Orthodox with the result they sought, expressed a political ideology closer to that of the ultra-Orthodox. Subscribing to a multicultural worldview, the dissent saw the ultra-Orthodox for what they consider themselves to be—a distinct community—and acknowledged their right to an autonomous communal sphere. The difference between the ultra-Orthodox and the dissenting Justices is, at least at first sight, simply over the question of where to draw the boundary lines of the communal sphere. They both are of the view that the ultra-Orthodox community should have an autonomous jurisdiction and disagree only as to what should be included in this jurisdiction. The dissent, then, appears to be ideologically closer to the ultra-Orthodox than the majority.

Intermediate conclusion: transparent liberalism and opaque multiculturalism This chapter examined two political theories—liberalism and multiculturalism—which were expressed in the *Bar-Ilan Road* case and the conceptions of space they give rise to. It concluded that liberalism, with its hostility toward entities intermediate between the state and the individual, does not recognize the existence of communities and therefore is also unable to conceptualize an autonomous jurisdiction for such communities. Instead, the liberal ideology dichotomizes space into either public or private spheres. Multiculturalism, on the other hand, acknowledges that society consists of a plurality of social groups, each of which deserves some recognition from the state. Thus, multiculturalism is more prone to accommodate the claim of territorial autonomy advanced by such social groups.

It is easy to notice the structural correlation between the opaque and transparent misconceptions of space, discussed in the previous chapters, and the politico-theoretical conceptions of space discussed in this chapter. The liberal conception of space is structurally related to the transparency misconception. A political theory that does not recognize intermediate entities will tend to refer to local jurisdictions as geographically defined delegates of centralized power without autonomous political significance.

> A view of political space as transparent necessarily devalues subcultural communities and community bonds, for most such communities are spatially defined and transmit their norms through small communal institutional and close personal interaction' (Ford, 1994, p.1889).

Correspondingly, the multicultural conception of space is homological to the opacity misconception. A political theory that sees the body-politic of the nation-state as an aggregation of social groups is more likely to treat local jurisdictions as autonomous entities that deserve deference because they are manifestations of local political communities, an unmediated democratic sovereignty (Ford, 1994).

Sacred Spaces—The Public/Private Distinction Deconstructed

Analyzing the political ideology of the ultra-Orthodox and its corresponding spatial conception is a somewhat confusing project. Although oftentimes using a set of terms familiar to a modernist audience, the meanings that are ascribed to these terms within the internal ultra-Orthodox discourse are quite different from those ascribed to them in modernist discourse.[26] In other words, familiar signifiers such as 'private sphere' and 'public sphere' signify one thing to a modernist audience and something quite different to members of the ultra-Orthodox community. For the modernist reader the public/private distinction is constitutive of her very perception of social reality. The distinction between the sphere of collective action and the sphere of individual self-regarding action is considered part of the natural order of things, thus setting 'fairly severe limits on the ways in which we can imagine the world and how we can change it' (Gordon, 1984, pp.109–110). Challenges to the public/private distinction within the modernist discourse usually take the shape of reclassification, namely classifying as 'public' (either entirely or for specific functions) entities hitherto considered as 'private' and vice-versa, remaining, in fact, within the structural framework of this powerful distinction. For the ultra-Orthodox, on the other hand, the public/private distinction, which they undoubtedly absorb from the 'outside', is constantly destabilized through religious and social practices to the point where it collapses altogether.

Two concepts illustrating the deconstruction of the public/private distinction will be analyzed. One is the concept of Eruv, exemplifying the privatization of the public sphere. The other is the concept of Parhesia, demonstrating the publicization of the private sphere. Taken together these two concepts blur the very distinction between the individual and the collective spheres and are indicative of the contingency of the public/private dichotomy as framed in the modernist mind.

An important caveat should be mentioned. My claim is not that the ultra-Orthodox have constructed a better and more liberating model than the one currently employed by the liberal-democratic state. If anything, the ultra-Orthodox model grants much less freedom to those subject to its rule. The liberating potential lies not in a specific model but in the chance to enlarge our scope of imagination and open up alternatives, thus setting us free from the conceptual chains imposed on us by the modernist discourse.

Privatizing Public Spaces: The Concept of Eruv

The concept of Eruv exemplifies the blurring of the public/private distinction through religious mechanisms. On the Sabbath, Jewish law forbids a range of practices, one of which is the carrying of objects beyond the home. The Eruv is a fictional Halakhic construct designed to cope with this injunction. Literally meaning 'to mingle', the Eruv creates a mingling of space, enabling a relaxation of the Sabbath carrying restriction. The physical manifestation of the Eruv is of almost no significance and involves using existing natural and artificial landmarks (such as the ocean, mountains or major highways), as well as the installation of a few poles joined by a thin high wire in places where the existing landscape cannot be used. The creation of an Eruv enables the transportation of objects to take place by symbolically transforming the space between private domains—which according to Jewish law is neither public nor private but classified as a third type of space called Carmelit—into a single private arena. By creating a bounded perimeter, which conceptually extends the private sphere, it provides a way for objects to be carried within a designated area (Cooper, 1998). Here the first conceptual confusion between the modernist and the ultra-Orthodox discourses comes into play. In Jewish law the notion of 'public sphere' bears a particularly narrow and restrictive interpretation. It applies only to a relatively small number of places, such as busy roads and parklands. Other spaces defined by the modernist discourse as 'public sphere' are classified in the Halakhic discourse as Carmelit, a domain that is neither public nor private but communal (Cooper, 1996). In fact, most places classified in the modernist discourse as 'public sphere' are, according to Jewish law, Carmelit. In this study Carmelit will be referred toas 'communal domain', distinguishing it from the liberal-modernist 'public sphere'.

Although originating in a technical Halakhic solution to Jewish law prohibition, the Eruv was transformed in modern times into a significant concept bearing important social functions. The sociological foundations of the recent revived interest in the Eruv was described by Davina Cooper (1998):

> Although eruvin go back many hundred of years, the modern movement gained force in the 1960s. Interest in eruvin has been linked to a growing Orthodoxy among young people, to the women's liberation movement, in particular, women's interest in participating more fully in religious life (eruvin allow them to push prams to synagogue or to place young children with families and friends while they attend); and more recently to demands for disability rights. Eruvin also function as a sign of increasing confidence among the Orthodox to communal structures and facilitate an improved quality of life (Cooper, 1998, p.125).

The single most important social function of the Eruv is the creation of a communal domain through a religious marking of the public sphere. The Eruv sets aside a portion of the public sphere and symbolically transforms it into a communal sphere. It allows the leaders of the religious community to demarcate the boundaries of their community and to develop 'a sense of community "which has a boundary… that comes into play on the Sabbath"' (Cooper, 1998, p.128). This function of the Eruv was observed in the United States, where the establishment of Eruv perimeters in Miami Beach, St. Louis and Baltimore, among other places, have been linked to the intensification of an Orthodox community identity. The Eruv evokes not only a sense of belonging among community members but sometimes also strong opposition among local residents who perceive the Eruv as territorializing and privatizing public spaces, thus transgressing the public/private distinction.[27]

The Eruv, however, has not only symbolic consequences but also material ones. The installation of an Eruv can potentially produce a demographic shift by encouraging Orthodox Jews to move into the area bounded by the Eruv, which, in turn, promotes the flight of non-Jews and non-Orthodox Jews from the area. This phenomenon has been noticed, for instance, in certain neighborhoods of the city of Baltimore (Cooper, 1998).

In their discussion of the ultra-Orthodox community of Jerusalem, Shilhav & Friedman (1985) acknowledged the socio-spatial importance of the Eruv as a mechanism of privatizing public space:

> The Eruv is a physical expression of the demarcation of the ultra-Orthodox territory... The territory included within the Eruv changes from time to time according to the spatial distribution of the ultra-Orthodox population and is published each year in the 'Kashrut Guide' of the Beith Din Tzedek of the ultra-Orthodox congregation. Although the Eruv bears almost no imprint on the landscape, it functions as an 'invisible boundary' well known to the members of the community, demarcating its territory and influencing its spatial behavior (Shilhav & Friedman, 1985, p.37).

According to Shihav & Friedman (1985), the Eruv, just like the closing of roads, marks the boundaries of the ultra-Orthodox ghetto. The extension of the boundaries of the Eruv over the years is indicative of the expansion process of the ultra-Orthodox ghetto.

The concept of Eruv is, however, still confined to the boundaries of the modernist discourse. While indeed blurring the public/private distinction, it seems to echo, at least to a certain extent, the multicultural conception of space discussed earlier. The following subsection discusses the concept of Parhesia that is even more problematic within a modernist discourse.

Publicizing Private Spaces: The Ethos of Parhesia

Parhesia is a key concept to understanding the socio-spatial ideology of the ultra-Orthodox community. It epitomizes a rejection of the principle of individual freedom and autonomy, on which the modernist discourse is premised. This modernist tenet is spatially expressed in the notion of the 'private sphere', a space in which the individual is free to pursue her particular conception of the good. 'Within her private sphere, the individual is free to decide upon the nature and content of her *good*. This includes deciding for herself how she will live her life, what she will pursue and deem as worthwhile, and how she will exercise her rights in attaining those ends' (Trakman & Gatien, 1985, p.4). This is also true for the weak version of the multicultural ideology employed by the dissent in the *Bar-Ilan Road* case. The dissenting Justices did not seek to replace the private sphere with a communal sphere (or an extended private sphere), but added the latter as an intermediate layer between the traditional liberal private and public spheres. The extended private sphere the dissent envisioned is, if fact, a reflection of the liberal private sphere on a communal level. It is a space in which the community, instead of the individual, is free to pursue its conception of the good. The community's extended private sphere extends, however, only to spaces considered in the liberal tradition as the public sphere, without encroaching on the freedom of individuals in their own private spheres.

The ultra-Orthodox, on the other hand, totally reject such a conceptualization of the private sphere. In their worldview, there is no place for a space in which the individual is autonomous and free to pursue his own conception of the good, independent from that of the community. The concept of Parhesia is the ultra-Orthodox substitute for the liberal public/private divide. It replaces the logic of territoriality, inherent, if sometimes only implicitly, to the public/private distinction, with the logic of communal solidarity. It signifies the lack of distinction between the interest of the individual and that of the community as a whole. Some scholars consider the concept of Parhesia as a key to understanding the internal logic of the ultra-Orthodox. 'Everything' wrote Amnon Levi (1988), 'occurs in the public sphere, in front of everybody, in Parhesia. The latter is a key word. It appears also in Huizinga as characterizing the medieval society. Undoubtedly, the relationship between what is considered the public sphere and what is called the private sphere is different in the ultra-Orthodox community and in the secular society' (Levi, 1988, p.13).

Parhesia, translated as 'in public' or 'publicly', whose antonym is 'secretly' or 'in private', means acting in public not in a spatial sense but in a communal sense, namely in the presence of other members of the community. The notion of Parhesia challenges the public/private divide because the classification of the space in which the action is carried out is of no importance. The only significant criterion is the presence of other community members. Thus, if a deed is done at home (the quintessential 'private sphere') but in the presence of other people—it was done publicly or in Parhesia. Similarly, if the same deed is done in the middle of a busy street (the 'public sphere') but nobody was there to watch it—it was not done in Parhesia.

The consequences of the public or private character of the act are quite significant. The desecration of the Sabbath, for instance, entails different repercussions if done in private or in public (in Parhesia). The desecration of the Sabbath in Parhesia is considered a much graver sin, punished by the expulsion of the sinner from the Jewish collective. Sagi & Zohar (2000) explain this apparent oddity by pointing to the harm done to the community by the very publicity of the act. 'Since the Sabbath is such an important and fundamental tenet of the collective's belief, its desecration severely harms the collective. The grievousness of the sin is derived from the degree of the harm felt by the collective as a result of the sinner's act. The Rabbis observed that the collective is harmed only when the desecration of the Sabbath was done in Parhesia' (Sagi & Zohar, 2000, p.17). The severity of the harm done to the community by the desecration of the Sabbath in Parhesia was stressed by ultra-Orthodox speakers throughout the various stages of the Sabbath Battles. In 1950, Rabbi Sha'ag, a Member of Parliament representing one of the ultra-Orthodox parties, said in the Knesset in response to the complaints against the ultra-Orthodox for rioting on the Sabbath and stoning vehicles crossing their neighborhoods: 'Whoever desecrates the Sabbath in Parhesia must be made aware that he is piercing the heart of the observant Jew as though with a sword.'[28] Similarly, almost half a century later, the ultra-Orthodox members of the Tzameret Commission stressed in their dissent the importance of preventing the desecration of the Sabbath in Parhesia: 'It is allowed', they wrote, 'indeed it is an obligation, to demonstrate in order not to lose the public domain and the Sabbath, the desecration of which in Parhesia is unbearable.'[29]

The notion of Parhesia, indeed the very idea that the severity of the sin is measured by criteria external to the sin itself such as the degree of harm to the collective, is very far from the Protestant ethos that emphasizes 'individual faith as the bedrock of religious integrity' (Boyarin, 1997, p.1542). The Protestant faith and individualism, Boyarin (1997) reminded us, facilitated the separation of the public sphere from the more autonomous private sphere.

For the ultra-Orthodox the fundamental modernist distinction between the psychological harm to an individual's feelings and the sociological harm to the collective, which lies at the foundations of the private/public distinction, does not exist. This is so because they lack the distinction between the interest of the individual and that of the community. In this respect, the similarity of the ultra-Orthodox community, governed by the ethos of Parhesia, to medieval society is striking. Gerald Frug (1980), eager to rehabilitate local power, has explored the legal status of the medieval city. His historical study revealed a society based on complete identification between the individual and the social group:

> The medieval town was not an artificial entity separate from its inhabitants; it was a group of people seeking protection against outsiders for the interest of the group as a whole... They achieved a freedom from outside control that was made possible by, and that allowed to be enforced, a strong sense of community within the town. It should be emphasized that the medieval town established the rights of a group that could not be distinguished from the rights of the individuals within the group. The status of the individual merchant was defined by the rights of the group to which he belonged, namely the medieval town (Frug, 1980, pp.1083–1084).

Frug (1980) concluded his discussion by stressing that in the medieval town the idea of the autonomy of the town and of its citizens merged. There was absent the distinctions that we recognize as fundamental between personal property rights and town sovereignty rights, between the town as a collection of individuals and the town as a collective whole. This is also true for the ultra-Orthodox community. The identification of the individual members with the collective is absolute. The absence of formal legal status for their collective increases the need to secure the volatile boundaries of the community and protect it against outsiders. The boundaries are created, enacted and protected through a multitude of socio-religious practices such as the Eruv, and social cohesiveness within these boundaries is maintained by the ethos of Parhesia, which is constitutive of the ultra-Orthodox community. As Friedman (1991) commented: 'the ultra-Orthodox ghetto is not only a residential neighborhood. It is first and foremost a framework in which the ultra-Orthodox culture can be expressed in Parhesia' (Friedman, 1991, p.122). Taken together the concepts we have explored, as well as other concepts we did not examine, are constitutive of an alternative political model that we shall call, after the ultra-Orthodox, the 'sacred community'.

The 'Sacred Community': An Alternative Conception of Political Space

In his article Decentering Decentralization, Gerald Frug (1993) stressed that the reason decentralization of political power to cities is undesirable in contemporary America is that 'the traditional account attributes to localities the power of self-assertion associated in our liberal culture with an autonomous individual. It presents localities as being able to do whatever they want: they can act in their own self-interest, cooperate with others on their own terms, and cause harm to those who disagree with them' (Frug, 1993, p.254). In other words, the traditional account ascribes to cities a centered sense of self. Gerald Frug's article is an attempt to imagine alternative subjectivities for local governments. Using postmodern theories and their critique of the centered subject, he seeks to replace the city's centered sense of self with alternative theories of the subject—the situated subject and the postmodern subject—that will make decentralization of power to cities desirable. In this section I accept the challenge put forward by Frug to 'help reframe local government law not by offering classic policy proposals… but by encouraging others… to generate their own ideas about how to revise the current entitlements of local government' (Frug, 1993, p.273). I use the internal structure of the sacred community, governed by the ethos of Parhesia, as an example of the situated subject, which provides an alternative model for current local government law.

Instead of a collective modeled on the centered subject, namely a collection of autonomous individuals who are allowed to act selfishly as if they had no neighbors, the sacred community offers a collective based on intersubjectivity or, what amounts to the same thing, a 'situated self' (Frug, 1993). The situated self is a self that is formed through the relationship with others. It is, in Charles Taylor's words, the recognition that 'our identity is always partly defined in conversation with others or through the common understanding which underlies that practices of our society' (Taylor, 1985, p.209). Intersubjectivity breaks the conceptual wall between the self and the other transforming 'self government' into a collective, instead of an individual, activity (Michelman, 1986).

The sacred community, based on intersubjectivity, challenges the distinction between the 'Self' and the 'Other' inherent in the liberal discourse. It also necessarily does away with the liberal conception of space that reifies borders between the 'Self' and the 'Other', a prime example of which is the boundary between private and public, the home and the street. This spatial reification can be and, as shown by Gerald Frug,

Richard Ford, Richard Briffault and others, is indeed translated at the local government level into the rigid and impenetrable boundaries between city and suburb, center and periphery, going all the way up to reify the borders between nation-states.

At the local government level the city/suburb distinction, as conceived in the popular consciousness, echoes the public/private divide. 'The suburb', asserted Richard Ford, 'is generally presented as a private and personal place for intimate associations, the formation of identity, and the transmission of cherished ideals and family values' (Ford, 1996, p.1178). The city, on the other hand, is projected in the popular culture as the instrumental and impersonal space, the market place driven by the laws of supply and demand, a hostile and alienated environment, the meeting place for strangers. In short, the city is the public space. These are not innocent popular metaphors. They are reflected in local land use planning, designed to preserve these values and attributes. In the suburb planning is used as a vehicle to preserve a private community style environment, while in the city 'land use planning is employed to facilitate the insertion of the environment into the stream of commerce, rather than to preserve a unique way of life' (Ford, 1996, p.1178). To sum up, the imagined metropolitan geography that corresponds to the sharp split between city and suburb encourages a view of local jurisdictional borders and the legal attributes that accompany them as natural and inevitable.

The sacred community offers an alternative model of space. It abandons the reified boundaries between public and private and replaces them with concepts of communal solidarity. If a community member harms another member by an action taken in her own private sphere, she is still held accountable. The rationale behind this socio-political regime is that what matters is not the reified space in which an action is carried out, but the effect of the act on other community members. This abstract idea, taken out of its immediate context and applied to other examples of self/other distinction, such as the city/suburb divide, offers a radically different point of view that might help produce a fundamental reform in local government law. It enables us to envision a relationship between city and suburbs that overcomes reified territorial boundaries and is based on solidarity that emerges from recognition of interdependency. A legal regime built on the recognition of the inextricable entanglement between city and suburb and an acknowledgment of the mutually constitutive nature of municipalities is bound to foster a sense of responsibility that is inherent to the consciousness of the situated subject (Frug, 1993). Solidarity and interdependency between city and suburb based on the ethos of Parhesia can be achieved by, for instance, implementing Richard Ford's suggestion to centralize the collection of tax revenue and redistribute it among localities on a need basis. 'In this way, localities would cease to view themselves as fiscally autonomous units competing for lucrative residents, business, and land uses, and instead see that the prosperity of each depends on the prosperity of the whole' (Ford, 1996, p.1188). Or alternatively by implementing the proposal of Richard Briffault (2000) to establish, in addition to the existing local governments, regional governments and vest in them the power to make land use and development policies for the region as a whole.

At the same time the claim of the ultra-Orthodox community to social and spatial separatism from Israeli society reminds us of the need to allow, as much as possible, local communities to control their own communal sphere according to their conception of the good. How do we reconcile the demands for both regional responsibility and local autonomy? It surely is not easy, but we will try to find a workable solution through reform of the current local government regime in the last chapter of this book.

Conclusion: Elusive Spaces

This chapter analyzed two political theories—liberalism and multiculturalism—and examined their spatial implications through an analysis of a Supreme Court decision involving a major highway in Jerusalem intersecting ultra-Orthodox neighborhoods. It concluded that underneath a conspicuous doctrinal disagreement among the Supreme Court Justices lies a more covert philosophical disagreement concerning the need to recognize the territorial autonomy of discrete communities. The majority, guided by a liberal conviction, was unwilling to reserve a distinct place for cultural communities, while the dissent, inspired by a multicultural ideology, recognized the existence of a communal sphere between the classic private and public spheres. Lastly, the chapter explored an alternative conception of political space that eliminates the public/private distinction and replaces it with communal solidarity.

Notes

1 *Haredim* is the term the ultra-Orthodox as well as Israeli society at large use to refer to the ultra-Orthodox community. The literal meaning of the Hebrew word Haredi is 'trembler' or 'fearful' originating in the verse 'Hear the words of the Lord, ye that tremble at his word' (Isaiah 66:5). I will use the terms 'Haredi' and 'ultra-Orthodox' interchangeably throughout this chapter.

2 Der Yid, June 15, 1983.

3 For an explanation of the concept of Eruv see below.

4 Groups of Haredi vigilantes that roam the streets of the ultra-Orthodox ghetto beating up women who do not conform to the strict dress code dictated by the Halakhic requirement for a high-level of modesty.

5 The ultra-Orthodox ghetto is an exception to Richard Ford's argument that due to technological advancements which have produced what some have called 'space-time compression' rendering physical distances less significant, communities are no longer dependent on physical proximity (Ford, 1997). Ford's argument applies to some types of communities, especially racial and ethnic ones, but it does not apply to 'nomos' communities of the kind described in this chapter.

6 From 51,615 in 1972, constituting 22.4 per cent of the Jewish population of Jerusalem, the

ultra-Orthodox community grew to 128,000 in 1995, making up 31 per cent of the Jewish population of Jerusalem. The growth rate of the ultra-Orthodox community is 3.3 per cent per year (Hoshen, 1983).

7 For the purpose of this study I examined four major newspapers representing different ultra-Orthodox groups: *Ha-Mahane Ha-Haredi* (the Belz Hasidic Court), *Yated Ne'eman* (the Lithuanian), *Ha-Modi'a* (the Gur Hasidic Court), and *Yom Ha-Shishi* (a general ultra-Orthodox newspaper that does not represent a specific group, but is operated by professional ultra-Orthodox journalists as a profitable business) in the time period between June 1996 and May 1997.

8 Sociologist Menachem Friedman, a prominent scholar of the ultra-Orthodox in Israel, reached a similar conclusion. After discussing the deep rifts and rivalries among the ultra-Orthodox groups he concluded:

'Notwithstanding the above discussion, the ultra-Orthodox community is still one community in the consciousness of its members. We should not jump to the conclusion that tomorrow this society might dissolve. The shared historic consciousness that produced the ultra-Orthodox community on the background of the crisis of the traditional east-European society in the mid-nineteenth century, the recognition in the value of Torah studies, and the necessity to defend, almost at all cost, the society of scholars, are sufficient to maintain, despite everything, a shared ultra-Orthodox identity as against the Israeli society' (Friedman, 1991, p.161).

9 A different but related struggle of the Haredim is the struggle to maintain a 'Jewish' character for the public sphere of the State of Israel in general, not only in their own neighborhoods. These struggles are conceptually distinct and, in most cases, can be easily distinguished. While the battle over their own public space is conducted through violent demonstrations and evokes strong emotions within the ultra-Orthodox, the struggle over the character of the Jewish State occurs mostly in the closed chambers of the parliament, through political lobbying and legislative initiatives. This distinction, however, becomes increasingly unstable as we get geographically closer to the ultra-Orthodox neighborhoods. The opening of movie theaters and other places of entertainment in Tel-Aviv, a city in which the presence of ultra-Orthodox is negligible, never evoked serious protest from the ultra-Orthodox community, but the opening of such places of entertainment in Jerusalem was the subject of heated, sometimes violent, debates. The story narrated here about the 'Sabbath Battles', as they are commonly called, includes some events that might be classified as struggles over the public sphere of the Jewish State, but are important to the unfolding of the story of the struggle over ultra-Orthodox communal spaces.

10 5 D.K. 2509 (August 8, 1950).

11 H.C. 174/62, *The League for the Prevention of Religious Coercion v. City Council of Jerusalem*, 16 P.D. 2665.

12 H.C. 531/77, *Barukh v. Traffic Inspector of the Tel-Aviv and Central Districts*, 32(2) P.D. 160.

13 H.C. 5016/96, 5025/96, 5090/96, 5434/96, *Lior Horev v. Minister of Transportation* (Jerusalem, 1997).

14 Report of the Commission for Investigation of Traffic Arrangements on the Sabbath and Jewish Holidays in Jerusalem (Jerusalem, September 1995).

15 Traffic Ordinance [New version], 1961, 7 L.S.I. 173.

16 Traffic Regulations, 1961, 1128 K.T. 1425.

17 1970 Yalkut Pirsumim 2281.

18 *Horev v. Minister of Transportation*, p.37.

19 *Horev v. Minister of Transportation*, p.37.

20 *Horev v. Minister of Transportation*, p.152 (Matza J. dissenting).

21 Id. pp.126–127 (Heshin J. dissenting). The majority rejected, as expected, such a conceptualization of the private sphere by arguing: 'A neighborhood's side streets are part of the "public sphere", and should not be regarded as the "private sphere" of its residents'. Id. p.151.

22 Id. p.129 (Heshin J. dissenting).

23 Id. p.158 (Dorner J. dissenting).

24 Id. p.87 (Or J. dissenting).

25 Id. pp.122–123 (Heshin J. dissenting).

26 By using the term 'modernist discourse' I refer to both the traditional liberal and the multicultural perspectives discussed in this chapter.

27 Davina Cooper describes a heated controversy engendered by attempts to install an Eruv in the borough of Barnet, suburban northwest London. Evoked by the puzzle how is it that 'a few poles joined by a thin, high wire' generated a fierce objection among local residents, Cooper's discussion concludes that objectors fought so intensely because in their view space was a finite container and the control of space a zero sum game. The symbolic privatization of space by the Orthodox community necessarily alienates it from the rest of society. Cooper ties this conception of space with the public/private distinction that constitutes the modernist-liberal perception of social reality (Cooper, 1996; Cooper, 1998).

28 4 D.K. 794 (2.14.50).

29 Tzameret Commission Report, p.4.

Chapter 5

Spaces of Identity: Zionist Ideology and the Social Production of Political Space

In the previous chapters we have explored three instances of the production and representation of political space in contemporary Israel. The first chapter examined the Arab-Jews using education law as a prism, the second chapter discussed the Bedouin in the context of urban planning and land use regulation, and the third chapter examined the ultra-Orthodox community through the lens of traffic management. These case studies revealed that, for the most part, political space assumed a very different role in legal analysis for each of the three social groups and that in each of these cases disparate conceptions of space organized legal analysis. In the case of the Arab-Jews, political space completely disappeared from legal analysis. It was misconceived as transparent; lacking any political significance or consequences of its own. In the Bedouin's case, the opposite was true. Space was resurrected in order to reify and justify a political community and to ground its boundaries in a political space that was seen as opaque, thus having a natural and prepolitical meaning. In the case of the ultra-Orthodox, political geography played an ambiguous and indeterminate role. The legal discourse oscillated between the spatial misconceptions of transparency and opacity, revealing the ambivalence of the Supreme Court as to the nature of the ultra-Orthodox community and its territory.

There is, to be sure, no self-conscious conception of space within legal thought. 'Space is implicitly understood to be the inert context in which, or the deadened material over which, legal disputes take place' (Ford, 1994, p.1857). It is precisely for this reason that in order to unearth the conceptions of space governing a society, the origins, development and demarcation of space (namely the characteristics that distinguish one political space from another) must be carefully studied and analyzed. This task was carried out in the previous three chapters. It is now time to tie all this together. This chapter is an attempt to understand the unifying logic behind the place of space in legal analysis by situating it within a broader political, historical and sociological context. It stresses the important role played by Zionist ideology and the ethnocratic regime it engendered in the production of the Israeli politico-spatial map and its legal manifestation—the territorial jurisdiction. In other words, this chapter aims at a critical exploration of the way received ideas about space and place within the Zionist ideological paradigm have shaped, and continue to shape, legal common sense which, in turn, reproduces and reinforces such spatial notions.

After engaging, in the first part of this chapter, in a brief theoretical discussion of the social production of political space, the second part of this chapter lays out the foundations for understanding the mechanisms through which Israeli political spaces are produced. The third part of this chapter engages in a short normative analysis of the pros and cons of geographical integration/separation, the only two options currently available in both public policy and the popular imagination.

The Social Production of Space: A Theoretical Synopsis

In his seminal work *The Production of Space,* the French philosopher Henri Lefebvre (1991), the pioneering theoretician of social space, stressed the importance of studying space in the social context within which it is produced. Social space, he argued, is a social product; a set of (material) social practices and, as a result, each society offers up its own peculiar space as an object for analysis and overall theoretical explication. This, of course, does not mean that 'space' is mere ideology and that the line between various nations, cities and districts are not 'real'. These lines are indeed very real, 'but they are real because they are constantly being made real, by county assessors levying property tax, by police pounding the beat (and stopping at the city limits), by registrars of voters checking identification for proof of residence. Without these practices the lines would not "be real"' (Ford, 1999, p.856). The social nature of space is successfully hidden behind its apparent natural form. Spatiality is reduced to its physical objects and forms (Soja, 1989). The evolution of space is conceived of as resulting from 'natural' forces such as 'economies of scale and market forces, aggregated individual preferences, and physical space itself—topography and distance' (Ford, 1994, p. 1858). Lost from view, under such a formulation, 'are the deeper social origins of spatiality, its problematic production and reproduction, its contextualization of politics, power, and ideology' (Soja, 1989, p.123).

Therefore, in order to understand the conception(s) of space governing a society, we must first examine the history of that society, its politics and constituting ideologies. It is impossible, for instance, to understand the rise of territorial sovereignty as the primary mechanism of government without describing its social origins as an offshoot of European feudalism (Ford, 1999).[1] It is equally hard to grasp the emergence of spatial-legal institutions such as lex mercatoria, whose behavior is regulated by interstate contractual and regulatory agreements established by multi-national agencies, corporations and banks, without taking into account the transition from mercantilist capitalism to the current stage of supra-state legality created by transnational capital (Santos, 1987).

Conceptions of space not only differ among different societies, they are also subject to controversy within each society. As David Harvey (1996) argued, 'the public sense of … space is frequently contested from within the social order' (Harvey, 1996, p.224).

Different subnational groups produce qualitatively different conceptions of space which must be negotiated with other subnational groups. 'Class, gender, cultural, religious, and political differentiation in conceptions of ... space frequently become arenas of social conflict' (Harvey, 1996, p.225). These conflicts, in turn, often produce and reproduce new definitions of political space through processes of intra-social negotiation, subordination and negation.

Zionist Ideology and the Geographies of Power

Zionism—the Jewish national movement advocating a geographic homeland for the Jews—sought to transform the Jewish people from a passive object of the historical process into an acting subject by establishing an independent nation-state. Jewish nationalism, which since the late nineteenth century found its political expression in the Zionist movement, was stimulated by a sentiment of attachment of an imagined community to a 'remembered' homeland and modeled on modern European nationalism (Horowitz & Lissak, 1989). Modern national existence requires the confirmation of a solid link between a delimited space (the state) and a people with an undivided culture and history (the nation) that together produce the modern nation-state. In other words, whereas the state is a political-territorial construct, the nation is based essentially on an ethnic sense of belonging to a distinctive cultural community. The modern state refers to a set of autonomous and abstract institutions within a given territory, while the modern nation refers to a sense of historic community associated with a unique 'homeland' (Smith, 1981). The political existence of modern states is predicated on their control over the access to a bounded territory, and over who has the right to live there (Handelman & Shamgar-Handelman, 1997). Similarly, the nation, although not primarily a political construct, does possess a vital territorial element. It is this element that links a cultural group, as defined by its unique heritage and its psychological sense of solidarity and destiny, to the world of politics. Where nations and states completely coincide, territoriality poses no problem. But where they do not, state and nation are liable to come into conflict over the extent, shape and control of a specific territory (Smith, 1981). Particular tensions arise in situations, such as that of the Jewish state, in which 'places that have been imagined at a distance become lived spaces' (Gupta & Ferguson, 1997, p.40).

It is by now self evident that a central component of the creation of communal, and especially modern national, identities is the setting off of the Other as the antithesis of the Self (Levine, 1999). Cultural anthropologist Claude Levi-Strauss (1997) suggested in his book *Tristes Tropiques* that throughout human history two prototypical strategies were deployed whenever the need rose to cope with the otherness of the Other: the anthropoemic strategy, and the anthropophagic strategy. The anthropoemic strategy consists of 'spitting out' or 'vomiting' the Other, which is seen as incurably alien. The extreme variants of the emic strategy are incarceration, deportation and, in extreme cases, murder of the Other. More refined and subtle forms of this strategy are separation, urban ghettos, discriminatory access to spaces and selective barriers to the use of space (Bauman, 2000). The anthropophagic strategy, on the other hand, consists of the 'disalienation' of the alien substance in the other; ingesting, so to speak, the foreign bodies and spirits so that they are made identical with the ingesting body. The phagic strategy has also taken a wide range of forms from cannibalism to enforced assimilation (Bauman, 2000). In other words, if the emic strategy is aimed at the exile or annihilation of the other, the phagic strategy is aimed at the suspension or the annihilation of his otherness.

In his book *Liquid Modernity* sociologist Zygmunt Bauman (2000) tied Levi-Strauss's anthropological insight to a theory of space. Levi-Strauss's dichotomy, he argued, is applicable to contemporary public spaces, namely spaces in which one is likely to meet strangers. These spaces are either 'interdictory spaces' designed to discourage strangers –an architectural rendition of the emic strategy—or 'consumer spaces' that deploy the phagic strategy by giving people the comforting feeling of belonging to a community. Both spaces, concluded Bauman (2000), respond in a different way to the same challenge—the task of coping with the likelihood of interacting with strangers.

Modern Israel's conceptual vision of space—a privileged connection between physical space and linguistic discourse—evolved through a dialectic interaction between the Zionist Self and its various Others.[2] The distinctiveness of these Others is predicated on the seemingly unproblematic assumption that Others occupy 'naturally' discontinuous spaces (Gupta & Ferguson, 1997). What follows is a description of the way racially, ethnically and religiously identified spaces were produced, and are still being reproduced, through positioning the Others of Zionism—primarily Arab nationals, but also Arab-Jews and Orthodox Jews, as the antithesis of the Self—the modern European Jew.

Arabs: The Nation vs. The State

The ideological origins of territorial indeterminacy The Jewish state has been characterized since its inception by territorial indeterminacy that stems from a non-congruence of territory, citizenship and national-ethnic identity. 'Most Jews live outside the State of Israel, while within Israel there is a considerable non-Jewish minority of Palestinian Arabs. For the individual, this creates a problem of identity; for society, that of defining its boundaries' (Horowitz & Lissak, 1989, pp.2–3). But the origins of contemporary territorial indeterminacy lie, in fact, much deeper in early Zionist consciousness. The fundamental indeterminacy of the Zionist utopian space is the product of an oscillation between two contradictory, yet complementary, discourses within the Zionist meta-discourse: the functional-positivist discourse and the organic-cultural discourse. The functional-positivist discourse 'sees the Diaspora as a *problem* and the territory as a *solution*' (Eisenzweig, 1981, p.263). Within this discourse, the desired space is presented as being unspecified, empty and purely functional. It is a necessary refuge for the Jewish people but it need not be specifically Palestine. In fact, according to this discourse, the true Zionist revolution is not the Return to Zion. 'On the contrary, the real change brought by Zionism ... is the *detour* leading to Zion via Argentine, Uganda, the United States and other locales' (Eisenzweig, 1981, p.261). The only prerequisite of the functionalist discourse is that 'the new Israel will be erected—can only be erected—on a vacant site' (Eisenzweig, 1981, p.265).[3] The organic-cultural discourse, on the other hand, has its roots in the attempt of the east European stream within Zionism (*Hibbat Ziyyon*) to find a language that could express politically the desire for a specifically Jewish solution to the Jewish problem. It is at the heart of the Jewish culture, preserved in eastern Europe, that the western language of emancipation would find a territory in which to take root—namely Palestine/Eretz-Israel. 'There is a cosmic element in nationality', wrote a Russian Zionist who immigrated to Palestine in 1904, 'which is its basic ingredient. That cosmic element may best be described as the blending of the natural landscape of the Homeland [Palestine] with the spirit of the people inhabiting it [the Jews]' (Hertzberg, 1997, p.379).

At first sight, these two discourses with regard to the nature of the Zionist space seem to be incompatible. In fact, however, although territorial indeterminacy, which is embedded in the functionalist discourse, was rejected by the adherents of the organic discourse, it was still useful to them. The functionalist discourse clears the way for the organic one by 'naturalizing' the space and emptying the territory of all troublesome presence. 'By negatively qualifying the dreamed-of space in regard to Palestine, it also inevitably does this in regard to any possible Palestinians' (Eisenzweig, 1981, p.265). Emptied of all otherness, the Zionist space is necessarily seen as Self. In other words, if the functionalist discourse is centered on the denial of the Other, then the vision of the organic discourse persists in a reconstitution of the Self. 'In fact, it is almost at the same moment that positivist Zionism realizes most concretely the exclusion of the Other from the "wilderness" that is Palestine, that [the adherents of the organic discourse] articulate... the emergence of Self in the heart of this nature' (Eisenzweig, 1981, p.283). The tragedy of Zionism is that it is able to deploy itself only in a discursive space where all otherness is absent or neutralized. The Zionist Self can realize itself only if the Other is kept out of sight. The spatial disappearance of all otherness from the Zionist landscape is nicely exemplified in an early slogan referring to the return of the Jews to Zion/Palestine as 'a people without a land returning to a land without a people'.

The territorial indeterminacy, which originated in the oscillation between the functionalist (which can be also referred to as 'synthetic') and the organic discourses, characterizes the Jewish State to this day. In contemporary Israel it is most clearly illustrated in the double identification of the state as both Jewish and democratic. This duality invokes the tension between the synthetic language of the modern liberal-democratic state, which is founded on civic equality and territorial sovereignty (namely territoriality as the basis of citizenship), and the organic notion of the Jewish nation, which is anchored in cultural particularism and tribal sovereignty (namely genealogy as the basis of citizenship). The result is a direct conflict between the 'state' and the 'nation' over the extent, shape and control of the territory and its people (Smith, 1981).

Despite arguments to the contrary, in my opinion, this tension cannot be resolved on a conceptual-theoretical level. The state cannot adhere at one and the same time to both liberal-universal and Jewish-particular values. The tension can only be ameliorated on a pragmatic level in individual cases. Hence, the presence of individual Palestinians in the Jewish space can be tolerated as long as this presence does not invoke their affiliation with a Palestinian collective. This silver lining, which is admittedly very hard to sustain, separates Israeli tolerance toward individual Palestinians from hostility toward the Palestinian presence as a phenomenon (Rabinowitz, 1997).

The dialectical politics of Othering The discursive expulsion of the Other from the Zionist space and the construction of a Self in its stead, is, in itself, a dialectical practice. The Zionist Self 'vomits' the Arab Other from the body-politic, but at the same time it needs that Other in order to define the Self as its imaginary opposite. This dialectical dependency on the Other is tied to the origins of Zionism in modernity and the European Enlightenment. It is impossible to separate the Zionist ideology in general, and the Zionist treatment of space in particular, from the larger ideological and material discourses of European modernity (LeVine, 1999). The project of modernity conjures up many meanings and visions, only a few of which need to be discussed here. Modernity, wrote Marshall Berman (1988, p.15):

> is a mode of vital experience—experience of space and time, of the self and others, of life's possibilities and perils—that is shared by men and women all over the world today ... Modernity can be said to unite all mankind. But it is a paradoxical unity, a unity of disunity: it pours us all into a maelstrom of perpetual disintegration and renewal, of struggle and contradiction, of ambiguity and anguish. To be modern is to be part of a universe in which, as Marx said: 'all that is solid melts into air'.

Modernity represents a new and accelerated mode of existence, stemming from the emerging dynamics of the capitalist market that grew alongside of the development of universal, positivistic and technocratic science, morality and law, the only tools powerful enough for the growing European bourgeoisie to grasp and control a world in which change, rather than tradition, had become ubiquitous and in which the past had become a burden from which humans needed to be freed (Harvey, 1990; Giddens, 1971). The invocation of the modern necessarily evokes an archaic past against which it is defined. As Latour (1993) stressed: '[The] modern is ... doubly asymmetrical: it designates a break in the regular passage of time, and it designates a combat in which there are victors and vanquished ... Other cultures became premodern by contrast' (Latour, 1993, p.39). Indeed, the modernity of the modern is dependent upon and defined by the exclusion of its opposite—the pre-modern, the barbarian, the irrational.

In the European case, the Other against which the modern Self is defined is, to a large extent, the imagined Orient. Orientalism, as conceptualized by Edward Said (1979), is a 'style of thought based upon an ontological and epistemological distinction made between "the Orient" and (most of the time) "the Occident"' (Said, 1979, p.2). The Orientalist discourse represents, or more accurately imagines, the Orient as a fixed entity that is exotic, obscured, disorganized and irrational; and Oriental societies as primitive, static and despotic. The Occidental Self is portrayed as the opposite of the Orient. 'European culture gained in strength and identity by setting itself off against the Orient as a sort of surrogate and even underground self' (Said, 1979, p.3). This process was most powerfully experienced in the space of the colonial city, as described by Mitchell (1988):

> The identity of the modern city is created by what it keeps out. Its modernity is something contingent upon the exclusion of its own opposite. In order to determine itself as the place of order, reason, propriety, cleanliness, civilisation and power, it must represent outside itself what is irrational, disordered, dirty, libidinous, barbarian and cowed. The city requires this 'outside' in order to present itself, in order to constitute its singular, uncorrupted identity... This dependence makes the outside, the Oriental, paradoxically an integral part of the modern city (Mitchell, 1988, p.165).

The Orient/Occident dichotomy is constitutive of the geographical imagination of Zionism. In the Zionist (and later Israeli) case, the Other can be identified more specifically as the Palestinian-Arabs—the indigenous inhabitants of Palestine. In order to maintain the barriers that keep the Arab-Other out of the Jewish space, it was essential to establish and sustain a system of spatial segregation that confines the Other to its own autonomous spaces, thus leaving the Jewish territories Other-free. This anthropoemic spatial strategy is justified, as was clearly demonstrated in the Bedouin case, by an appeal to the cultural otherness of the Other (that in fact constitutes its essence), thus rhetorically transforming forced segregation into a respect for difference. The dialectic dependence of the Self on the Other for self-definition was also illustrated in the case of the Bedouin: 'Nomadism, associated with chaos and rootlessness, is the perfect mirror image of modern law, which assumes and demands the ordering of populations within definite spatial and temporal boundaries... The basic sanction for nomadism is exclusion from the social realm and the positioning of the nomad on the side of nature' (Shamir, 1996, pp. 236–237). The result of these discursive mechanisms is that Zionism asserted its identity as a modern Western project by resisting the backward-looking and chaotic East.

The Bedouin, however, are only one example for a much larger institutional spatial policy of 'separate and unequal', targeting the entire Israeli-Arab minority. In 1960, an agreement between the Jewish National Fund (JNF)—a Zionist body controlled by world Jewry through the World Zionist Organization—and the State of Israel transferred administration and effective control of all JNF lands to the state, through its agent—the Israel Land Administration (ILA). Following the agreement, the ILA controlled over 93 per cent of Israel's land, of which the JNF owned only about one third. Nevertheless, the JNF was granted equal representation on the board of directors of the ILA and therefore has significant control over the allocation of all ILA-administered land (which is called 'Israel Land'). Most importantly, the JNF prohibited the selling or renting of Israel Land to non-Jews. As a result, the Arab citizens of Israel remain almost completely excluded from public land allocation and, as of 1995, they were allocated only approximately a quarter of one per cent of all public lands (Yiftachel & Kedar, 2000; Dalal, 2000).

Jewish spatial control is illustrated not only in ownership of land and discriminatory land allocation but also in various other spatial mechanisms. Despite the fact that Arab citizens make up more than 18 per cent of the Israeli citizenry, 97.5 per cent of Israel's sovereign territory is under Jewish municipal control (Yiftachel & Kedar, 2000). In addition, the highly centralized Israeli statutory planning system grants local governments only limited autonomy and discretion. Rural local governments (regional councils) have even less control over planning at the local level than do urban local governments. As a result, Arab local governments, which are overwhelmingly rural (in contrast to Jewish localities which are largely urban), have very little control over planning and land use regulation even within their municipal areas (Yiftachel, 1992).

From a Zionist to a post-Zionist conception of space? A recent decision, delivered by the Supreme Court in March 2000, seems at first sight to depart from the Zionist conception of racially identified spaces, and to open the door for future spatial integration between Jews and Arabs. In *Qaadan v. Israel Land Administration*[4] the State of Israel allocated land to the Jewish Agency, a quasi-governmental entity controlled by the World Zionist Organization, in order to establish a Jewish community settlement—Katzir—in the Galilee region, where Palestinian-Arabs constitute 75 per cent of the population. The Qaadans, a Palestinian-Israeli family, attempted to acquire land in Katzir but were refused on the basis of their Arab nationality. Prior to the Supreme Court's decision in the *Qaadan* case, it was the state's declared policy that Arabs could not acquire land in settlements administered by the Jewish Agency. In October 1995, the Association for Civil Rights in Israel (ACRI), which represented the Qaadan family, filed a petition with the Supreme Court arguing that the decision not to allocate land to the Qaadans in Katzir based on their 'Arabness' constitutes unlawful discrimination. Chief Justice Aharon Barak, joined by Justices Zamir, Or, and Heshin, ruled that when allocating state lands the state is not allowed to discriminate on the basis of religion or nationality. Therefore, the state could not have allocated state land to the Jewish Agency for the establishment of Katzir on the basis of discrimination between Jews and non-Jews. The Court refrained, however, from granting the petitioners the relief they requested, which was an order that their application to reside in Katzir be determined on its merits without taking into account their nationality. Instead, the Court merely instructed the state to consider whether on the basis of the equality principle, and taking into consideration factors concerning the Jewish Agency and the settlers in the place, it could allow the petitioners to establish a home in the confines of the Katzir community settlement.

Despite some reservations with regard to the operative part of the decision, the Supreme Court's decision was hailed by the liberal-left camp as a groundbreaking decision. Kedar (2000) praised the decision as representing 'an essential shift in the Court's position' that 'signals a transition from a collective and "settling" into more individualistic and "liberal" jurisprudence' (Kedar, 2000, p.3). Kedar admitted that the decision is not 'a categorical transformation', but nevertheless argues that it is 'a big leap, from the "Jewish/Zionist" toward the "Democratic/equality" pole within the "Jewish-Democratic State" legal tenet' (Kedar, 2000, p.3). In a like manner, sociologist Ronen Shamir called the decision the first post-Zionist decision written by the Supreme Court. 'This is a post-Zionist decision', explained Shamir, 'because it severs the equation between the concept "state lands" and the concept "nation lands"' (Shamir, 2000b, p.27). But is this true? Does the *Qaadan* case indeed represent an epistemological break in the Supreme Court's ideology? In order to answer this question we have to analyze carefully the rationale leading the Supreme Court to its decision.

We begin with the Court's description of the Qaadan family: 'The petitioners are a couple with two daughters. They are Arabs who currently live in an Arab settlement. They sought—and still do—to reside in a place in which the quality of life is different from the one they currently experience.'[5] According to the Court, the Qaadans are a middle class family—husband, wife, and two children, who seek to raise their quality of life. The (largely middle class) audience of the Supreme Court can easily identify with them. The Arabness of the Qaadans is presented as incidental, almost insignificant. They are depicted as individuals, abstracted of any collective identity. Not a word is mentioned about the long history of discrimination against the Palestinian-Arabs in Israel. Despite the fact that the case centered on the issue of discrimination against the Arabs as a distinct racial-national group, the Court focused on the individual level. The Court was very keen on repudiating history. Chief Justice Barak, delivering the opinion of the Court, repeatedly emphasizes that the decision 'looks forward into the future', as if wanting to tell us that 'there is great fear in looking to the past' (Shamir, 2000b, p.27).

There were some obstacles in the Supreme Court's efforts to ignore history. The respondents—the Jewish Agency, the Israeli Farmers' Association and the Katzir community settlement—insisted on introducing the Zionist-nationalist narrative, with all its structural discriminatory implications, into the case. They argued that the settlement was a link within a chain of Lookout Settlements (Mitzpim) designed to retain the landscape of Israel for the Jewish people. The existence of Katzir, they added, was predicated on the need to settle Jews throughout the country, and in particular in rural areas in which the Jewish presence was sparse, to disperse the Jewish population and to increase Israel's security. The presence of Arabs in Jewish settlements might cause the Jewish residents to flee, thus transforming settlements designed for Jews into Arab settlements. The Qaadans contributed their fair share of disturbances by introducing into the case the negative social effects that the policies advocated by the respondents had on perpetuating the social gap between powerful and weak populations in Israel (Ziv, 2000).

The Supreme Court rejected all the attempts to draw it into the ideological conflict between the 'state' and the 'nation'. The respondents' arguments, the Court stressed, raised difficult and complicated issues. Nevertheless, there was no need to cope with these issues in the framework of the petition. 'The petition does not involve the totality of Jewish settlement in all its aspects; the petition does not deal with the various actions of the Jewish Agency. This petition is limited to a specific community settlement, whose establishment does not invoke all these issues.' 'The respondents', continued the Court, 'do not dispute the right of the petitioners to live ... in a neighborhood built by the Housing Ministry ... why, then, would their living in the community settlement, two kilometers from this neighborhood, justify a violation of the equality principle.' This paragraph is striking for both the individualizing and the trivializing effects that it has on the dispute. The Supreme Court did not for a moment question the Zionist tenet of Jewish settlement or the justification of the segregationist practices of the Jewish Agency, but in fact praised them.[6] The Court insisted, however, that in this case these issues did not arise. It was just this one settlement, not the policy of Judaizing the Galilee; it was only this individual middle-class family, not the entire Israeli-Arab population. History evaporated and the national conflict between the Jewish and the Arab peoples was transformed rhetorically into a trivial question of two kilometers.

Having erased history, the Supreme Court allowed the Qaadans to enter the Jewish space as abstract individuals. They had a private biography, but no tribal history (Feldman, 1995). Penetration of the Arab-Other into the Jewish space was tolerated within the Zionist paradigm as long as the Arab was stripped of any group identity. This is the pragmatic compromise between the liberal-democratic (synthetic) and the Jewish-nationalist (organic) components of the Jewish State described above.

The decision, then, despite its positive outcome, is a far cry from being post-Zionist, rather it follows mainstream Zionist thinking. It enables the Court to have its cake and eat it too; to hold on to the Zionist tenets, while at the same time paying lip-service to the liberal-democratic values and to the liberal and civil-rights organizations from which the Court draws its status as well as its moral and political support. Indeed, 'the decision is very suitable for liberal Jewish thought on equal rights for individuals, and less so for inter-group thought on the layered structure of oppression existing in Israel' (Shamir, 2000b, p.30). It is not beyond the realm of possibility, however, that *Qaadan v. Israel Land Administration* may open the door for a future post-Zionist jurisprudence, in the same way that *Brown v. Board of Education*,[7] despite its cautious style, furthered the United State's civil rights movement.

Arab-Jews: The Unfulfilled Promise of Assimilation

Inspired by the utopian ethos of the 'ingathering of Exiles' and the 'melting pot', the official Zionist ideology with regard to Arab-Jews was, and still is, that of integration or, more accurately, assimilation. The Zionist claim is that it is an emancipatory movement for all Jews, no matter where they came from. In reality, however, Zionism has been primarily a liberation movement for European Jews and despite its claim to provide a homeland for the entire Jewish people that homeland was not offered to all with the same largess (Shohat, 1988). The gap between ideology and reality, vision and praxis, explains the conspicuous reality of ethnically-based spatial segregation on the one hand and its complete erasure from legal texts on the other.

The Jewish victims of Zionism The Zionist repudiation of the Orient left its mark on the attitude of the Zionist establishment toward the Arab-Jews. The Arab-Jew represents a problematic entity for European Zionism. Although Zionist ideology collapses the Arab-Jews and the European Jews into the single category of 'one people', the Arab-Jews' Oriental 'difference' threatens the European ideal-ego which fantasizes Israel as a prolongation of Europe 'in' the Middle East, but not 'of' it. In a Zionist Orientalist system, built on a clear dichotomy between East and West, an Arab-Jewish identity represents a real conundrum. The Arab-Jews are ambiguous and indeterminate creatures that undermine the ordering of the world: they are genealogically and religiously Jewish and therefore part of the Zionist Self, but they are culturally Arab and therefore also part of the Other. The 'cultural difference' of the Arab-Jew was particularly disturbing to secular Zionism, whose claim to represent a single Jewish people was premised not on a common religious background but on common nationality. The strong cultural, linguistic and historical links that Arab-Jews shared with the Arab world, which was in many respects much stronger than those they shared with the European-Jewish Zionists, threatened the conception of a homogeneous nation akin to those on which the European nationalist movements were based (Shohat, 1988).

In anthropological terms the Arab-Jew invoked among the Zionists the fear of the 'stranger', who conjured up the horror of ambivalence. 'Ambivalence', wrote Zygmunt Bauman, 'the possibility of assigning an object… to more than one category, is a language-specific disorder: a failure of the naming (segregating) function that language is meant to perform' (Bauman, 1991, p.1). According to Bauman, the world is divided into friends and enemies, inside and outside, that stand in opposition to one another. The friend/enemy opposition organizes reality into neat categories. It sets apart truth from falsity, good from bad, beauty from ugliness, and right from wrong. It dispels doubt and makes the world readable and thereby instructive. The 'stranger' is set against this stable antagonism. The stranger is an anomaly. He is neither a friend nor a foe. The stranger occupies an indeterminate space, neither inside nor outside. He stands for the fallibility of order, the vulnerability of the inside.

> The stranger undermines the spatial ordering of the world—the fought-after co-ordination between moral and topographical closeness, the staying together of friends and the remoteness of enemies. The stranger disturbs the resonance between physical and psychical distance: he is physically close while remaining spiritually remote. He brings into the inner circle of proximity the kind of difference and otherness that are anticipated and tolerated only at a

> distance—where they can be either dismissed as irrelevant or repelled as hostile (Bauman, 1991, p.60).

The Zionist ambivalence toward the Arab-Jewish 'stranger' is apparent in many journalistic, political and academic writings. David Ben-Gurion, the first Israeli Prime Minister, repeatedly expressed his contempt for the culture of the Arab-Jews: 'We do not want Israelis to become Arabs', he stressed. 'We are in duty bound to fight against the spirit of the Levant, which corrupts individuals and societies' (Smooha, 1979, p.88). And in an article entitled The Glory of Israel, Ben-Gurion lamented that 'the divine spirit left the Jews of the East and their role in the Jewish nation receded or disappeared completely' (Segev, 1986, p.156). Yet, on another occasion, Ben-Gurion insisted that 'even the immigrant from North Africa, who looks like a savage, who has never read a book in his life, not even a religious one, and doesn't even know how to say his prayers, either wittingly or unwittingly, has behind him a spiritual heritage of thousands of years' (Segev, 1986, p.156). Over the years many Israeli leaders repeated and reinforced this ambivalence toward the Arab-Jews and candid hostility toward Arab culture—the marker of their difference. Abba Eban, the former Israeli Foreign Minister, argued that 'the goal should be to infuse [the Arab-Jews] with a Western spirit, rather than allow them to drag us into the unnatural Orientalism' (Eban, 1957, p.76). 'One of the great apprehensions which afflicts us', he added, 'is the danger lest the predominance of immigrants of Oriental origin force Israel to equalize its cultural level with that of the neighboring world' (Smooha, 1979, p.44). Prime Minister Golda Meir also expressed her fear that Israel would fail in its mission to 'elevate these immigrants to a suitable level of civilization' (Smooha, 1979, pp.88–89). Academic discourse was quick to follow suit. In the early fifties, Israel's most celebrated intellectuals wrote essays addressing the 'ethnic problem'. Prof. Karl Frankenstein suggested that the Arab-Jewish immigrants could be compared to the primitive mind of children, the retarded, or the mentally disturbed (Segev, 1986). And Prof. Yossef Gross was of the opinion that the new immigrants from the backward Arab countries were suffering from 'mental regression' and 'a faulty development of the ego' (Segev, 1986, pp.157–158). The ambiguous and prejudicial view of the status of the Arab-Jews did not remain confined to the corridors of the Parliament and the academic ivory tower, but trickled down into all layers of society.

The Zionist immigration scheme was designed initially for European Jews only. The founding fathers of Zionism did not plan on enlisting Jews of Arab origin for their project. It was only after the failure of European Jewish immigration, in the post-Holocaust era, that the Zionist establishment decided that it had no choice but to bring in Arab-Jewish immigrants en masse (Shohat, 1988). Arab-Jewish immigration, described in the official historiography as a grand rescue mission performed by the Zionist establishment in order to save the Arab-Jews from the harsh rule of their Arab captors, was intended, in fact, to save Zionism from possible economic and political collapse. Throughout the 1950s, the heyday of Arab-Jewish immigration, Zionist officials continued to demonstrate ambivalence toward the mass immigration of Jews from the Arab countries. However, economic and demographic necessities—such as settling the periphery of the country with Jews, securing the borders and having laborers to work and soldiers to fight—did not leave them much choice (Shohat, 1988). Arab-Jewish settlements, which were primarily aimed at settling the peripheral territories of the new state (a policy called 'population dispersal'), created and reinforced an unequal social division of space between European-Jews and Arab-Jews. An unwritten pact between the state and the mostly European bourgeoisie left the urbanized and economically developed central region of the state to private capital, while the state's public housing projects, populated overwhelmingly by Arab-Jews, focused on the underdeveloped peripheral areas (Kallus & Law-Yone, 2000). These policies led to the concentration of many Arab-Jewish immigrants in the country's periphery and suburban areas, and thus served as an instrument of residential segregation by class and ethnicity (Gonen, 1995).

One nation under God? Israeli law, as illustrated in the first chapter of this book, is, and has always been, completely blind to the conspicuous reality of the social and spatial segregation of Arab-Jews. The legal system has been operating under the assumption that the Israeli Jewish population is not divided along ethnic lines. Without an acknowledgment that Israeli society is divided based on ethnic affiliation, there can be no ethnic segregation. Any segregation that exists is explained away as freely chosen by individuals, and alternative explanations are denounced as dangerous attempts to 'divide the nation' or to 'extract the ethnic genie out of the bottle'. The source of this oversight, I submit, is the ideological commitment of Zionism to the cultural assimilation of Arab-Jews; to changing their status from 'strangers' to 'friends'.

The inventory of reactions to the stubborn presence of strangers follows, according to Bauman (1991), 'the logical yet implausible strategy of separating again what the anomaly, pregnant with semantic ambiguity, blends; and that of removing the resistant residue out of sight—either physically or spiritually' (Bauman, 1991, pp.65–66). This can be done in one of two ways: (1) by forcing the stranger to leave; reestablishing order through bringing together personal and spatial estrangement, thus transforming the stranger into a foe, or (2) by assimilating the stranger; removing from him all foreign features, thus turning the stranger into a friend. These strategies are oftentimes implemented in the course of nation-building projects, which are a 'deliberate effort to construct an over-arching collective political identity based on belief in common culture, ethnic origin and homeland' (Yiftachel, 1998, p.34) in which a group attempts to 'draw the boundaries of the community of friends and chart the location of enemies' (Bauman, 1991, p.69).

In Israel nation-building efforts were characterized primarily by an attempt to construct the collective political identity of the 'new Israeli' through cleansing Oriental features from both the Jewish people and the Jewish space. While the Palestinian-Arabs were physically expelled from the Jewish space (yet allowed and even encouraged to foster their collective identity that mark their otherness), Arab-Jews were forced to repress their Arab identity and culture, which were consistently stigmatized as an evil to be uprooted. Zionism brought a painful binarism into the formerly peaceful Arab-Jewish identity. Arab-Jews were prodded to choose between anti-Zionist 'Arabness' and a pro-Zionist 'Jewishness', which for the first time were posed as antonyms (Shohat, 1988). 'Distinguishing the "evil" East (the Moslem Arab) from the "good" East (the Jewish Arab), Israel has taken upon itself to "cleanse" the Sephardim of their Arab-ness and redeem them from their "primal sin" of belonging to the Orient' (Shohat, 1988, pp.7–8). The melting pot ideology required the Arab-Jews to disassociate themselves from all idiosyncratic cultural elements and assimilate into the hegemonic Ashkenazi Western culture, thus fulfilling the utopian Zionist notion (intended initially to include only European Jews) of 'one people' reunited in its ancient homeland (Lissak, 1999). While European Jewish immigrants underwent a process of 'absorption' upon their arrival in Israel, the immigrants from the Muslim Arab countries were required to undergo a process of 'absorption through modernization', which included 'desocialization'—an erasure of their cultural heritage—and of 'resocialization'—assimilation to the Ashkenazi Western way of life (Shohat, 1988).[8]

Since having Arab characteristics led to rejection, many Arab-Jews internalized the Western perspective and tried very hard to assimilate into the Ashkenazi culture. Attempting to conform to European norms, Arab-Jews came to repudiate their own language and culture. Used to viewing themselves through the West's distorting mirror, Arab-Jews were eventually taught to see the Arabs (and as a corollary also their own culture) as Others (Shohat, 1988). The nation-building project was a success. The Zionist melting pot produced an overarching collective political identity based on a 'common' Western culture. The ethnic gap, indeed the very categorization of Jews into ethnic groups, was declared a thing of the past, and with it disappeared also the notion of ethnically identified spaces. Or did it?

Assimilation is an elusive project, fraught with inner contradictions. The liberal call to assimilate ideally sounds a death knell to stigma. The message of cultural assimilation amounts to a standing invitation to all and everybody to leave behind them their inferiority and attain the highest, worthiest and hence most coveted values. It offers not just hope but a clear plan for its realization (Bauman, 1991). On closer scrutiny, however, an inner contradiction is revealed that renders this offer as misleading as it is tempting. 'The offer of assimilation (assimilation is always a one-directional process) obliquely reaffirms what was to be proved—the superiority and the benevolence of the native rulers' (Bauman, 1991, p.70). Ethnic, religious and cultural strangers are all too often tempted to embrace the liberal vision of group emancipation through assimilation (erasing the collective stigma). They go out of their way to get rid of and to suppress everything that makes them distinct from the rightful members of the hegemonic community—and hope that a devoted emulation of hegemonic ways will render them indistinguishable from their hosts and therefore guarantee their classification as insiders entitled to the benefits that 'friends' routinely receive. But as hard as they may try, they never make it to the finish-line. When it seems within their grasp, a dagger of racism suddenly emerges from beneath the liberal cloak. 'What they mistook for a game of emancipation is in fact the game of domination' (Bauman, 1991, p.71). A 'conservative curse', argued Sander Gilman (1986), hangs over the liberal project: 'The more you are like me, the more I know the true value of my power, which you wish to share, and the more I am aware that you are but a shoddy counterfeit, an outsider' (Gilman, 1986, p.2). The stranger cannot cease to be a stranger. 'The best he can be is a former stranger, "a friend of approval" and permanently on trial, a person vigilantly watched and constantly under pressure to be someone else than he is, told to be ashamed of his guilt of not being what he ought to be' (Bauman, 1991, p.72). This is the fate of the Arab-Jews. As hard as they try to assimilate to the Ashkenazi-European ways, and rid themselves of all Oriental markers, they cannot cease to be strangers. The Israeli sociopolitical formation, at the same time that it claimed to embrace the Arab-Jews as equal, one with the Zionist Self, continually generated their structural inferiority and underdevelopment (Shohat, 1988).

To sum up, the disappearance of ethnically identified spaces from legal analysis, despite their persistence in reality, is a result of a gap between the Zionist promise and its non-fulfillment. As part of the Zionist nation-building project, Arab-Jewish spaces were discursively integrated into the larger space of the Jewish nation-state. Inspired by the Zionist discourse, the Supreme Court does not conceptualize space in ethnic terms. The only relevant political community is the Jewish nation, which represents 'one people' with a homogeneous culture. As a result, the only organic jurisdiction of this political community is the territorial boundaries of the nation-state. Any internal division within the nation-state is conceptualized as a bureaucratic convenience—a synthetic jurisdiction. The group defined by such synthetic jurisdictions has no moral relevance (Ford, 1999). As a result, ethnically identified spaces within the nation-state become politically insignificant.

The Zionist integrationist ideology indeed erased all signs of spatial segregation from the legal text, but not from the social reality underlying it. The law creates political geography even as legal doctrine denies its relevance. In reality, ethnic segregation is, as we have seen, the norm, with devastating social consequences. There is no need for deliberate segregationist policies, which indeed do not exist as a matter of law. The historical patterns of residential segregation (concealed as a 'population dispersal' policy) are perpetuated by both economic forces and individual prejudices. Ethnically identified spaces, reinforced by ethnically-neutral laws, both create and perpetuate ethnic segregation.

Ultra-Orthodox Jews: The Unredeemable Strangers

The relationship between Zionism and Judaism qua religion is dialectical and ambivalent. On the one hand, since its inception Zionism has been a secular ideology, which was bitterly opposed by the religious establishment (Prior, 1999). Zionism, and particularly western European Zionism, 'share[s] the Enlightenment belief that modernity is becoming progressively wiser than "tradition"' (Boyarin, 1994). Tradition, embodied in Jewish orthodoxy, was thought to be an impediment to the realization of the Zionist dream of a Jewish sovereign state. This is reflected in the writings of the founding fathers of Zionism, such as Theodore Herzl, Moshe Hess, Max Nordau, Eliezer Ben-Yehuda, and Leo Pinsker, who called for Jewish nationalism without religion. The pioneering Hebrew lexicographer, Eliezer Ben-Yehuda, for instance, argued that 'total liberation from the burden of Torah and the commandments [mitzvot] was a mandatory step in the struggle to revive the Hebrew language' (Luz, 1988, p.13). The Jewish religion, Ben-Yehuda insisted, was the source of the Jew's excessive spirituality that usurped the role of land, language and state—the three pillars of every people's national identity and life. The secular posture of Zionism was consistent with mainstream historical opinion to the effect that modern nationalism must be based on the secularization process.

On the other hand, Zionism feeds on the Jewish tradition, which is embedded in the Jewish religion. Nationalist movements, revolutionary as they may be, are always an attempt to revisit the past and reinterpret it in light of present national needs. Since religion is a foundational dimension of the history of many people, nationalist movements must deal with the religious dimension of its past in a creative and formative way (Avineri, 1998). Zionism, the national movement of the Jewish people, is no exception to this. Its symbols, constitutive texts and cultural institutions are all drawn from the reservoir of the Jewish religion. The Jewish Menorah, the Temple, and the Star of David became powerful symbols of the Jewish national renaissance. The Bible was redeemed as a historical text providing invaluable knowledge as to the history (and implicitly also the future) of the people of Israel. The Sabbath became the official day of rest and the Jewish holidays were instituted, with some secular interpretations, as the official holidays of the Jewish State (Avineri, 1998).[9]

The ultra-Orthodox present the Zionist establishment with a real challenge. The ultra-Orthodox oppose Zionism as a nationalist ideology and believe that the establishment of a Jewish State was contrary to the stricture that the Jewish people's redemption must be a divine rather than human act. They further believe that the establishment of a secular-liberal state in the Holy Land is heresy. As a result, not only are members of the ultra-Orthodox community not interested in assimilating into Israeli society, but they also view their own culture and way of life as an alternative to the Israeli secular-Zionist culture (Friedman, 1991). The ultra-Orthodox feel that they have succeeded where Zionism failed in establishing an ideal society that embodies the values of modesty, family stability, personal responsibility and mutual assistance, and 'many Israelis are prepared to accept this statement as true' (Friedman, 1991, p.ii). The ultra-Orthodox distinguish themselves from the rest of Israeli society in every way possible: they dress differently (in traditional east-European clothing), speak a different language (Yiddish instead of Hebrew), live in segregated neighborhoods, do not serve in the army and do not observe non-religious national holidays (such as Independence Day). On the other hand, they do participate in national politics, a platform from which they challenge the basic values and culture of the Israeli society as a whole and compete for its political and economic resources. It is no wonder, therefore, that 'many of the adherents of [the secular-Zionist] culture regard the ultra-Orthodox as a significant threat to its existence' (Friedman, 1991, pp.i–ii). The ultra-Orthodox undermine not only the secular way of life, but also the very legitimacy of the Zionist State. They challenge the belief in a 'natural' association of a culture (Israeli-Zionist culture), a people (the Jewish people) and a place (Israel), that lies at the foundations of Zionist nationalist thought (Gupta & Ferguson, 1997).

Some strangers, Bauman (1991) argued, are not just 'as-yet-unclassified' as enemies or friends, but are in principle 'unclassifiables'. These are the true hybrids that put into question the very distinction between the inside and the outside, the good and the bad. They unmask the artificiality of this division and stretch the temporary inconvenience of 'not knowing how to go on' into a terminal condition; a state of internal confusion. The ultra-Orthodox are a paradigmatic case of such unclassifiable strangers. They are a hybrid. They have elements of both the core Self (Jews of European origins), and of the complete Other (bitter enemies of Zionism). They cannot be assimilated, but as Jews of European origins neither can they be totally expelled from the body politic. They, therefore, cannot be redeemed from their status as strangers. They are destined to occupy a space of ambivalence and uncertainty which invokes an anxiety among the Zionist Self, 'an acute discomfort that we feel when we are unable to read the situation properly and to choose between alternative actions' (Bauman, 1991, p.1).

This state of ambiguity and uncertainty is reflected in, and in turn constructed by, the legal treatment of ultra-Orthodox spaces. The Supreme Court, as we have seen in the *Bar-Ilan Road* case, is divided on this issue. The Court's majority employed a liberal conception of space that includes the ultra-Orthodox within the Zionist Self, but ended up closing the road on the Sabbath thus reinforcing in reality the segregation of the ultra-Orthodox and their exclusion from the Zionist body-politic. The dissent, on the other hand, employed a multicultural conception of space that excludes the ultra-Orthodox from the Zionist Self, but ended up prohibiting the closure of the road, thus contributing to the notion of ultra-Orthodox inclusion within the Self. This paradoxical state is due to the ambiguous status of the ultra-Orthodox within the Zionist thinking as simultaneously both insiders and outsiders.

Intermediate Conclusion: The Segregated Spaces of Zionism

To sum up what we have seen thus far: legal analysis has treated political space in very different, and even contradictory ways, depending on the social group involved. The Supreme Court was unwilling to recognize Arab-Jewish spaces, and any existing ethnically homogeneous jurisdiction was treated as a synthetic jurisdiction bearing no moral or political significance. On the other hand, it treated Bedouin townships as organic jurisdictions that marked the boundaries of a distinct political community. Attempts to trespass on these organic jurisdictions were harshly suppressed by the Court. The territorial jurisdiction of the third social group—the ultra-Orthodox—did not receive unified and consistent treatment.

This disparate treatment of political geography reflects a deep tension in Israeli-Zionist political thought. Political spaces are produced through dialectical processes of interaction (negation, negotiation and subordination) between Zionism, as an institutional ideology, and its various Others. The Supreme Court, as part of the Zionist establishment, engages in a tacit nation-building effort. These efforts, however, take many different forms, depending on the social group involved. The desire to secure national citizenship propelled the Court to deny recognition to Arab-Jews as an ethnic subgroup, treating them instead as mere individuals. The same desire, however, propelled the Court to recognize the Arabs as a distinct subgroup, which justified their spatial expulsion from the body-politic. The ultra-Orthodox—as unredeemable strangers—received an inconsistent and ambivalent treatment by the Court, reflecting an inherent inability to determine whether they should be included in the nationalist project (and thus be denied subgroup status) or excluded from it (and thus be recognized as a distinct subgroup).

This conclusion is somewhat counterintuitive. What is commonly described by both the right and the left as a benevolent recognition of cultural difference that justifies, or even requires, some sort of geographic separatism is explained here as an attempt to deny the group a place in the body-politic. In other words, segregationist practices are rhetorically transformed into respect for cultural difference, which are spatially expressed in separate organic jurisdictions. On the other hand, denying a social group the status of subgroup and refusing to recognize its independent spatiality is explained here as stemming from the desire to include the group within the Zionist national project (which can be, as we have seen, no less oppressive).

Despite the differential treatment of political space, however, the result in all cases is similar. Regardless of the spatial mechanisms involved, all three social groups—Arab, Arab-Jews and the ultra-Orthodox—live respectively in racially, ethnically and religiously identified spaces. Arab segregation is due to explicit state policies coupled with strong sentiments of cultural and jurisdictional autonomy among members of the group. Arab-Jews have been segregated due to facially ethnic-neutral legal rules and institutions built on historical patterns of ethnic segregation. The ultra-Orthodox are spatially separate because of their strong subgroup solidarity and self-segregationist ideology.

Segregation, in fact, cuts much deeper. The social groups discussed are internally divided into different subgroups that live in separate jurisdictions. Thus, for instance, the Arab social group is further divided into Palestinians (Christians and Muslims), Bedouins, Druse and Circassians, who all live in different settlements. Arab-Jews are internally divided into different sub-groups according to their country of origin. And the ultra-Orthodox are fractured into Ashkenazim and Sepharadim, Lithuanians and Hasidim, as well as among the different Hasidic groups.

Cultural Communities and Jurisdictional Autonomy

The map of Israel is a mosaic of different settlements, each having a distinct ethnic or cultural identity. Even in the larger cities, the different neighborhoods consist of homogeneous groups of residents (Benvenisti, 1998, p.800).

Israel's segregated political spaces, supported as they are by public policy and legal rules, raise an important normative question: is living in racially, ethnically or religiously defined spaces necessarily a bad thing? Is geographical separatism an evil to be eradicated at all cost or is it a reflection of subgroup solidarity and therefore a good to be pursued? Or is it, alternatively, an imperfect or even wrong conceptualization altogether?

Geographic Separatism

Geographical separatism does not have the same political and economic impact on all social groups. Jurisdictional autonomy can cut both ways. It can protect the group's rights and guarantee its autonomy, but it can just as easily facilitate stereotyping and the targeting of an unpopular group. Experience teaches us that subordinated groups, such as African-Americans and Native Americans in the United States or Arabs in Israel, are likely to be adversely affected by segregation. Territorial identification provides such groups with no safe haven from outside influence and is often politically oppressive and economically disempowering. Segregation 'involves more than simply the relationship of individuals to other individuals; it also involves the relationship of groups of individuals to political influence and economic resources … Segregated minority communities have been historically impoverished and politically powerless' (Ford, 1994, p. 1844). Despite its idealistic association with 'territorial homeland', a sanctuary of cultural belonging which led many progressive scholars to articulate claims for social justice in terms of territorial separation, jurisdictional autonomy in fact helps promote a separate and unequal distribution of political influence and economic resources. As Ford (1999) concluded, 'in many cases people fought hard to establish [territorial jurisdictions] as minority enclaves. The hope was to create a safe place in which the minority group can flourish and enjoy autonomy. But "local autonomy" has not served historically subordinated groups well' (Ford, 1999, p.916).

Non-subordinated minority groups, on the other hand, are more likely to benefit from jurisdictional autonomy and, therefore, oftentimes seek geographical separatism. Without the politico-economic sword of Damocles hanging above their heads, these groups can freely enjoy the benefits of territorial autonomy, such as increased solidarity among the members of the group and effective participation in the political process, without suffering negative repercussions of segregation.

As a result, 'the ethics of provincialism'—the vision of cultural pluralism managed by geographic autonomy—as a political solution for cultural minority groups can be either liberating or oppressive depending, among other things, on the nature of the group. Equal treatment of jurisdictional subdivisions of subordinated minority groups and of non-subordinated groups might yield a totally different, sometimes opposite, political outcome. While the legal recognition of jurisdictional autonomy for the ultra-Orthodox resulted in community empowerment, similar 'recognition' in the Bedouin case resulted in political and economic disempowerment.[10] Unfortunately, most minority groups are, at least to a certain extent, subordinated and thus their loss from jurisdictional autonomy outweighs their gain.

Geographic Integration

Equally difficult problems arise if we attempt to impose spatial integration on the different subgroups that comprise Israeli society through the dissolution of jurisdictional boundaries. There are good arguments that support the claim that in some cases spatial desegregation is indeed warranted, especially when the subgroups share religious traditions, a common language and geographical landmarks and resources as, for example, Arab-Jews and European-Jews do. In other cases, however, spatial integration is uncalled for and if implemented might have a seriously damaging impact on minority groups. This is the situation when distinctions such as religion, language and geography have historically separated a subgroup from the dominant or ruling group (Ford, 1997), as Arabs in Israel are separated from the Jews. Should such minority groups, interested as they are in separate spheres in which to practice their own culture and religion, be denied such jurisdictional autonomy? Moreover, if we are to allow geographical 'exit' to some social groups, how can we deny it to others?

Overcoming Dichotomies: The Elusive Jurisprudence of Political Space

Democratic regimes constantly negotiate a contradiction between the need to accommodate and contain differences through the creation and protection of geographically defined ethnic/cultural enclaves on the one hand, and the need to avoid social fragmentation and inter-group antagonism and to maintain national unity through the dissolution of boundaries, on the other (Ford, 1997). The former evokes the Tocquevillian ideal of the local community, which is thought to enhance democratic participation through subgroup solidarity, while the latter is thought to increase subgroup integration and individual rights in the spirit of the Madisonian extended sphere of government. Since both desires are important, our goal should not be to choose one or the other, but rather to negotiate a more informed modus operandi that would mediate the tensions between the two desires. This negotiation can and should open up alternatives to the dichotomies between integration and segregation, togetherness and separateness, sameness and difference, which currently dominate both public policy and the popular imagination (Frug, 1999).

The reason that we object to segregated territorial jurisdictions is less because of the intent that lies behind their creation (which might be innocent and at times even noble) than because of their contemporary social meaning, as well as their political and economic consequences (Ford, 1997). Accordingly, the goal of legal reform should not be to eliminate residential segregation, a goal that is both impractical and normatively doubtful, but instead to alter its political and economic consequences. 'We must not forget', Ford (1994, p.1878) reminds us, 'that in order to reject segregation, we need not unreservedly accept integration. Indeed, especially for racial minorities, some degree of separatism may represent the best or only avenue to empowerment and fulfillment.' We should focus on formulating such a model that when cultural communities choose to live in autonomous jurisdictions, this will not disadvantage them politically, economically or otherwise. And, what amounts to the same thing, we have to make sure that attempts by the ruling majority to marginalize certain social groups by confining them to segregated localities, thus promoting a 'separate and unequal' distribution of political influence and economic resources, will not prevail.

We should seek, in other words, to amend the social and political meanings of space, rather than physical space itself. If space is a social product, as has been repeatedly argued, we should be able through a carefully thought-out legal reform to consciously transform the meaning and function of space without physically moving even one person from his place of residence. That is, we should be able to desegregate political spaces while leaving physical spaces intact. In order to be effective, the proposed model must challenge the mechanisms by which current political spaces are created and maintained, which, in turn, challenges one of the mechanisms by which racial and cultural hierarchies are perpetuated. Where jurisdictional boundaries under the current system intentionally divide society into racially, ethnically and religiously homogeneous groups, those boundaries should be conceptually altered to provide for an integrated political process.

Yet, although the reform does not call for a planned program of spatial integration, we can expect that the desegregation of political spaces would result in fewer racially and ethnically homogeneous spaces for two main reasons. First, since the political and economic benefits that dominant social groups reap from the current system of segregated political spaces would no longer exist, the incentive to maintain spaces would significantly weaken. Second, and more importantly, political space does not only reflect but also produces political and social identities. Territorial jurisdictions define the identity of the people that occupy them. Therefore, any change in the political significance of space is bound also to transform the identity of the cultural community itself (Ford, 1994).

Notes

1 Whereas early modern European sovereignty was either 'tribal sovereignty', which was based on a claim of right over people not a territory, or 'imperial sovereignty', which made a claim to control over the entire world, after the rise of feudalism the sovereign began to perceive itself as standing in the same relation to the soil as a baron to his estate (Ford, 1999).

2 'Zionism' should be understood, in this context, not as the historical socio-political movement, but as a distinct ideology which is embedded in contemporary Israeli institutions, among them the legal system, and fulfilled through a wide array of social practices.

3 The functionalist discourse is reflected in the works of west European Zionists such as Theodore Herzl and Leo Pinsker. Theodore Herzl: 'It is true that the Jewish State is conceived as a particularly modern structure on unspecified territory. But a state is formed, not by piece of land, but rather by a number of men united under sovereign rule' (Herzl, 1946, p.137); Leo Pinsker: 'We must, above all, not dream of resorting to ancient Judaea. We must not attach ourselves to the place where our political life was once violently interrupted and destroyed. The goal of our present endeavors must be not the "Holy Land", but a land of our own. We need nothing but a large piece of land for our poor brothers; a piece of land which shall remain our property, from which no foreign master can expel us' (Pinsker, 1997, p.194).

4 H.C. 6698/95, *Qaadan v. Israel Land Administration*, 54(1) P.D. 258.

5 *Qaadan v. Israel Land Administration*, ¶4.

6 'Of course, it is impossible to ignore the special status of the Jewish Agency in the State of Israel and the many credits owed to it in the development of the state and the fulfillment of its destiny as a Jewish state, in addition to its being a democratic state ... The Jewish Agency played a highly important role in the fulfillment of the Zionist vision, in the ingathering of the Exiles and the flourishing of the state. The Jewish Agency has not completed the role designed for it. It still serves as a "voluntary body", an emissary of the Jewish people in the development of the country as a Jewish and democratic state.' *Qaadan v. Israel Land Administration*, ¶36.

7 347 U.S. 483 (1954).

8 The Jewish landscape underwent similar processes of cleansing and adaptation to Western standards. Zionism has never had a clear physical image of the territory it occupied. It aspired to create a new landscape for a new society—a space suitable for the 'new Jew', but the exact shape of this landscape or the model according to which it was to be built was never contemplated. The existing landscape (the 'old' space) signified for the Zionists the backwardness and hostility of the Arab Other. It was the landscape of the indigenous, an Oriental space that was filled with the Middle Eastern culture of the enemy. The architecture of the public housing projects, designed during the 1950s, challenged the landscape, erasing from it any Oriental characteristics. Its western European expressions were violent enough to subdue the Arab landscape. The public housing projects, built in the state's periphery and populated by Arab-Jewish immigrants, promoted two complementary goals: the molding of the Oriental immigrants' identity into the form of the West, and the imprinting of the marks of the Jewish State's sovereignty on the previously Arab rural landscape; thus integrating the two projects of 'nation building' and 'state building' (Kallus & Law-Yone, 2000).

9 Zionist attempts to completely replace Judaism, by creating secular alternatives to religious institutions, have failed. One such attempt to create a national secular alternative to the Jewish religion is provided in the book *The Colonies of Law* by sociologist Ronen Shamir. Shamir

(2000a) tells the story of an abortive attempt by a group of Zionist jurists in the 1920s to establish a national-secular legal system—the Hebrew Law of Peace—that would operate independently of both British state law and traditional Jewish law. They ran a set of community based tribunals that were designed to employ relatively informal, yet 'new Hebrew' ways to solve disputes. The project was rejected by the ultra-Orthodox community that operated the Rabbinical courts under the auspices of the colonial government, as well as by religious Zionists and the Jewish legal profession and ceased to exist, in the mid-1930s.

10 This basic truth escapes the Supreme Court, as well as many commentators such as Benvenisti (1998) and Margalit & Halbertal (1994), who draw a parallel between the Bedouin-Arab and the ultra-Orthodox due to the basic fallacy of multiculturalism discussed in the previous chapter. Multiculturalism assumes that there are significant cultural differences that fracture society and define identifiable social groups, and that these cultural characteristics have moral weight for both the subgroup and the society as a whole. However, by describing vexing social problems in terms of 'cultural difference', multiculturalism underplays 'hard' material-economic and political concerns, replacing them with 'soft' symbolic, cultural and aesthetic concerns, which results in an inability to distinguish between subordinated and non-subordinated social groups.

Chapter 6

Toward a Reform of Local Government Law

This book is a socio-legal essay on the historical production of political spaces, not a study of Israeli local government law. Nevertheless, the role of local government law, as currently structured, in the reproduction of segregated spaces, and the potential it has, if thoughtfully reformed, to mend many of the shortcomings inherent in the current system of political space requires an initial exploration into local government law.

Local governments are significant to our study of political space because an important source of segregation, and of the isolation and oppression of minorities that accompany it, is the autonomous political subdivision that forms an ethnically, racially or religiously homogeneous jurisdiction (Ford, 1994). Jurisdictional boundaries do much more than separate territories; they also separate groups of people and produce political and social identities (Ford, 1999). This chapter demonstrates how contemporary local government law perpetuates the historically imposed patterns of ethnic and racial segregation. On the one hand, the law prevents localities from exerting any meaningful power; local governments have only those powers delegated to them by state law which were traditionally curtailed by judicial interpretation. On the other hand, local government law nourishes a privatized version of local autonomy that separates local governments from one another and prevents any form of cooperation among them. Due to a gap between 'law in the books', that vests local governments with very limited powers, and 'law in action', which grants extensive discretion to local governments that can afford to use it, the current system creates and perpetuates inequality between affluent and fiscally independent localities, located mostly in the central part of the country, and poor and dependent localities, located on the state's periphery. The result is a system of segregated local governments that form autonomous political units with dramatically disparate powers, whose internal political processes tend to reproduce the existing power hierarchies.

After examining, in the first part of this chapter, the historical roots of the structure of contemporary local government and describing its operative legal mechanisms, as well as its social and political shortcomings, the second part of this chapter lays out three theoretical models of local governance and examines their respective strengths and weaknesses. The third part of this chapter is an attempt to match a suitable structure of local government law to the unique social and political conditions of Israel.

The Structure of Local Government in Israel

There are approximately 267 local governments in Israel, ranging from cities with a population of over 200,000 inhabitants to small localities consisting of less than 500 inhabitants. Israel has a one-tier local government system divided into two types of localities: urban localities and rural localities. Urban local governments are divided internally into two categories—cities and local councils, which are governed by different legal rules.[1] A settlement with a population exceeding 2,000 inhabitants is generally deemed entitled to the status of independent local council. City status is generally granted to a settlement that has attained a minimum size threshold of 20,000 residents. All other small settlements are grouped within a framework of about 54 rural regional councils.[2] These rural local governments vary greatly in terms of area, population size and composition. Larger regional councils cover an area of over one million dunams and provide services to more than 40 settlements, while some of the smaller regional councils encompass less than 50,000 dunams and contain as few as three settlements within their jurisdiction. Altogether, regional councils control over 80 per cent of the land of Israel but less than 10 per cent of its population (Newman & Applebaum, 1995; Razin & Hasson, 1994).

Between Utopia and Reality: A Short History of Local Government

The structure of local government was formalized during the first decade of statehood. The system adopted was based on municipal patterns that had began to emerge in the pre-state period, combining Zionist communal-rural utopian ideology with British local government structure that served as an operational model for the Mandate authorities. The period of transition from the phase of pre-state to independent statehood and the pressing need to translate many of the ideas and philosophies of Zionism into a tangible reality left its mark on the structure of local government. The newly independent state and its institutions were meant to reflect the unique input of a Zionist utopian world-view, while, at the same time, providing for an efficient apparatus for the management and administration of a state (Newman, 1995).

Israel's structure of local government embodies two sets of contradictions, reflecting a deep-seated tension between the Zionist utopia and the Israeli reality: (a) Zionist ethos of local autonomy on the one hand, and a perceived need for a strong centralist state on the other; (b) ideological rejection of the city in Zionist thought on the one hand and the concentration of the majority of Israel's population in urban centers, on the other.

State of Schizophrenia: Centralist State and Localist Ethos

1. The Zionist Ethos of Local Autonomy

The ethos of local autonomy—the belief in the autonomous status of communities with internal processes of self-definition—is deep-seated within Zionist political thinking. The Zionist settlements which were established in the pre-state period conceived of themselves as virtually autonomous communities, populated by like-minded people who professed a similar ideological commitment. The first local governments in Palestine, incorporated by the Jewish settlers under the laws of the British Mandate, were designed to give the settlements as much autonomy from outside intervention as possible. As one commentator observed, 'local self-government was the first vehicle for asserting the national goals of the Zionist movement. The first Zionist colonies were created as self-governing covenant communities not dissimilar in the fundaments of their political organization from the early Puritan settlements of New England' (Elazar, 1988a, p.8). This notion of 'organic' political communities evolving naturally into local jurisdictions which are the 'outgrowth of circumstances, conditions and principles that, morally, preexist the state' (Ford, 1999, p.859) appears also in the report of the State Commission on Local Governments ('Sanbar Commission') (Elazar, 1988b). According to the Sanbar Commission, the State of Israel is a mixture of different communities gathered in various localities. The basic building blocks of the state are the 'many local groups that founded settlements which, only at a later date, united into a national community, which, still later, became a state' (Elazar, 1988b, pp.379–380). In this sense, the Sanbar Commission concluded, similarly to Switzerland and the United States, Israel is a country that 'evolved upwards from its local communities' (Elazar, 1988b, p.380). Local communities are the fundamental element from which the Israeli democratic regime has developed.

Local governments appear, under such a formulation, as a matter of right. They are perceived as a natural outgrowth of social and political communities that pre-existed the state and therefore their autonomy and right of self-determination are not questioned. Indeed, the conclusion of the Sanbar Commission was that state-local relationships should not be based on a hierarchic model in which local governments function as an administrative arm of the state, but rather on a decentralized model in which local governments are equal in status and responsibility to the central government (Elazar, 1988b).

2. Centralist State: Making a Virtue out of Necessity

At the same time, Israel is characterized by a hyper-centralist regime. Since the early days of statehood, political power has been concentrated in the hands of the central government, while local governments were left with the role of 'subcontractor'; the mere recipients of power delegated to them by the state (Dery & Schwartz-Milner, 1994). Local governments are weak entities, despite the strong Zionist ethos of local autonomy, due both to the legacy Israel inherited from the colonial powers that ruled Palestine until 1948 and to the political, social and economic challenges arrayed against the state during the first decades of independence. Under the Ottoman regime, local governments were largely insignificant. 'Measured by modern standards they were non-existent. The only tasks which the Turks entrusted to the local authorities of the country were the removal of refuse and the illumination of a few main streets' (United Nations, 1963, p.44). The marginal status of local governments was unchanged throughout the British Mandate (1917–1948). As expected from a colonial ruler, the British introduced a centralized form of government into Palestine, which was carried over into the phase of Israeli statehood (Dery & Schwartz-Milner, 1994).

During the first two decades of statehood, the young state was faced with numerous challenges—economic depression, mass immigration and recurrent military campaigns. These challenges led to a perceived need, both in the public and among policy makers, for a strong centralist government that would be able to respond swiftly to all the problems the country faced. The nation-building project the state engaged in, accompanied as it was by a 'melting pot' ideology, contributed to the powerlessness of local governments since local autonomy was conceived of as encouraging factionalism and social fragmentation. As a result, a notion of local government contrary to the 'organic' notion was developed—local government as 'synthetic'. According to the synthetic conception, local governments do not naturally evolve out of pre-existing social groups, but are instead imposed on groups from 'outside' or 'above' (Ford, 1999). There is no independent rationale for the existence of such synthetic jurisdictions; they exist only for the convenience of the institutions that they serve and are at their mercy. 'Synthetic jurisdictions may have some degree of formal autonomy to make decisions and alter arrangements, but such autonomy is granted only in order to advance a goal of the central government, such as responsiveness to changing circumstances or efficiency' (Ford, 1999, p.861). The synthetic notion of local government was very prominent throughout the 1950s and 1960s and is reflected in many political writings from that period: 'In the small State of Israel', wrote one commentator,

> which is, in its entirety, at a state of development and [immigration] absorption, it is hard to distinguish between the local-municipal and the central-state realms. Without coordination between the two realms it would be impossible to absorb immigrants, develop the country, and build economic and social infrastructure: the municipal government is nothing but the administrative arm of the central government (Ze'ev Goldberg, 1967, p.51).

'In a country such as Israel', stressed Pinhas Lavon, a leader in the ruling Labor party, 'which is equal [in size] to one or maximum two electoral districts in the United States, a state of discordance between the local government and the central government is bound to become a focal point for conflict and instability whose result is chaos all over the place' (Lavon, 1967, p.45). 'With all due respect to local services', added another commentator,

> [such as] water supply, sewage, sanitation, lighting, paving roads and sidewalks—they are not the most important things on our municipal agenda at this stage of state-building, when all our deeds must be harnessed to one fundamental goal—immigrant absorption, countywide economic development, employment supply, and social and spiritual ingathering of the exiles. Absent a complete coordination between the local and the central governments we will not withstand this test (Gury, 1967, p.44).

'Coordination' means, in this context, full control by the central government over processes occurring at the local level.[3]

To sum up, two contradictory conceptions of local government, reflecting the tension between the Zionist utopian ideology and the Israeli reality, are evident in early Israeli political thinking. One is the organic conception, according to which local governments are autonomous sovereigns; the natural outgrowth of political communities that preexisted the state, whose source of power is the will of their citizens. The other is the synthetic conception, which views local governments as mere recipients of delegated state powers; administrative subdivisions without autonomy or independent political significance.

Urban-Rural Conflict and the Origins of Israel's Jurisdictional Map

1. Urban-Rural Conflict

In no sphere of activity was the clash between ideology and practice as pointed as in that of settlement policy. The classic forms of Zionist rural settlement, which had evolved during the first half of the twentieth century, were the ultimate expression of the practical implementation of Zionist ideology. Rural communities were not simply a form of settlement, but represented a social and economic utopia aimed at creating a new form of society (Newman, 1995). The early preference for the rural sector was a product of the Zionist ideological framework that viewed the return to the land as the core of national revival. The city, on the other hand, had traditionally been looked upon in Zionist thought as a necessary evil. As summarized by Erik Cohen (1970), the author of *The City in the Zionist Ideology*:

> Pioneering Zionism has been characterized by a strong pastoral or agricultural bias stemming mainly from the belief that ... society [is] rejuvenated by creating a healthy peasantry... The tendency of Zionist leaders, and particularly of the leaders of the pioneering socialist movement, which dominated the Jewish community, was to disregard the city completely.

There were also pragmatic reasons for preferring the rural sector. Prior to the establishment of the state, the Zionist movement's main concern was gaining control over disputed lands and a physical presence in remote areas was an important element of land nationalization (Torgovnik, 1988). As a result, the rural-cooperative sector gained vast political power, which it managed to retain long into the phase of statehood.

Successful absorption of the new immigrants, who flooded the country throughout the first decade of independence, required that the new immigrants be placed mainly in urban centers rather than in agricultural settlements. The rural sector could not realize the Zionist dream due to natural constraints (such as a shortage of water and fertile land) and the lack of employment opportunities in agriculture. In addition, the new immigrants had been predominantly city dwellers in their countries of origin and were not inclined toward rural living (Gradus & Stern, 1980). The rural-cooperative settlements, on their part, refused to absorb the new immigrants who came from Arab countries. In order to avoid the formation of large urban agglomerations in the already overcrowded central region of the country and to achieve the national-political goals of 'population dispersal' in the southern region and 'Judaization' in the northern region, it was decided, as a compromise between utopia and reality, to create a network of small to midsize urban centers in the state's periphery, which would be interlinked with the rural settlements ('New Towns') (Shachar, 1998; Gardus & Stern, 1980).[4]

2. The Ideological Origins of Local Boundaries

The political dominance of the rural-cooperative sector led to a complete separation of rural and urban local governments. Regional councils were originally set up to service the needs of the rural-cooperative sector within the settlement system. As such, within their jurisdiction the regional councils included only the classic forms of Zionist cooperative settlements—the kibbutz (collective settlement) and Moshv (cooperative settlement). Non-cooperative rural settlements, such as the Moshavot—the private enterprise agricultural communities—were excluded from the regional councils, since they were not based on collective or cooperative principles. As a result, non-cooperative settlements, even those with exceedingly small populations, were awarded independent municipal status, leaving them, in many cases, as small enclaves within the regional councils' jurisdiction (Newman, 1995). Moreover, in many cases attempts were made to set up homogeneous regional councils in which all the settlements were of the same organizational type (i.e. cooperative, non-cooperative), resulting in an internal system of segregation within the rural sector. Efficiency and functional criteria, not to mention social justice considerations, were often ignored in the demarcation of local jurisdictions if they were in conflict with the ideological and political imperatives of the governmental and quasi-governmental settlement agencies (Newman, 1995).

The practice of separating rural from urban and cooperative from non-cooperative settlements continued throughout the first decade of statehood, when the present structure of local government was consolidated. The New Towns, established in the remote rural regions of the country during the 1950s and populated mostly by new immigrants from the Arab countries, instantaneously received independent municipal status even when completely surrounded by rural regional councils (Razin

& Hazan, 1995). Although originally it had been planned that these towns would become hubs for their rural surroundings, the cooperative organization of the rural settlements used its political power to avoid any kind of municipal cooperation with the urban sector (which included the New Towns). The rural regional councils provided settlements in their jurisdiction with a full range of services, including a segregated educational system and industrial zones occupied by agricultural processing plants owned by the rural settlements (Hasson & Razin, 1990).

A shift in the political, ideological and economic realities, which had been taking place since the 1970s, triggered a decline in the rural-cooperative sector's power and led to a growing number of boundary conflicts between urban localities (that house most of the population) and rural localities (that include most of the land).[5] Despite the weakness of the regional councils, most attempts by urban local governments to annex rural land have ended in either compromise or failure (Razin & Hazan, 1995). Local boundaries, once established, are difficult to alter and the Minister of the Interior, although possessing the power to change jurisdictional boundaries at will, has been reluctant to use his power without the consent of all parties involved (Razin, 1997; Elazar, 1988a). As a result, the jurisdictional map that objectified and geographically inscribed the balance of power in the first decades of statehood has not changed much since the 1950s.[6]

The Legal Structure of Local Government

Local government law is the product of an attempt to mediate the tension between utopia and reality, between the deep-seated Zionist ethos of local autonomy on the one hand, and the perceived need to centralize power to allow the state to effectively meet its challenges on the other. As a result, doctrine involving local government law oscillates between two different conceptions of local government—synthetic and organic—which are informed by two contradicting misconceptions of political space—space as transparent and space as opaque. The misconception of space as transparent—the view that political boundaries are a mental construct that have no social or political significance – corresponds to the synthetic conception that sees local governments as mere delegates of state power. The misconception of space as opaque—the view that political boundaries define natural and pre-political association of individuals—corresponds to the organic conception of local government that sees local governments as autonomous sovereigns, unproblematically unified and self-validating entities with rights against the central government (Ford, 1994).

City powerlessness: The illusion of transparency Local governments are generally treated by Israeli law as 'creatures of the state'. Their official legal status is that of mere administrative agencies of the central government, which are completely subject to state authority. The power to establish local governments and to define and change their jurisdictional boundaries is at the sole discretion of the central government, with only limited input by local communities.[7] Local governments are dependent on the central government in almost every respect, with relatively little discretion over their own affairs (Ben-Zadok, 1993). Severe restrictions on local power are supplemented by firm state control over local decision making. State law grants the central government far-reaching powers to oversee local government activities, including to amend, abridge or overrule any of their decisions and, in some cases, even to retract their power and exercise it on their behalf (Vinograd, 1998).

The powers possessed by local governments are those expressly granted to them by the Municipal Corporations Ordinance.[8] Actions taken by local governments without explicit statutory authorization are ultra-vires and therefore invalid. The application of the ultra-vires doctrine to local governments, which is the quintessential expression of the synthetic notion of local government as delegate of state power, was articulated for the first time in the 1951 landmark case *Hat v. Municipality of Haifa*.[9] A local government, the Supreme Court stated, is a legal entity created by state law, which has no existence outside the law.

> State law defines its powers, and any act beyond the scope of the powers granted is null and void (ultra-vires)... The general rule for determining whether a certain act done by the local government is beyond the scope of its powers is not whether the [law] forbids the act either explicitly or implicitly, but rather whether it is expressly permitted. In other words, it is not enough that the act is not forbidden; it must be explicitly permitted in order for it to be proper in the eyes of the law. The law does not leave any empty space that [the local government] is allowed to fill at will.

The Supreme Court reinforced this position in a series of decisions in which it invalidated actions taken by local governments without an explicit authorization in state law. One example is *S.Z.M. v. Mayor of Jerusalam*,[10] involving the power of business licensing. In *S.Z.M.* the municipality of Jerusalem refused to grant a license to a business that displayed and sold sex products and magazines. The municipality based its decision on a democratic argument—the will of its local citizens. It argued that the city's population is comprised of many religious people, Jews, Christians and Muslims, who are offended by the operation of such a business within the city's jurisdiction. The Supreme Court invalidated the municipality's decision. The issue at hand, the Court stressed, is that of limiting the freedom of occupation. In such cases, the law must be strictly applied and narrowly construed. The courts will uphold a decision not to grant a business license only if the authority to deny a license is explicitly within the powers granted to the local government by state law. 'With all the sympathy of the Court to the righteous and desirable goals of the municipality of Jerusalem', the Supreme Court concluded, 'the law does not grant local governments the power to protect the feelings of their citizens', and therefore its decision is void. In another case—*Da'abul v. Mayor of Ramat-Gan*[11]—the Supreme Court clarified: 'it is clear that no local government has a natural authority to assume upon itself the role of the guardian of its citizens' morality, be they young or adults. Such an authority must be based on state law, which law does not exist'.

According to these cases, the source of municipal power is not the will of its citizens, but rather the central government through the legislative process. Cities are powerless to act on behalf of their inhabitants without an explicit authorization, which is granted at the will of the state. Local governments are simply administrative agencies of the central government that exist at its pleasure and for its administrative convenience.

This conclusion is strengthened when examining the law concerning local governments' jurisdictional boundaries. The authority to create local governments and to define their boundaries is within the sole discretion of the central government. Requests for boundary changes are filed with the Minister of the Interior, who can either turn them down or appoint a boundary commission to evaluate the proposal. After studying the commission's recommendations, the final decision lies with the Minister, who has no legal obligation to accept the commission's recommendations. When the jurisdiction involved is not a city, but rather an urban local council or a rural regional council, the Minister can resolve the issue without even appointing a commission, although it is customary to do so (Razin & Hasson, 1994).

In a series of cases that challenged the Minister's discretion, the Supreme Court held unequivocally that the discretion of the Minister of the Interior to define and alter local government boundaries is very broad. The Court made it clear that rarely would it be appropriate for the courts to interfere with the Minister's decision: 'The only question that we may ask is whether the Minister knew what he was doing and intended to do so and whether there was no unlawful motive behind his decision. If the answer to both questions is positive—it is not our place to intervene.'[12] Although the 'will of the majority of the city's citizens' is mentioned explicitly in the Municipalities Corporation Ordinance as one of the reasons for appointing a boundary commission, the Court held that the Minster has no obligation to accept the commission's recommendations.[13] In fact, if no administrative or procedural error has been made, the Minister's decision is valid even if it stands in stark opposition to the expressed will of the citizens of the local governments involved in the boundary dispute.[14]

The absolute power vested in the central government to draw and modify jurisdictional boundaries of local governments is compatible with the idea that local governments are merely political subdivisions of the state. This view assumes that local boundaries are politically insignificant and fungible. Under this conception of political geography, 'spatiality is reduced to a mental construct alone, a way of thinking, an ideational process in which the "image" of reality takes epistemological precedence over the tangible substance and appearance of the real world' (Soja, 1989, p.125). The shape of local political geography is perceived as insignificant to the fulfillment of citizenship and democratic participation (Ford, 1994). In other words, local political space is 'transparent' and therefore subject to change by the central government, through whatever mechanism it deems fit.

If we take the synthetic/transparent conception to its logical conclusion, that conclusion must be that there is no autonomous sphere of local sovereignty. All local concerns are actually state concerns, all local policies are in fact state policies, all local citizens are simply state citizens, and all local elections are sub-state elections. Citizens, therefore, have no right to reside in a particular locality, to control its character or even to elect local representatives. If local governments are mere delegates of state power, no fundamental right is breached if local representatives are nominated by the central government instead of being elected by local citizens. The autonomy of local communities cannot, according to this logic, serve as a basis for upholding local policies, since local government policies are, from a legal point of view, state policies. As we shall see shortly, however, this logic was not always employed. In fact, the Court was often guided by very different, indeed contradictory, conceptions of local government and political space.

Local autonomy: The illusion of opacity Although local governments are officially defined as delegates of state power, at times the courts treat local governments as autonomous sovereigns with rights against the central government. The view of localities as autonomous legal entities suggests that local governments derive their power not (or at least not only) from state law but rather from the will of their citizens.

The notion of local government as autonomous sovereigns can be found in some cases involving local elections. For example, in *Muasy v. Minister of Interior*[15] the issue was whether the central government has authority to defer local elections beyond the five-year period prescribed by law. Due to serious mismanagement, the elected members of the local council of Baqa El-Garbiah were dismissed one year after their election and replaced by members appointed by the Minister of the Interior. The appointed members served until special elections took place in Baqa El-Garbiah two years later. Almost five years after the special elections, when the new local council's term of office was about to end, the Minister issued a directive postponing elections in Baqa El-Grabiah until the following local elections, which was scheduled to take place one and a half years later. The Minister based his decision on the principle of 'efficiency and administrative convenience', which requires that all local elections be held concurrently. The residents of Baqa El-Garbiah challenged the ministerial directive in court, arguing that the Minister of the Interior had no authority to defer the elections beyond the five-year period prescribed by law.

The majority of the Supreme Court sustained the challenge. The right of citizens in a democratic state to elect local representatives at preordained times, the Court reasoned, is a fundamental right. When the central government interferes with such a fundamental right, it must bear in mind:

> the obligation to behave respectfully toward both the elected representatives of the local governments and their constituency, and remember that the paternalism of the past is long gone. When interpreting laws concerning state–local relationships, both the court, as the interpreter

> of the law, and the central government... should be guided... by the principle of local government autonomy... 'The autonomy principle' implies a direct link between the local government and the law, without the mediation of other governmental authorities.

The Court stated that considerations of efficiency and administrative convenience are important and should be applied whenever possible. In this case, however, applying these considerations necessarily meant infringing on local government autonomy, and respecting the autonomy of local governments and their elected representatives is more important than either efficiency or administrative convenience.

The conception that guided the Supreme Court in Muasy is evidently not the synthetic notion of local governments as administrative agencies of the state, but rather an organic notion of local governments as autonomous sovereigns. Under the synthetic conception, citizens have no fundamental right to vote in local elections (which are in fact sub-state elections) and therefore the Minster's decision, driven by the principles of efficiency and administrative convenience, should have been upheld by the Court. However, in Muasy the Court recognized that the central government does not have unlimited authority over local government, but rather that there is a sphere of local autonomy that the central government must respect. This suggests that local power is not simply delegated state power but rather is derived from some other source—the will of local residents.

Not all local governments, however, are treated equally. Some types of local governments seem more suitable, in the eyes of the law, for the organic description and therefore more deserving of deferential treatment than others do. This is reflected in *Yanovitz v. Verbin.*[16] The factual circumstances of *Yanovitz*, which involves the power of business licensing, are quite similar to those of *S.Z.M. v. Mayor of Jerusalem* discussed above. The local council of Ramat Ha-Sharon, a rich suburb of Tel-Aviv, refused to license a business displaying and selling sex products and pornographic magazines on one of the city's major streets. The local council justified its decision by appealing to the inherent power it possesses to protect the morality of its citizens. The local council argued that a sex shop operating in the city's main street would become a source of temptation for young people passing by, and particularly for schoolchildren who attend nearby schools. The Supreme Court upheld the locality's decision not to grant a business license. To do so, it had to distinguish this case from prior cases that had struck down similar local government resolutions based on the morality principle. The Court did so by emphasizing the difference between cities and local councils:

> Local councils, as distinguished from cities, have extensive general powers to prohibit the establishment of businesses. The rationale for this difference in scope between the power of local councils and that of cities is that local councils accommodate relatively small and homogeneous populations. The extensive discretion [granted to a local council] enables it to take into account in its decisions the uniqueness of the population within its jurisdiction and to protect... its special character.[17]

In the *Yanovitz* case, the Supreme Court accepted as a premise that local government boundaries define discrete and autonomous communities that have a right to self-determination.[18] The notion of local government as circumscribing a community conflicts with the conception of local government as a subdivision of the state and invokes instead the notion of local government as 'imperium in imperio' (Ford, 1994). The conception of political geography underlying such a notion of local government is different as well. Rather than being politically insignificant and fungible, as perceived under the transparency conception, local boundaries under this alternative conception of political space—space as 'opaque'—are viewed as natural and inevitable. Local boundaries are imagined to have been developed naturally around preexisting political communities that therefore deserve legal recognition of their autonomy.

As already noted, however, not all local governments are equally deserving of autonomy. The Supreme Court made a distinction between two types of localities: the city, the locus of strangers, and local councils, the locus of communities, echoing the Zionist preference for small rural communities and its antagonism toward the city. The local council, like its counterpart the American suburb, conjures up romantic images associated with the notion of community. 'It invokes the idealized feeling of belongingness, oneness, solidarity, and affective connection that, it is imagined, were once fostered in traditional, face-to-face villages' (Frug, 1999, p.57). The local council is presented as representing homogeneous communities that share common norms and values. It is a private and personal place for intimate associations, a safe haven from the instrumental and impersonal space that is the city. It is a 'place' rather than a mere 'space'. The city, on the other hand, is coded in the popular political geography as alienating, impersonal, and dangerous. It is the locus of strangers, and the disorder, violence and crime associated with them in popular imagination. The city is in a constant state of flux and is therefore insecure and unreliable; in need of continuous supervision and control (Ford, 1996).

As a result, cities have been subjected to greater state intervention than local councils (Vinograd, 1998). The imagined metropolitan geography that corresponds to the split between city and local council 'encourages a view of local jurisdictional borders and the legal attributes that accompany them as natural and inevitable' (Ford, 1996, p.1177), and therefore contributes to the growing fragmentation of metropolitan areas.

The fragmentation of the Israeli metropolis into autonomous and self-contained local governments is illustrated in *Rosenberg v. Ministry of Construction and Housing.*[19] At issue in *Rosenberg* was whether the state could favor residents of a local government in allocating housing within the jurisdiction of that same locality. The government, in cooperation with the local council of Ramat Ha-Sharon, embarked on a joint project to construct subsidized residential housing in Ramat Ha-Sharon and sell them to low-income individuals and families. The state was responsible for the financing of the project, while the local government directed the constructing and marketing of the units. The units were marketed to the residents of Ramat Ha-Sharon. Only remaining units, after all the participating local residents had been allocated housing, could be distributed among the public at large. The appellant, a resident of Tel-Aviv, who, as a single mother, would have otherwise qualified for participation in the project, challenged the residency requirement, arguing that it constituted an unlawful discrimination in the allocation of state land.

In a majority opinion the Supreme Court rejected the appellant's argument. According to the Court, the favoring of Ramat Ha-Sharon residents did not amount to unlawful discrimination but rather constituted a lawful differentiation. The justification for the residency requirement is the 'bond people develop toward their place of residence, which is comprised of the totality of the familial, social, cultural and sometimes also occupational relationship to their environment and community'. Local government is portrayed by the Court as an autonomous political community with an inherent right to exclude outsiders. Geography is invoked in order to reify and justify a political community, delimited by the boundaries of the local government and to ground these boundaries in a political space that is left unexamined; that is seen as opaque (Ford, 1994). The Supreme Court, in other words, justified local power and local boundaries by reference to geography itself. In upholding the residency requirement, the Court employed the misconception of space as opaque, which masks the tautology of community definition: it assumed that residency in a local government is a necessary prerequisite to participation in a political community which is presumed to preexist the local government, but is, in fact, defined by the jurisdictional boundaries of that very local government.

Justice Heshin, in a powerful dissent, pointed to the fallacy and arbitrariness of the residency requirement (especially when dealing with local governments within the same metropolitan area), thus tacitly criticizing the conception of political space as opaque and the corresponding notion of local government as organic:

> In the past, one would 'plant' himself in a certain place of residence and would not leave it but for exceptional circumstances. Whoever lived in Tel-Aviv lived in Tel-Aviv, whoever lived in Jerusalem lived in Jerusalem, whoever lived in Herzliya lived in Herzliya, and whoever lived in Haifa lived in Haifa. These days are long gone... Nowadays people, both individuals and families, move from place to place with relative ease... It is possible, for instance, for a person to live in Tel-Aviv and work in Ramat Ha-Sharon or Herzliya only because the rent in Tel-Aviv is cheaper than the rent in those other localities... Ramat Ha-Sharon borders on several local governments—greater Tel-Aviv, Herzliya and Hod Ha-Sharon. If we add to these local governments other localities whose distance from Ramat Ha-Sharon is measured by hundreds of meters—Givataim, Ramat Gan, Kefar Saba, Ra'anana, Petah Tiqwa, Rosh Ha-Ayin, Bney Beraq—we must conclude that Ramat Ha-Sharon is but one locality within a cluster of adjacent localities that constitute territorial continuity, as if they were one local government.

For these reasons, the dissent concluded, the exclusion of some citizens from participating in a governmental project executed within the territorial jurisdiction of a local government of which they are not residents is 'arbitrary through and through' and therefore amounts to unlawful discrimination.[20] The opinion of the dissent reflects a recognition that local governments, as political spaces, are not insular entities but instead part of a larger political community, which they affect and are affected by and to which they owe consideration (Ford, 1994).

What lies beneath: The consequences of the misconceptions of political space The juridical consequences of the oscillation between the two misconceptions of political space, space as opaque and space as transparent, which lie at the philosophical foundations of the contradictory notions of local government as either organic or synthetic, are far-reaching. Although the two misconceptions are in opposition to each other both place geography outside the scope of legal review. Geography is either natural and pre-political, and therefore inevitable and not subject to change by legal means, or it is irrelevant and therefore not worth considering at all (Ford, 1997). As a result, the Court never examined how local jurisdictions were created. Local government boundaries were left unexamined. They were assumed to be 'a fact of the case rather than a subject of the dispute and a proper object of the law' (Ford, 1994).

Contemporary Local Government Law: A Critique

Under the current legal doctrine, Israeli local governments are at the same time both too weak and too strong with repercussions detrimental to a large segment of the Israeli population, as well as to society as a whole. This part of the chapter critiques contemporary local government law by examining the social, economic and political consequences of that body of law.

All too weak: Local government and political participation Local governments are weak in the sense that many important aspects of local life are left outside the reach of local citizens. Local governments have, for instance, very little control over their financing. Any decision to increase local taxes (mostly property taxes) or to borrow money from financial institutions must be authorized by the central government (Vinograd, 1998). The central government has traditionally used this power to increase the dependency of local governments. It has restricted the internal income of local governments by capping the amount of local taxes that can be collected directly by local governments, while contributing to their income at a rate of between 25 and 75 per cent of their total budget (Kalchheim, 1997). The reason for this practice is that 'the more finance is supplied by the central government from nationally raised taxes the less tends to be the discretion allowed to the local government. Conversely, the greater the ability of a local government to raise finance from its own sources then the less able the central government to control the local government' (Hepworth, 1970, pp.14–15).

Local governments are limited in many other ways as well. Under the current system the citizens of local governments have a limited ability to influence their environment, their quality of life and the future of their children. As argued by Dery & Schwartz-Milner (1994, p.11):

> Municipal road systems and the highway safety measures adopted in them, the view that one sees from his window, the quality of air that one breathes, the quality of school and kindergarten teachers, assistance to the elderly, the protection of property, and employment opportunities—these and many other quality of life aspects of Israeli localities are all dictated, to a large extent, from above, far beyond the direct influence of citizens and the local representatives that they have elected.

The problem with local government's powerlessness is that it empties the notion of political participation of any significant meaning and devalues local bonds. Local governments have long been celebrated for their role as schools for democracy. As Alexis de Tocqueville wrote, 'local institutions are to liberty what primary schools are to science; they bring it within the public's reach, they teach people how to use and enjoy it. Without local institutions, a nation may establish a free government, but it cannot have a spirit of liberty' (Tocqueville, 1863, p.76). John Stuart Mill also stressed that participation at the local level is the 'practical part of the political education of the free people' (Mill, 1991, pp.121–122). Democracy requires that citizens have opportunities to participate in the political process, and active political participation is much more likely to occur in small polities than in larger ones. In other words, limited size is a prerequisite to the ability of ordinary citizens to truly participate in public life. Local governments provide citizens with opportunities for participation in public life that are unavailable at the state level (Briffault, 2000). The costs of participation in the political process, in terms of money, time and energy, are likely to be lower in smaller political units, and the prospects of influencing the political outcome are likely to be much higher (Dahl & Tufte, 1973).

Political participation will occur, however, only in cases in which it can indeed affect the lives of local citizens in a meaningful way. As argued by Gerald Frug, 'no one is likely to participate in the decision making of an entity of any size unless that participation will make a difference in his or her life. Power and participation are inextricably linked: a sense of powerlessness tends to produce apathy rather than participation, while the existence of power encourages those able to participate in it exercise to do so' (Frug, 1999, p.23).

All too strong: Local government and the power to exclude Local governments have too much power in the sense that, once created, they obtain broad powers to exclude outsiders (defined in positivist-geographical terms as anybody who lives outside its jurisdiction) and very few incentives to include outsiders or to cooperate with other local governments. The nostalgia for pure space, for the pastoral ideal of homogeneous communities inherent in the Zionist utopian dream, has led Israel to fragment its local governments, 'to turn them into patchwork quilts made up of separate enclaves, each defined by a seam that binds as well as divides them' (Ford, 1994, p.1907). The ideal of community expresses the desire for the fusion of subjects with one another. It values and enforces homogeneity on the one hand and denies and represses any sign of social difference, on the other. As a result, the ideal of community operates, in practice, to exclude those experienced as different, those with whom the group does not identify. By invoking the ideal of community as a description of the life of local governments, contemporary local government law reproduces the problems of exclusion that this ideal poses (Young, 1990).

Local government law treats localities in individualistic terms. The boundaries that separate cities from each other are treated as comparable to the boundaries that separate one property owner from another. This understanding of local boundaries results from the equation of local power with local autonomy—that is, with the ability to act like a self-interested individual, albeit on a collective basis (Frug, 1999). The law not only allows but also encourages self-interested behavior on the part of local governments. It portrays local governments as autarkic markets, governed by what Gerald Frug has aptly called a 'fee for service mentality' (Frug, 1998, p.42)—the understanding that the residents of local governments are paying taxes that should then be reinvested in their community in the form of municipal services.[21] Services across the border, substandard as they may be, are of no concern to local residents. Local boundaries, in other words, limit the scope of residents' concerns and create a psychological separation among residents of close-by localities that is very difficult to bridge. By tying political participation, service provision, tax-base, and land use regulation to local borders, the current system narrows local residents' range of vision to an extent that they are often unable to recognize that they are affected by the actions of other localities and have a stake in the well-being of their residents (Briffault, 2000).

One of the problems arising from such a notion of local autonomy becomes apparent when examining the actual nature of contemporary local governments and the negative externalities they generate. Local boundaries exclude not only people who are uninfluenced by the decisions made and powers exercised within the boundaries of the locality, but also many who are profoundly affected by local decisions and practices. The imaginary lines defining local boundaries do not correlate with the influence of municipal actions. A local government's decisions inescapably affect individuals working in the city, living immediately outside its border, or traveling through its jurisdiction, as well as other local governments in the region. Local governments are not insular communities; they are part of a larger political space. Cross-border spillover undermines the 'homogeneous community' rationale for local autonomy since such a rationale must assume that the consequences of local action are borne solely within the acting locality, which of course is rarely the reality (Briffault, 1996). Local borders generally generate some spillover. In the past, however, local governments were set apart from each other by unincorporated land, and people, who were less mobile, focused more on their activity within the territorial boundaries of their locality. As a result, the spillover effect may have been slight. The spillover problem became much more acute with the expansion of metropolitan areas, in which local governments 'abut one another, and oftentimes you would not know when you left the boundaries of one locality and entered the jurisdiction of another'.[22] In contemporary metropolitan regions, 'local governments are sure to generate externalities and area residents are sure to be excluded from participating in the decisions of many localities that have direct implications on their lives' (Briffault, 1996, p.1133).

The only way to overcome the spillover problem, within the conceptual boundaries of the current legal regime, is intercity collaboration. Contemporary local government law, however, has made collaboration among local governments possible only to the extent that each participant believes that it would be in its self-interest to cooperate with other localities. The only legal mechanism that allows for intercity cooperation is the 'cities confederation' (Razin, 1994).[23] Cities confederations are special purpose districts created by two or more adjacent urban local governments (cities and local councils) in order to undertake specific municipal services, usually services that are based on economies of scale (Elazar, 1988a). Existing cities confederations range from the Dan region sanitation and garbage disposal district to the Sharon region mosquitoes extermination district, and also include several sewage, fire fighting and water districts. Although the establishment of a cities confederation requires the formal approval of the Minister of the Interior, it is based, for the most part, on the voluntary agreement of all the local governments that join the special purpose district (Vinograd, 1998; Razin, 1994).

Cities confederations are, in reality, an obstacle not a vehicle for meaningful cooperation among local governments. They allow small local councils to combine with each other and with cities in order to fund infrastructure they can not afford individually, without ceding local political autonomy over other matters. The structure and design of these special purpose districts minimize the intrusion of local government autonomy: the services cities confederations provide (fire fighting, water supply, sewage system, refuse disposal, etc.) usually lack broader implications for the economic and social demography of local communities. They supply, in other words, 'engineering solutions to technical problems, and are not directly involved in area-wide social or political policymaking' (Briffault, 1990, p.376). Lastly, the largely voluntary nature of cities confederations forestalls any attempt to use this mechanism to force local governments to solve regional problems generated by local autonomy in issues such as land use planning and tax-base disparities. As a result, a local government can maintain political independence while still sharing in the economies of scale provided by infrastructure services organized and funded on a regional basis (Briffault, 1990).

Local government law and the reproduction of social hierarchies The detrimental social consequences of the current structure of local government cuts deep into the fabric of

Israeli society and can be understood only against the backdrop of the patterns of residential segregation that characterize the Israeli polity. By draining localities of any significant political power on the one hand, and insisting on their autonomous existence on the other, local government law perpetuates the historically segregated political spaces and reproduces the power hierarchies that accompany them.

As established in the previous chapters, a combination of public policies and private choices, generously assisted by legal rules and institutions, has operated to transform Israel into a mosaic of segregated and economically unequal local governments. Public policies, such as population dispersal, that forced Arab-Jews into remote localities, complemented by the separation of peripheral urban (mostly Mizrahi) and rural (mostly Ashkenazi) localities, governmental 'deference' to the alleged will of Arab minority subgroups to live in separate jurisdictions, and the individual choice of members of cultural and religious communities to concentrate in homogeneous enclaves have all contributed to the division of Israel into a patchwork of segregated localities.

Segregation is oppressive and disempowering, not because there is something inherently immoral in living in homogeneous communities, but because segregation involves more than simply the relationship among various social groups; it also involves the relationship of social groups to political influence and economic resources. It creates a structural inequality that distributes political power and economic resources in a way that systematically benefits one social group at the expense of others. As a result, 'segregated minority communities have been historically economically impoverished and politically powerless' (Ford, 1994, p.1844).

The present structure of local government silently and more effectively performs the job that was done in the past by explicitly segregationist legal rules and public policies. Facially neutral legal rules and institutions, set against the historical backdrop of state action in the service of racial and ethnic segregation, perpetuate and entrench the conditions of segregation, and the socio-economic stratification that accompanies it, even in the absence of any de jure segregation. Local government law serves precisely this function. Political space—the function of jurisdictional boundaries—advances and legitimizes the conditions of segregation, and the system of unequal distribution of political power and economic resources that comes with it.

By stressing, on the one hand, a self-centered notion of local autonomy, contemporary local government law does the work of maintaining 'separate and unequal' jurisdictions, while its underlying conceptions of political space disguise its role in perpetuating segregation, representing it either as the delegation of state power and therefore politically inconsequential, or as natural and therefore inevitable. The legally encouraged local fragmentation institutionalizes the dominance of a favored minority, by preventing any sort of cooperation among economically disfavored localities who could otherwise forge a region-wide or even statewide coalition. Under the current regime, it is impossible for the citizens of an atomized polity to recognize, much less pursue, a mutual destiny with people outside their local political jurisdiction, who are perceived as 'Others' (Cashin, 2000). By insisting, on the other hand, on local powerlessness, local government law guarantees that the structural inequality in power, wealth and political access, built into the system of segregation, is perpetuated. The power of localities and their citizens to affect any structural change through their internal political mechanisms is significantly curtailed. This problem is exacerbated by an existing gap between 'law in the books', that leaves local governments with very limited powers, and 'law in action', that grants local governments who can afford it extensive leeway. As noted by Kalchheim (1997, p.23):

> Despite the great centralization of the governmental structure, expressed in legislative powers, financial resources and service development—one should not conclude that the autonomy of local authorities is shriveled. On the contrary, the large number of 'addresses' of state and public institutions, the lack of coordination among them, the absence of supervision on their behalf, and their insufficient mastery of the details of local occurrences ... enlarge the opportunities of local governments to achieve their goals beyond the formal boundaries.

As a result, the conditions of economic and political inequality between affluent and fiscally independent local governments, located mostly in the central part of the country, and poor and dependent local governments, located on the state's periphery, are sustained and perpetuated (Inbar & Choshen, 1994).

To sum up, contemporary local government combines the worst of both worlds: formal local powerlessness that results in structural inequality among local governments, together with a romantic notion of autonomous communities that works to segregate and fragment them as well as to prevent any inter-local alliances. Moreover, the condition of structural inequality fuels and reinforces the segregative effect of political boundaries in a vicious circle of causation, that results in a deepening of the gap between rich and poor local governments, easily identified in ethno-class terms.

We must find a way to break this vicious circle and change its course. Whereas the current system encourages exclusionary behavior while limiting the political power of local communities, a beneficial system of local government would enable localities to turn into a modern Agora—the locus of democratic life—without fueling exclusionary sentiments. We must reject the conception of local government as either subdivisions of the state (the synthetic misconception) or as autonomous sovereigns; insular forums for registering the private preferences of the people that inhabit them (the opaque misconception) (Barron, 1999). Neither is tenable, as explained by Ford (1994, p.1886):

> If local government is a mere delegate of a larger democracy, the relief that it theoretically is to provide from the potentially oppressive nature of majoritarianism and the distance of centralized bureaucracy is lost. But if local government is an autonomous sovereign, the boundaries that define the government require a prior and external justification to avoid circularity... Localities are neither sovereigns nor delegates, neither freely chosen nor wholly imposed; rather they are altogether distinct political agent, and as such require a distinct theory of law and justice.

The following section of this chapter provides a synopsis of the contemporary normative debate on local government structure, which will serve as a basis for the discussion in the third section, which offers a provisional map for reform of Israeli local government law.

Theoretical Models of Local Governance

Theoretical models of local governance abound. They range from total centralization—entrusting all governmental functions in the hands of the state (Sharkansky, 1997)—to complete decentralization of powers that places local governments on an equal footing with the central government (Nozick, 1974).[24] It is possible, however, to classify existing theories of local government into three ideal-types: public choice models that advocate complete decentralization, regionalist models that emphasize the benefits of regional centralization, and political decentralization models that try to overcome the centralization/decentralization dichotomy by deconstructing the philosophical premises on which it is based.

The normative debate on local government is characterized by tension among four main considerations, which often stand in opposition to one another. These considerations are: (a) economic efficiency, (b) democratic participation, (c) community building, and (d) social justice. We shall now proceed to a brief discussion of the three models and examine how each of them attempts to mediate the tensions among the various normative considerations.

Public Choice: The Case for Decentralization

Charles Tiebout's pure theory of local expenditures In his groundbreaking article *A Pure Theory of Local Expenditures,* urban economist Charles Tiebout (1956) hypothesized that a market type solution exists to determine the optimal number of local governments, as well as the level and mix of services to be provided by each. His theory, which came to be known as the public choice approach, is based upon individualistic premises and utilitarian philosophy, and proceeds from the assumption that a diversity of individual preferences needs to be matched by a diversity of goods and services. Local government is seen under this model as a mechanism for allowing individuals maximum scope of choice rather than as a political system for collective decision making; or, in other words, as corporate management rather than as democratic sovereignty. Accordingly, public choice theorists support local government structure that approximate free markets as closely as possible, allowing individuals to make choices about their preferred mix of services, taxes and other policies. Efficiency is seen as best promoted by competition among service providing units, allowing people and capital to find their preferred and most profitable location undistorted by government regulation (Keating, 1995).

Local residents, labeled by Tiebout (1956) 'consumer-voters', shop around for a jurisdiction that provides them the mix of services and taxes that best suit their preferences. Some want to live in a locality that provides good schools, others prefer cultural institutions, and still others look for parks and low-density housing. Local governments compete for consumer-voters by offering different packages of public goods that they believe will be attractive to them. The larger the number of local governments, the more options exist for consumer-voters to choose from. The multiplicity of local governments, combined with the freedom to move among them, creates a market in public services, which, in turn, generate the efficiencies that result from inter-local competition. According to this model, 'the optimal number of governments is the point in the space where citizens enjoy the greatest satisfaction of their preferences' (Cooter, 2000, p.103). Considering there are almost as many preferences as there are people, the public choice model supports a fragmented system of local government, composed of a multitude of small-scale localities. Moreover, the multiplicity of local governments would not promote efficiency unless each could set its own fiscal policies and regulate its own land use. Therefore, public choice theorists support local authority over taxing, spending and regulatory decision making (Briffault, 1990).

The power of local government is justified, under this model, neither by its responsiveness to the democratic notion of political participation nor by its attentiveness to community values, but by the notions of free choice and political 'exit'. The mechanism Tiebout identified as most crucial was the mobility of consumer-voters: 'moving or failing to move', he noted, 'replaces the usual market test of willingness to buy a good' (Tiebout, 1956, p.420). Consumer-voters are assumed to have agreed or disagreed with the particular benefits and burdens of local citizenship by their presence or absence.

'Reality Bites': A critique of public choice In order to make his model work—that is, in order to create a mechanism that generates an efficient allocation of public goods—Tiebout had to rely on a set of simplifying assumptions 'so patently unrealistic as to verge on the outrageous' (Frug, 1999, p.168). He had to assume that people are fully mobile and that mobility is costless, ignoring the obvious objection that people's choice of residential location is based on work as well as on non-economic factors such as family and community bonds, emotions and sentiments, rather than purely on the bundle of local services. In other words, 'Tiebout's model assumes that neither physical distance nor political geography constrain individual decisions regarding residence' (Ford, 1994, p.1882). He also had to assume that residents are fully knowledgeable of the differences among the various localities and that the public goods and services supplied have no adverse impact on neighborhood communities (the spillover problem) (Frug, 1999).

In reality, however, people are not equally mobile, and 'exit' is not an option for all residents. Mobility between jurisdictions is not cost free, but is constrained by a variety of economic and social factors that tend to affect poorer people much more than affluent ones. Exclusionary zoning, such as the exclusion of multifamily and subsidized housing, drives up the cost of housing in many jurisdictions, denying many potential movers a meaningful choice of place to live. Since access to jobs and access to homes are often interrelated, zoning decisions often make the communities adjacent to attractive working places, such as new manufacturing facilities, offices and industrial parks, economically inaccessible to all but relatively affluent people, effectively denying the less affluent both housing and employment opportunities or forcing them to endure long commutes (Briffault, 1990).

The importance of social and economic inequalities in problematizing the normative value of the Tiebout model cuts however much deeper than the class and wealth based distinctions that affect a consumer-voter's ability to exit. The public choice model assumes that service, tax and regulatory differences among local governments are the result of a variation in 'tastes' among different people. In theory, one locality may prefer municipal parks, another may favor better schools, a third might opt for new roads and a fourth might decide to cut taxes and spend less on local services. In reality, however, local taxing, spending and regulatory decisions are, more often than not, based not on idiosyncratic tastes but on the stark differences in local fiscal capacity that divide localities within the same metropolitan area. Wealthy communities spend much more per capita on local services, but can still tax their residents at much lower rates than poorer communities, which typically tax at high rates but can still manage to provide only a low level of local services. There is general interest among local residents in a high level of local services such as good schools, safe and clean streets, and paved roads. Given these common concerns it is likely that inter-local taxing and spending differences are less a result of differences in taste than of broad fiscal disparities among local governments, which can be easily identified in class, ethnic and racial terms (Briffault, 1990). In sum, the public choice model, for all its intuitive power, fails to provide a satisfactory normative basis for local autonomy.

Post-Tieboutian public choice theories More recent public choice approaches to local government structure, which are built on Tiebout's assumption about matching individual preferences with service provision through market mechanisms, have devoted themselves to refining this model so that it could be applied to a more realistic version of the world. Robert Cooter (2000), for instance, confronted the problem of spillovers, inherent in Tiebout's model, arguing that power over public goods should be assigned to the smallest possible unit of government that can internalize their effects. Whenever, he continued, the effects of a public good spill over local jurisdictions, a special district should be established to provide the public good and control its bad effects.

James Buchanan's model of local governance is another example of a post-Tieboutian public choice theory. Unlike most public choice scholars, Buchanan (1971) acknowledged that people are not equally mobile and that the decision of the wealthy to move out of a jurisdiction has serious adverse effects on the middle and low-income residents left behind. Because of this negative impact, Buchanan argued, it is in the interest of everyone in the jurisdiction to keep the affluent people from exiting. This can be done either by 'punishing' them for leaving, making sure that non-residents cannot enjoy the benefits offered by the central city without contributing to the internal fiscal surplus, or by striking a 'deal' with the rich, offering them better schools, parks and protection than those available to others in the jurisdiction in exchange for their willingness to stay. These 'bribes' admittedly violate traditional equity norms, but as Buchanan himself argued, his theory 'has nothing to do with the "deservingness" of the high-income or the low-income groups, or with "justice" or "equity" as an abstract ethical norm' (Buchanan, 1971, p.14).

Regionalism: Local Government in the Age of the Metropolis

From regionalism to new regionalism Since the early 1950s, most advanced industrial states have been faced with a perceived need to enlarge the units of their local government in order to cope with major changes, both demographic and conceptual, at the local level. The demographic change was expressed in considerable post-second-world-war growth of urban centers well beyond their existing jurisdictional boundaries. The conceptual change involved the expansion of the service responsibilities of local governments, both in relation to the new spatially determined functions related to urbanism and to the expansion of the state itself and its new role as a modifier of market allocation. The enlarged demographic units and the new local services, which often involved high fixed costs, raised questions about the adequacy of the existing local government structure, in terms of economies of scale and externalities, and gave rise to a regionalist movement that advocated increasing the scale of local governments as the only way to meet these problems properly (Sharpe, 1995).

The extent of the response to regionalism has varied considerably among the Western states from the United States at the one extreme, where it has been non-existent—indeed the number of local units has only increased—to the United Kingdom, where local governments have been transformed into the largest units in the entire Western world.[25] Since the mid-1970s, and more so during the 1980s, the regionalist model has suffered a significant decrease in prestige. This change reflected a general decline in faith in the institutional capacity of governmental institutions that found its most extreme expression in the widespread privatization movement. As Smith (1985) observed: 'the values of decentralization seem to have wide appeal, regardless of ideology or political theory. It is fashionable to deplore the over-centralization of contemporary government' (Smith, 1985, p.3). Another major blow to the regionalist movement was the decline in the importance of planning as a central mechanism of government. Planning as the pinnacle of urban government was an intellectual fashion in the 1960s and was rejected in the 1980s, partly as a reaction to some of the planning products of the 1960s. As a result, regional governments in several European metropolitan areas (most notably Barcelona, Rotterdam, Copenhagen and London) were abolished (Sharpe, 1995).

The last decade has witnessed an upsurge of interest in regionalism, arguably due in part to disillusionment with the social and economic effects of decentralization. What follows is a discussion of the notions of local government advanced by new regionalist scholars.

New regionalism: Localism for metropolitan areas Regionalism, argued Richard Briffault (2000), is in fact localism for metropolitan areas. The theoretical case for local autonomy rests on a set of arguments about the role of local governments in promoting efficiency, political participation, and community values. Local government law has traditionally been associated with the organization and powers of discrete and relatively small localities, whose residents had a high level of interaction with each other and a low level of interaction with outsiders. A notion of local autonomy that enables the people who live within such discrete communities to organize themselves into distinct political units and gives those units power to make decisions with respect to a range of public policies and services worked well in such a system. In contemporary times, however, the vast majority of the population does not live in discrete communities, but rather in sprawling metropolitan areas (Briffault, 1996). The economically, socially, and ecologically relevant unit in such metropolitan areas is not so much the locality as it is the region as a whole. People who live in metropolitan areas do not—indeed cannot—concentrate their daily lives within any one locality but, rather, regularly cross local jurisdictional boundaries. 'A person may live in one locality, work in another, shop in a third, seek entertainment or engage in a cultural activity in a fourth, and move through a large number of other localities during the course of his or her daily rounds' (Briffault, 2000, p.3). Regions, not localities, function as the primary units of reference for metropolitan residents in terms of housing and labor markets, environmental resources and cultural activities. Therefore, if we apply the traditional notion of local government—a group of people who have common place-based interests, a relatively high level of interaction with each other and much less intense interaction with residents of other localities—to contemporary metropolitan regions, then, in David Rusk's words, the real city is the total metropolitan area (Rusk, 1995). As a result, in the metropolitan context, concerns about efficiency, democracy, community and social equality, ought to lead to a shift of some of the powers away from the existing localities to new structures and organizations that promote decision making on a regional level.

- Efficiency—In metropolitan areas, negative externalities and spillover effects can be avoided, free mobility protected and the opportunity of poorer localities to supply decent public services secured only at a regional level. Therefore, in the metropolitan context the efficiency arguments provided as a justification for decentralization actually indicate the need for some kind of regionalism (Briffault, 2000).
- Democracy—A central value of democratic participation is that it enables people affected by governmental decisions to participate in the process by which those

decisions are made. The pervasive externalities that undermine the efficiency argument, however, mean that many of the people affected by a locality's decision live outside its jurisdictional borders and therefore are unable to participate in its decision-making processes. In particular, local land use decisions regularly affect people outside the locality. Only a regional forum can make sure that more citizens affected by a decision will have an opportunity to voice their opinion in a fully democratic process. A second assumption of the democratic argument for decentralization is that only in small and autonomous units of local government can citizens participate in the political process in an effective way and make a real impact. This argument is undermined, however, by the limited ability of many local governments to effectively address critical issues of local significance, such as adequacy of the local tax-base, economic development and urban sprawl. The individual may have a larger role in the formulation of local policies, but in the metropolitan context local governments are powerless to solve many critical problems. Thus, as with efficiency, the democracy argument in fact supports the case for some form of regionalism (Briffault, 2000; Cashin, 2000).

- Community—The localist argument for community assumes that localities are not simply a group of people who happen to live in relatively close proximity, but are, instead, territorially-based associations of people who closely interact with each other, have common interests and concerns, and are in some sense bound to each other. In metropolitan areas, however, localities are not communities within the traditional romantic sense. In the age of the automobile culture, localities are not the focal point of most of the activities of their residents, who work, shop, and engage in social activities across jurisdictional boundaries. In addition, most localities lack any public fora that could promote face-to-face contact among citizens. Therefore, neither the locality nor the metropolitan areas are communities in the traditional sense of the term (Briffault, 2000). More importantly, if the desire for 'community' effectively means the desire for racial, ethnic and socio-economic homogeneous localities, which is in many cases what the term community is translated to mean in reality, its normative justification loses much of its legitimacy (Cashin, 2000; Young, 1990). Lastly, it should be remembered, regionalist scholars argue, that local communities are, to a great extent, not the source but the product of the current structure of local government. The existing structure prevents metropolitan residents, who live in separate localities, from recognizing their shared interests and interdependence and thus also from becoming part of a regional community. In order to foster a notion of regional community, we have first to change the legal structure governing the region. Regional growth management laws, regional tax-base sharing or regional governing councils would be the means to bring the regional community into being (Briffault, 2000). The central deficiency of local autonomy, however, is that the efficiency and democracy benefits of local governments are not equally available to all metropolitan area residents, and as a result residents of poorer localities are treated as less than equal members of the metropolitan community. The existing structure reflects and reinforces inequalities in mobility opportunities, tax burden and municipal services among residents of different local governments. Affluent local governments that benefit from the status quo have, of course, no interest in changing it, and the only way to overcome the self-interested nature of local politics is by imposing on it some sort of regional government (Briffault, 2000).

Different models of regional governance Regionalist ideas on the structure of metropolitan governance take many shapes and forms. While in the 1960s, the heyday of the old regionalist movement, the preferred types of regionalism were either the unitary model or the two-tier model, new regionalists advocate radically different models, ranging from regional tax-base and service sharing mechanisms to a 'mix strategy', combining regional and local power. The unitary model advocated the creation of a metropolitan-wide authority simply by extending the boundaries of the existing local government to cover whatever is deemed to be the real extent of the metropolis. In this way the structure of government remained unitary. The unitary model suffered, however, from many shortcomings, not the least of which was political—it was, in most cases, politically impossible for central cities to obliterate and absorb the municipalities surrounding them.[26]

The two-tier model leaves the existing pattern of municipalities intact, superimposing a metropolitan authority over it. Advocates of the two-tier model argue that it can help resolve the eternal tension within local government between the values of democratic participation and local identity on the one hand and efficiency and social equality on the other (Sharpe, 1995). As David Harvey argued, what is required is 'a territorial organization which is hierarchical in nature and which allows maximum participation while at the same time ensuring a closer to optimal provision of general urban services' (Harvey, 1973, p.94).

Contemporary new-regionalists advocate yet a third model of regional governance that is even less invasive in the local sphere than the two-tier model. Regional policy making, it is argued, does not necessarily require regional institutions. What is needed, instead, are mechanisms that would be able to articulate regional concerns and formulate and implement regional policies. Policy proposals can come from sources as varied as existing local governments, public interest groups or individual citizens. Tax-base and service sharing can be administered by the state. In short, the mechanisms for regional coordination and cooperation can take any form, as long as regional issues are considered and policies responsive to the concerns of the residents of the region as a whole are implemented (Briffault, 2000).

Political Decentralization: The Promise of an Emancipating Political Space

The third approach to local governance, labeled by some 'political decentralization', shares much of the criticism leveled by regionalist scholars against decentralization as envisioned by public choice scholars. Advocates of political decentralization also agree with regionalist scholars that the current structure of local government law, which fosters metropolitan fragmentation and local selfishness, has an adverse effect on social equality and therefore is untenable. They shy away, however, from embracing centralization, in the form of regional government, as the cure for the system's ills for both ideological and pragmatic reasons. The ideological argument is based on the values of participatory democracy and community building. 'Participatory politics cannot thrive in a mass democracy', wrote Richard Ford (1994, p.1908). 'If anything, local units need to become smaller to make meaningful political participation feasible. A centralized regional authority that encompass several localities leaves little opportunity for politically empowered cultural communities to form and to thrive.' From a pragmatic standpoint the reliance on centralization is, according to Gerald Frug (2000), highly problematic because:

> the prevailing conceptual framework that now dominates thinking about metropolitan governance presents local governmental power as the exercise of freedom and centralized decision making as the exercise of coercion ... Regional government is usually understood as simply one more form that this centralized coercion would take. As a result, 'almost no one favors metropolitan government', as Anthony Dawn put it, 'except a few political scientists and intellectuals' (Frug, 2000, pp.32–33).

Instead, political decentralization scholars propose an alternative definition of decentralization that is radically different from the one embraced by public choice scholars or by contemporary local government law. The notion of decentralization that they advocate is based neither on a zone of immunity from state control nor on the power to exclude outsiders, but on the reestablishment of the importance of cities to the lives of their inhabitants. The 'community' that they envision is nothing like the traditional community, which devalues social difference and defines itself in opposition to other groups. On the contrary, they seek to avoid the romantic sense of togetherness traditionally associated with the term 'community', replacing it with an understanding of community as a 'being together of strangers'. The purpose of 'community building', according to Frug (1999), is to increase the capacity of metropolitan residents to live in a world composed of people different from them:

> Neither cities nor the individuals who live within them need to rely for their protection on fortifying the boundary lines that separate them from others in the region. But they also do not have to fuse with these others into a larger whole Instead, they can develop the kind of relationship with each other that has historically characterized city life, one built on the ability to find an accommodation with those who inhabit the same geographic area, no matter how dissimilar they may be (Frug, 1999, pp.115–116).

What follows is a description of two models of local governance that apply these original notions of 'community' and 'decentralization', attempting to achieve a decentralized yet just local sphere.

Regional legislator: Gerald Frug's model Gerald Frug (1999) suggested shifting the power to define the legal authority of the metropolitan region's cities from the state government to a regional legislature. The purpose of the regional legislature, he explained, is not to have regional bodies replace local governments as the principal decision-making entities, as suggested by regionalist scholars, but to inject a regional voice into local decision making by requiring localities to take into account in their decisions the interests of other localities within the region. The task of the regional legislature would be confined to defining the powers and specifying the legal entitlements of the local governments within its jurisdiction. Since almost any local power has some effect on the region as a whole, the regional legislature, rather than individual cities, must have the power to determine the scope of the issues to be decided by it. The legislature, however, would not exercise its power to impose any decisions on the local governments, but would serve, instead, as a forum for inter-local negotiations about how to decentralize power. The very act of empowering a regional legislature to determine city entitlements, argued Frug, would transform the meaning of the decentralization of power. The objective of decentralization could no longer be the advancement of a parochial self-interest because no locality could achieve its goals without convincing fellow localities that its vision of decentralization was a good idea. Once cities learn, through battles in the regional legislature, what the regional impact of their decisions is, they will begin to internalize a more regional perspective and apply it in their own local decision making.[27]

Permeable boundaries: Richard Ford's model Richard Ford (1994; 1996) proposed semi-autonomous local governments with permeable boundaries. His model is based on decoupling local citizenship from local residence, thereby creating a more fluid notion of citizenship and more permeable local boundaries.

Under Ford's proposal local governments would retain authority over most services currently conceived of as local, including land use regulation, but jurisdictional boundaries would be rendered permeable in two ways. First, local elections would be open to all members of the metropolitan region or even to all citizens of the state rather than only to local residents. All local elections would be held on the same day and voters would receive a number of votes equal to the number of open seats. They would be able to cast the votes in any locality they wished, either casting all their votes in one election or spreading them around in order to weigh in on several elections. In this way voters would in fact draw their own jurisdictional boundaries, decide which local governments were most important to them, and allocate their votes accordingly. Second, revenues currently defined as local (mainly property taxes) would not be retained by any particular locality. Instead, the state or a regional administrative body would distribute the tax collected from all the localities in the region according to egalitarian principles of need or state-prescribed goals of the common good. In this way, localities would cease to view themselves as fiscally autonomous units competing with each other for tax-base generating residents and businesses and instead would recognize their interdependency.

This proposal, Ford argued, allows local governments to retain autonomy in decisions that directly affect community character, such as land use and planning decisions, but makes sure that such decisions will have no effect on tax revenues or political inclusion. A system of desegregated political space, concluded Ford, would probably result in more physical integration. It is different, however, from the classic model of spatial integration in two important ways:

> First, it does not impose a particular pattern of integration, but rather removes the impediments to a more fluid movement of persons and groups within and between political spaces. Second, this model does not accept the current manifestation of political space and simply attempts to 'shuffle the demographic deck' to produce statistical integration, but instead challenges the mechanism by which political spaces are created and maintained, and by extension, challenges one of the mechanism by which racial and cultural hierarchies are maintained (Ford, 1994, p.1914).

Toward a Reform of Local Government Law

Having surveyed various theoretical models of local governance, in this section I propose a blueprint for reform of local government law for Israel. This proposal consists of preliminary ideas for a possible reform, roughly sketched out. The proposal is offered not as the last word on the subject, but, on the contrary, as an introductory note for what would hopefully become an ongoing discussion about the way to structure a better local government law for Israel. It suggests that a structure of local government that could reverse the vicious circle described above by fostering regional equality and social justice, without giving up the values of community building and democratic participation, indeed exists.

A Provisional Map for Reform of Local Government

The reform of local government law proposed here was inspired, primarily, by the models envisioned by new-regionalist scholars such as Richard Briffault, Iris Marion Young and Sheryll Cashin, but was also influenced by the ideas of political decentralization scholars such as Gerald Frug and Richard Ford. My proposal seeks to reduce the significance of local boundaries and create regionally bounded elected governments to address issues of regional significance, while leaving local governments a reduced, yet meaningful, sphere of local empowerment. It proposes the establishment of a regional government structure that would wield power over areas that transcend local borders, such as regional planning, land use regulation, mass transportation, and schools, while allowing local communities to retain some political power over matters of local concern. Under the new model, small local governments, in some cases smaller than the local units existing today, would remain the principal political units for decision making on issues that have insignificant or minor economic and political externalities. Yet, general purpose regional governments, with fiscal and land use planning powers, would provide a forum for metropolitan-wide deliberations, democratic participation, and the structuring and implementing of regulations and policies designed to meet the needs of the region as a whole.

Establishment of metropolitan-based regional governments At the core of my proposal lies the establishment of a two-tier municipal structure with strong upper-tier metropolitan governments, which would assume responsibility for all matters transcending local borders such as taxation, regional land use planning, and growth management, and less strong, yet meaningful, lower-tier local governments with powers over local matters. A regionalist approach, with powerful metropolitan governments at its center, is needed in order to overcome local selfishness, and foster a sense of regional interdependence among metropolitan localities. Regional tax-base sharing and a central forum for land use decision making, inherent to the regionalist model, would mend the structural economic inequality among local governments. Similarly, the romantic notion of local autonomy that currently works to fragment and segregate local governments as well as to prevent them from engaging in any inter-local cooperation would also become a thing of the past.

Specifically, four general-purpose regional governments for the four main metropolitan regions of Israel—Tel-Aviv, Jerusalem, Haifa, and Beer Sheva[28]—would be formed to accommodate some 90 per cent of the Israeli population presently residing in these four urbanized regions (Sharkansky, 1997) (Map 2). Each of the four metropolitan areas has special needs as well as unique advantages and functional specialization that should be attended to and nurtured by the regional government. Tel-Aviv is the center of commerce, high-tech industry, and cultural activities; Jerusalem is the locus of political power and national administration and offers also tourist attractions and strong research institutions; Haifa's economy is based on heavy industry as well as food and lodging services; and Beer Sheva contains a wide range of natural resources and is characterized by very low population density, thus providing the largest land reserve in the country (Shachar, 1997). Under the current regime, municipal fragmentation makes it impossible to develop those regional advantages efficiently, due to lack of cooperation among localities and fierce competition over tax-base generating sources; no attention is paid to the negative externalities such competition imposes on the region. Powerful regional governments with authority over taxing and land use would be able to overcome those inefficiencies and generate economic growth for the benefit of the region as a whole.[29]

It should be noted that my proposal is not the first initiative aimed at establishing regional governments for Israel's metropolitan areas. Already in the early 1970s, a state commission, chaired by Professor Ben-Shachar, supported the establishment of a multi-purpose municipal district that would serve the inner parts of the Tel-Aviv metropolis. The commission's report identified the acute problems of municipal fragmentation, such as lack of coordination among localities, lack of comprehensive land use planning and economic disparities between city and suburbs. The Ben-Shachar commission recommended the establishment of an upper-tier metropolitan government that would be granted extensive powers. The recommendations were never implemented (Razin, 1994). The 1980s have witnessed a general decline in the appeal of regionalist schemes which affected Israel as well. It led to the unfortunate recommendations of the Sanbar Commission on further decentralization of powers to local governments, and the granting of extensive fiscal powers, without any consolidation of existing local governments (Elazar, 1988b).

The political climate changed once again in the 1990s, and is now much more favorable to a regionalist-type reform. In fact, Israel is moving, slowly and unwittingly, toward a quasi-metropolitan governmental scheme, although, admittedly, there is a long way to go. Since the early 1990s Israel's national planning has undergone significant changes. The most significant policy departure from the pre-1990s planning phase was the abandonment of the population dispersal policy, replacing it with a more efficiency-oriented (and therefore metropolitan-oriented) approach (Shachar, 1998). The policy of population dispersal, which served as the major rationale for the building of a large number of small- to mid-size towns and villages in the state's periphery, has had a burdening effect on the country's economy in terms of capital investment, infrastructure, public housing and public services. The declining importance of political space in national planning combined with a transformation in the economy that made spatial aspects much less significant relative to efficiency considerations, highlighting the many inefficiencies inherent in the existing system of local government. The numerous small local governments, many with 3,000 residents or less, are unable to support themselves from internal sources (Razin, 1999). In 1996, the government appointed a commission, chaired by Arie Shachar, to look into the matter of local government consolidation. In its report the Commission for the Consolidation of Local Governments (the 'Shachar Commission') recommended forbiding the establishment of settlements under 10,000 residents by law, and consolidating all existing localities with a population under 3,000 with neighboring cities. The Shachar Commission further recommended the consolidation of medium size and even large cities, within the framework of a comprehensive reform that would significantly reduce the number of local governments in Israel. The Minister of the Interior adopted the recommendations and there are some indications that the government is moving to implement them, although, at this stage, only on a case-by-case basis.[30]

Uniform legal status to all local governments In order to avoid a conflict of authority, as well as differential legal treatment of similarly situated localities, all local governments—currently divided into cities, local councils and regional councils—would be granted a uniform municipal status irrespective of their size, nature and organizational belonging.

1. Abolishment of Regional Councils

   The establishment of the new regional governments would make the existing regional councils, which constitute the basic organizational unit of small rural settlements, obsolete. In fact, the justification for the existence of regional councils is questionable even under the current regime. The sharp decline in the formerly dominant ruralist ideology, as well as the increasing blurring of the distinction between rural and urban settlements, eliminates the need for separate planning and administration for the urban and rural sectors and thus undermines the very raison d'etre of the regional councils. The collectivist ideology has lost much of its influence in shaping the life and organization of rural communities, thus opening them up to new institutional arrangements that resemble in many respects those of Israel's urban communities. A growing number of kibbutzim and other cooperative settlements have abandoned the communal-agricultural life and have become involved in the booming real estate market, establishing joint ventures with private capital to promote the development of housing estates and industrial business facilities. Most Arab villages located in the rural areas had been forced to urbanize, transforming much of their labor force into commuters to the metropolitan labor markets. In addition, many exurban residential communities were established in recent years in formerly rural areas, further blurring the already tenuous distinction between rural and urban spaces. These processes have propelled regional councils to become more and more like urban local authorities and to take on the same responsibilities as urban local governments (Shachar, 1998). Unless the current structure of local government is reformed, the continuing advent of residential, industrial and other non-agricultural land uses into rural space would lead to an increasing municipal fragmentation of the urban-rural fringe. Regional councils must, therefore, be abolished and their underlying settlements should receive city status.

2. Abolishment of Local Councils

   The existing legal distinction between local councils and cities is also harmful since it creates an unjustified differential treatment of functionally similar local governments. Cities and local councils within contemporary metropolitan regions are indistinguishable in terms of the services they supply and the role they play in the life of their citizens. Nevertheless, as we have seen, the legislature and the courts still treat cities and local councils differently, reflecting an idealized and romantic notion of local councils as the locus of organic communities and long-lasting Zionist disdain for and fear of the city. Indeed, some local councils, such as Ramat Ha-Sharon, that long ago reached the size threshold for city status, refuse to change their legal status, probably due to the favorable legal treatment received by local councils (Peled, 1988). Since there is no justification, economic, moral or otherwise, for sustaining such a distinction, it should be abolished.

Cities should be granted meaningful powers Participatory politics is, admittedly, hard to sustain in a mass democracy. A centralized regional government of the kind proposed here leaves little opportunity for politically empowered communities to form and to thrive. Although we should expect some form of 'regional community' to evolve out of a regionalist scheme, if we sincerely wish to nourish cultural difference we will need to grant smaller communities some degree of control over their public sphere as a haven for cultural subgroups (Ford, 1994). Regional governments need not—indeed should not—wholly replace local governments. There is a place within our model for reduced yet significant local power to be exerted. It is important, however, as Iris Young (1990 p.249) argued, 'to distinguish local empowerment from local autonomy'. Autonomy, she explained, primarily emphasized exclusion; the right to keep others out and prevent them from interfering in local decisions and actions. Empowerment, on the other hand, is defined as 'participation of an agent in decision making through an effective voice and vote' (Young, 1990, p.251). Unlike Iris Young, who is willing to cede to local communities only powers that affect no one, thus in fact stripping them of any meaningful power, I believe that in order to empower local communities we must grant them some power to determine conditions under which other agents are compelled to act, albeit only in matters that are, fundamentally, of local concern.

The division of powers between regional governments and local governments is an issue which is hard, if not impossible, to resolve analytically. There are, of course, powers that can be rather easily classified as either regional or local in nature. Master planning, public transportation, environmental protection, and taxation are all easily classified as powers that have major regional effects and therefore should be exercised by the regional government. Local cultural activities, and parking and traffic regulation of side streets and internal roads can be identified as matters of local concern. There is, however, no clear distinction between local and regional matters. Small-scale land use decisions, the police power, as well as unique public services that target the needs of a local community, are issues that fall within the 'gray area'. In fact, almost every local power can be shown to have some regional effect. We should not, therefore, attempt to answer in advance what powers would be exerted by each of the entities. Instead, I propose a procedural mechanism to decide the 'hard cases' that fall within such a gray area.

The initial authority to determine the scope of local power would be granted to the regional governments. The regional governments would not have, however, the final word. A quasi-judicial mechanism for resolving regional-local disputes over the scope of their powers would be established under the auspices, but not the control, of the Ministry of the Interior, in which both local and regional interests would be represented (the

'Tribunal'). The panel of the Tribunal would be comprised of seven judges—two local representatives from localities with similar characteristics to the one involved in the dispute, two representatives from regional governments other than the one involved in the dispute, one representative appointed by the Minister of the Interior, and two experts specializing in urban planning and local government. Proceedings in the Tribunal would take the form of negotiations rather than adversarial litigation and the rules of evidence and civil procedure would not apply. The decisions of the Tribunal would be final and no appeal to further legal authorities would be allowed. The decisions of the Tribunal would serve as precedents in future disputes, but would not bind the Tribunal. The Tribunal would have the authority to fine or otherwise penalize localities for submitting frivolous claims, or regional governments for instigating them.

We should expect a large number of disputes during the initial phase of the reform implementation. After a while, however, when the dust has settled and the Tribunal has delivered a set of decisions, the division of powers between the new regional governments and their localities would be much clearer to all parties involved.

Local boundaries should be more easily amended in order to respond to community needs
The proposed reform does not include restructuring the current map of local governments (namely, changing the number or size of existing local governments). However, since some decisions that affect local communities would continue to be made at the local level, the shape of local boundaries would remain important. As Richard Ford (1994) argued, reified conceptions of community or local government that remove the placement of boundaries from democratic control are incompatible with cultural desegregation. The authority to define local boundaries should be placed, then, in the hands of local communities, employing a procedure that would guarantee the dissolving of boundaries which no longer reflected active communities and the establishing of new boundaries as new communities form.

I propose that no-fault, nonconsensual secessions would be granted. By 'nonconsensual secession' I refer to the right of citizens who live in a territorially bounded area to form a separate political jurisdiction without first having to seek the approval of any authority outside their own community. More specifically, a group of local residents who live in one or more territorially-connected neighborhoods, with a minimum of several hundred residents, would be allowed to secede from an existing locality, with the consent of a super-majority of their residents, and form in its stead a separate locality. The secession should be allowed even when the existing municipality has fulfilled every duty and caused no harm to the group that nevertheless wants to secede. Such 'no-fault' secession should be granted because it is based not upon fear of 'the tyranny of the majority', but upon a community's desire to express individuality that it cannot express while remaining in the existing municipality (Poindexter, 1997).

Once we make sure that such secessions would affect neither tax revenue and wealth distribution nor significant land use decisions, they become much less threatening to the goals of democratic inclusion and social equality, but would still have a significant empowering effect on subcultural communities. It is reasonable to assume that only communities that truly share a worldview and practices that significantly diverge from those of the rest of the local citizens would bother to secede, when the benefits of secession would be expressed neither in economic terms nor in terms of control over land resources, but mostly in cultural terms.[31]

Elections to regional governments—one person/one vote Elections to the regional government would be open to all residents of the metropolitan region. Elections to the regional government and all its underlying local governments would be held on the same day, and voters would cast votes for the chair and council members in both their locality and the regional government.

The elections would be based on a one person/one vote system. Many advocates of regionalism, including all former proposals for metropolitan government in Israel, recommend deviation from the one person/one vote rule, basing representation at the regional level on preexisting local subunits (the 'federative model'). Richard Briffault, for instance, proposed a federative model for regional government elections, arguing that 'moderating the stringency of one person/one vote for regional governments is less than a deviation from democratic norms' (Briffault, 1993, p.417). A federative regional government model is justified, according to Briffault, because it is unlikely that the burden of the government would be borne differently by different subunits. 'Residents of subunits subject to the regional government would also, by definition, be residents of the region and, thus, the region would be the jurisdiction for the application of strict scrutiny to deviation from population equality' (Briffault, 1993, p.416).

The logic of this argument escapes me. I fail to see how a regional government, based on preexisting local subunits, would be able to prevent deviation from a fair electoral process, while governed by the same local governments that benefit from this deviation. In fact, experience teaches us otherwise. Political jurisdictions and the indices used for weight voting have often been manipulated in order to disenfranchise minority groups. Moreover, in a system like the one proposed here, in which secessions are voluntary, a federative model might encourage secessions into small local units in order to obtain more power in the regional government. Only a universal one person/one vote rule can guarantee fair and equal representation for all the communities in the metropolitan region. This is all the more true in the Israeli situation in which minority groups have been traditionally underrepresented in all governmental and administrative bodies. More than half the Bedouin population, for instance, who live in 'unrecognized villages' both in the southern and the northern regions of Israel, would be denied a voice under a federative model. As a result, a stringent one person/one vote must be applied.

Why Regionalism?

The reasons for preferring the regionalist scheme to the two other models—decentralization and political decentralization—should be spelled out:

Why not decentralization? The decentralization model was rejected due to its detrimental effect on social equality. Decentralization of the kind suggested by Charles Tiebout and other advocates of public choice would not solve the problems of the current structure of local government discussed earlier, indeed it would only make them worse. Greater local autonomy is likely to produce even more exaggerated forms of the inequities that the current system produces: the concentration of needy people in those local governments that are least capable of providing proper social and welfare services would intensify, while other municipalities would continue to turn their back on what they consider as not their problem. The already large socio-economic gaps between rich and poor localities, easily identified in racial and ethnic terms, would intensify and segregation would become even more common.

Why not political decentralization? The Israeli situation does not lend itself to the implementation of the political decentralization model either. Gerald Frug and Richard Ford's prescription is greatly influenced by a disputable notion of community and is very much tied to the American sociopolitical context. Ford rejects any notion of local community independent of the territorial boundaries that created it. His proposal, he stresses, "is premised on the idea that local citizens, like local governments, are made not found... The boundaries define the local self; no preexisting local self creates the boundaries' (Ford, 1996, p.1191). Under such an assumption it is indeed possible to 'redefine ... that political boundaries define, to a great extent, the local self; indeed my proposal is based on such an assumption as well. I would not go, however, so far as to argue that there is never a preexisting self that defines local boundaries. In fact, my discussion of the ultra-Orthodox stresses precisely that communities sometimes preexist and define local boundaries. The process is a dialectical one in which political boundaries on the one hand and cultural communities on the other define and redefine each other.

Moreover, in order for the political decentralization scheme to work there is a need for a broad integrative category that binds all the distinct sub-national groups together. In America such a category exists and 'groups are different within a larger paradigm of sameness, namely national citizenship' (Ford, 1997, p.1437). Blacks, Caucasians, Asians, and Latinos define themselves first and foremost as Americans. Such a sentiment does not exist in the Israeli context. Israel is made up of a multitude of racial, ethnic and religious groups that oppose integration and are quite hostile to each other. Minority groups would rather suffer the consequences of segregation, if the only alternative presented to them was assimilation to the Israeli Jewish-Ashkenazi society. The Arab citizens of Israel, for instance, making up some 18 per cent of the entire population, do not consider themselves part of the national whole, but, on the contrary, affiliate themselves with the Arab nations. Another 10 per cent of the population—the ultra-Orthodox community—is also, in many respects, alienated from any substantive notion of national-democratic citizenship (as distinguished from a genealogical notion of Jewishness). A growing number of Arab-Jews (although not many) consider themselves to be culturally Arab, and reject what they consider as attempts of the state to strip them of their cultural identity.

Even in the American case some commentators express serious concerns that the political decentralization model, if implemented, would lead to loss of local control by local communities, whose political will would be frustrated by 'outsiders'. This model, they argue, would end up discouraging, instead of encouraging, political participation on the local level, and the groups that would be harmed most severely are cultural and racial minorities who need local autonomy as a safe haven from the rule of the majority (Briffault, 1996). Such concerns would be almost a certainty in the Israeli case. The animosity among the different groups is so great that the majority, if given the opportunity to interfere with the affairs of minority sub-groups, would not hesitate to do so, imposing its notion of the good on such groups thus frustrating the purpose of the reform.

Why not the state? The last question left to answer is why should we not just leave control over the local sphere at the state level? If we decide that centralization is the right way to go, we might as well go all the way and entrust local control to the state government. This would not even require structural reform, since the current structure of local government law enables the state to exert power over localities just about whenever it wishes to do so. Indeed, such an argument has been made. Ira Sharkansky (1997) claimed that a gradual process of urban expansion has resulted in the integration of the various urban centers into a 'mega-metropolis', which transformed Israel into, what he called, a 'metropolitan nation-state'. This process of metropolitan integration has resulted, in turn, in a convergence of local and national policy-making, and the creation of a governance system marked by 'responsiveness, accountability, democracy and metropolitan coordination', which renders unnecessary proposals for reforming the Israeli regime through decentralization of power to local or regional entities.

This argument is erroneous both empirically and theoretically. First, the state government has already been proved incompetent with regard to this mission. The central government is unable to exert the omnipotent powers to oversee local governments entrusted to it by law. The fact that almost any action by the local government requires approval in advance by the central government results in inadequate supervision over local activities (Ben-Elia, 1995). Strong localities that can take advantage of the central government's weakness and expend their realm of operation become even stronger, while weak localities that cannot enjoy this freedom for lack of financial and administrative capabilities are further weakened.

More importantly for our discussion, even if the state had proved itself functionally capable of overseeing local government activities, it would still be an untrustworthy agent because of its lack of ability to develop either a local or a regional perspective. The state has its own national agenda to pursue that is often in direct conflict with the well being and development of localities or even regions. Thus, for instance, nation and state building projects that for many years have been governing national decision making, dictating policies such as Judaization of remote territories as well as deliberate population dispersal, stand in direct conflict with the well being of at least some local governments and their residents (Yiftachel, 1997).

The result of the 'convergence of local and national policy-making', praised by Sharkansky, is that the balance of power in the state government is reflected at the local level. The strength of the ultra-Orthodox parties, for example, as the political group holding the balance of power between the Right and the Left, enables them to influence the policies governing localities all over the country, despite the fact that most local governments serve primarily non-Orthodox residents. Thus, for instance, most local governments prohibit public transportation as well as the operation of businesses on the Sabbath, including even localities that are entirely devoid of Orthodox residents (Gavison, 1998). Similarly, Arab localities have been traditionally discriminated against in budget allocation as well as physical infrastructure, reflecting power relations between Jews and Arabs in the state government.

Conclusion: The Benefits of Regionalism—The Case Studies Revisited

In conclusion, I will briefly revisit the case studies discussed in the first three chapters and illustrate how a regionalist reform of the kind proposed here would solve the problems inherent in the current system of political space.

Metropolitan-wide school desegregation Metropolitan-wide school desegregation has been proved, according to several commentators, both feasible and durable in a number of large metropolitan areas in the United States (Orfield, 1996; Powell, 1996). Metropolitan integration strategies that transcend municipal borders have been more successful at promoting and maintaining a greater level of school desegregation than citywide approaches, since they reduce the link between residential and school segregation (Powell, 1996).

The current structure of local government law has resulted, as we have seen in the first chapter, in perpetuating school segregation by treating local education authorities, whose jurisdictional boundaries trace the boundaries of local governments, as discrete and autonomous entities. Such a legal structure, on the background of the prevalent ethnic-based residential segregation, frustrated implementation of any significant school desegregation efforts.

The four regional governments, established under my proposal, would assume the power over education, currently vested in local governments, and function as a unified school district for the region as a whole. A metropolitan-wide school district would be able to overcome the problem of segregation, created by the historic unequal division of political space between Arab-Jews and European-Jews, by severing the link between residential segregation and school segregation.

Political and economic empowerment of minority groups Regional governments would serve to empower subordinated minority groups in two interrelated ways: first, by the amalgamation of regional powers that the current system of local government significantly curtails, and second, by the opening of new venues for grassroots coalition building across ethnic and racial lines.

The Palestinian-Arab minority, which makes up about 20 per cent of the entire Israeli population, is largely concentrated in two regions: the northern region, in which it constitutes about 40 per cent of the population, and the southern region, where more than one quarter of the population is Bedouin (Shachar, 1997). These regions, if officially recognized as significant political units, could realize a liberating potential for Arab minority groups.

The current system of local government, with its engineered fragmentation of regions into a multitude of secluded and powerless localities, has seriously hampered this possibility and, as a result, no such regional entities have been developed (Yiftachel, 1997). The proposed reform would deliberately create regional entities and vest them with significant powers, thus serving to change the political and economic power structure and giving much more weight to regionally based minority groups, such as Palestinian Arabs and the Bedouin.

Moreover, the balkanization of the metropolitan population into separate jurisdictions, increasingly stratified by income as well as by race and ethnicity, fosters an ill-conceived conception of self-interest that blinds local citizens to the real potential benefits of collective alliances across jurisdictional boundaries. Fragmentation has enabled a political order in which a narrow class of interests (middle and upper class Ashkenazi interests) dominates state decision making and most institutional processes that allocate public resources.

One of the aims of the regional government would be to energize coalitions of citizens and interests currently hampered by local jurisdictions. Coalitions across jurisdictional boundaries, and thus also across racial and ethnic lines, would change the political division of power dramatically. Under a regionalist system, the various New Towns in both the southern and the northern regions would be able to join forces in the regional government to change their fate. They might also realize that they have a lot in common with the Arab villages and Bedouin townships, which, like them, are located at the bottom of the socio-economic ladder, and together reassert democratic majoritarianism in institutional decision making.

Local autonomy without exclusion Small cultural communities, such as the ultra-Orthodox community in Jerusalem, which are geographically concentrated yet not large enough, under contemporary local government law, to form separate local governments, would be able, under the new regime, to incorporate as an independent locality and wield some powers over their jurisdiction, such as control over local religious and cultural institutions, and the regulation of local traffic. As a result these communities would be able to shape, to a certain extent, the public life of their locality according to their own system of belief, but would lack the power to exclude others who wish to join them.

At the regional level, however, such cultural communities would not be able to amalgamate a significant regional power and therefore their ability to influence the life in localities in which they do not constitute a majority would be significantly curtailed, to the benefit of the residents of these localities.

Notes

1 Cities are governed by the Municipal Corporation Ordinance (New Version); Local Councils are governed by the Local Councils Ordinance (New Version).

2 Regional Councils function through a two-tier system. Each individual village has its own settlement committee, elected by the local residents, which is responsible for the provision of various cultural and minor economic ventures. Each local committee sends at least one representative (depending on population size) to the management committee of the Regional Council, which is responsible for the provision of municipal services. Until 1990, the chairperson of the Regional Council was elected by majority vote from among the management committee representatives. As of January 1990, however, this election mechanism was replaced by direct elections in which all the residents of the region's villages directly elect the chairperson. (Newman, 1995).

3 To complete the picture, changes in the political climate, erosion in the status of the central government, and the economic growth that took place since the early 1970s entailed a transformation in the role of local governments. This process, which was not a planned one, did not involve any major change in the legal structure of local governments. Instead, the process was one of 'decentralization by default', with local governments feeling the vacuum created by the decline of the central government's influence (Ben-Elia, 1996). The only significant legal reform that did take place in the mid-1970s was the direct election of mayors. Prior to the reform, local elections were held exclusively on a party basis, with the party winning the elections nominating the mayor. As a result local officials were accountable primarily to their party. The idea behind the reform was to free mayors from the need to appeal primarily to their party, and thus facilitate the rise of independent candidates. Having mayors elected directly and, therefore, directly accountable to the public, substantially changed the typical local politicians (Janner-Klausner, 1994).

4 A factor shaping the planning doctrine of Israel from the 1950s to the 1980s was the role of settlements, both urban and rural, which were used to achieve political goals. 'The goals had different manifestations over the course of this period, two of which merit special attention.

One was the establishment of a maximal presence in vacant or semi-vacant parts of the country in order to repel any challenges to Israel's sovereignty over them. The principle was applied mainly in the Negev, the southern region of Israel. The second manifestation had as its aim the increase of the proportion of the Jewish population in certain regions. This principle was applied most actively in the Galilee, the northern part of Israel' (Shachar, 1998, pp.210–211).

5 While in a ten-year period between 1970 and 1979 only 62 boundary conflicts involving regional councils were filed, 73 such claims were filed between 1985 and 1989, and 41 claims in the year 1990 alone (Razin & Hasson, 1994).

6 The emergence of many small exurban residential communities in the rural areas of Israel in recent years, as well as the industrialization and urbanization of many of the formerly agricultural communal settlements (kibbutzim and Moshavim), blur the urban/rural distinction and might therefore serve as a catalyst of change in Israel's local government map (Shachar, 1998; Newman & Applebaum, 1995).

7 'The authority to change local boundaries is in the hands of the Minister of Interior. When a request is filed, the Minister can either turn it down or appoint a boundary commission to evaluate the proposal. After studying the commission's recommendations, the final decision is at the Minister of Interior's discretion. When no city (usually over 20,000 inhabitants) is involved, but rather smaller urban local councils and regional councils, the Minister is not obliged to appoint a commission, although it is customary to do so. Nevertheless, in some of these cases only a single investigator is nominated. The Minister can even rely on an agreement reached by the municipalities concerned, and decide without any formal enquiry. This legal framework has remained intact for decades' (Razin & Hasson, 1994, at 50). For Supreme Court decisions that restate and reinforce the magnitude of the Minister of the Interior's discretion in drawing jurisdictional boundaries: H.C. 51/68, *The Local Council Azur v. The Minister of Interior*, 22(2) P.D. 226, 228; H.C. 94/97, *The Municipality of Rishon-Lezion v. Minister of Interior*, 28(2) P.D. 711, 716; H.C. 489/94, *Municipality of Kiryat Ata v. Rabin, The Prime Minister and the Minister of Interior*, 38 Dinim Elyon, 182.

8 There are similar restrictions on the power of local councils and regional councils in the Local Councils Ordinance and the Local Councils Ordinance (Regional Councils) respectively.

9 H.C. 36/51, *Hat v. Municipality of Haifa*, 5 P.D. 1553.

10 H.C. 230/73, *S.Z.M. v. Mayor of Jerusalem*, 28(2) P.D. 113.

11 H.C. 287/71, *Da'abul v. Mayor of Ramat-Gan*, 26(2) 821, 824.

12 H.C. 94/97, *Municipality of Rishon-Lezion v. Minister of Interior*, 28(2) P.D. 711, 717.

13 H.C. 5445/93, *Municipality of Ramla v. Minister of Interior*, 50(1) P.D. 397.

14 H.C. 5139/92, *Sa'ida v. Minister of Interior*, 32 Dinim Elyon 147.

15 D.N.G.Z 1913/97, *Muasy v. Minister of Interior*, Takdin Elyon 98(1) 227.

16 H.C. 809/86, *Yanovitz v. Verbin*, 41(4) P.D. 309.

17 The Court qualified its decision saying that the outcome of the case might have been different if the petitioners had sought to open the sex shop in one of the side streets, instead of the main street. In a concurring opinion, Justice Bach went even further and rejected the distinction between a town's main streets and its side streets. Justice Bach wrote that it is beyond his comprehension why local councils, as opposed to cities, should be denied the power to limit and prohibit certain businesses, if most of the council members are of the opinion that such a prohibition is advisable for educational, moral or other reasons. 'The question is

not what would have been our decision if we had served as council members, but whether there is a justification for our interference with the decision of elected local officials, who represent a majority of the local citizens and who can be replaced by them at time of elections if they are not pleased with their decisions.'

18 The organic notion of local government is also illustrated in another business licensing case: H.C. 166/71, *Awad v. Local Council Usffiah*, 25(2) P.D. 591 (the local council of the Arab village of Usffiah refused to allow a coffeehouse opened in the village to play Western music. The Court affirmed the local council's decision: 'We do not think it is our place to frustrate the will of the elected body of local citizens to preserve the unique character of their village… according to the spirit and culture of the majority of its citizens').

19 R.C.A. 5817/95, *Rosenberg v. Ministry of Construction and Housing*, Takdin-Elyon 95(3) 1368.

20 It is important to note that Justice Heshin's dissent is tailored to the facts of the case, which are the exclusion of non-local-residents from participating in a project financed by the central government within the jurisdiction of a certain local government. It is quite clear from several remarks made by Justice Heshin that his opinion would have been different if the project had been financed and carried out by the local government. However, the logic of Justice Heshin's dissent reaches beyond the specific facts of the case.

21 This 'fee for service mentality' is reflected in many cases. For example, C.A. 1842/97, *Municipality of Ramat Gan v. Menahemy Migdaley David Ramat Gan L.T.D.* ('Local government resembles an autarkic market for income and expenditures'); H.C. 6741/99, *Yekutiely v. Minister of Interior* ('Local government operates, in principle, only within its jurisdictional boundaries, and within this jurisdiction it bears all the costs involved in administering the community and supplying environmental and communal services to community members').

22 *Rosenberg v. Ministry of Construction and Housing*, p.1376 (Heshin J. dissenting).

23 There are also examples of inter-local tax sharing agreements among various localities. However, these agreements are put in place only when they provide benefits to all the parties involved. In addition, the transfer of revenues from one municipality to another stands on shaky legal grounds and has not yet been tested in court (Razin, 1997).

24 Nozick denies the state any role in promoting a substantive conception of the common good. Instead, he argues, the state should serve as a mere framework for small utopias—voluntary communities that pursue their own vision of the good life—enforcing contracts between individuals and communities and mediating disputes between communities).

25 While the number of local government units in the U.S. rose between the years 1972 and 1987 from 22,185 to 29,532, the number of local units in the U.K. decreased from 1391 localities in 1972 to 415 in 1987 (Sharpe, 1995).

26 David Rusk is an example of a contemporary regionalist scholar who advocates implementation of the unitary model. Rusk (1995) urges in his book Cities Without Suburbs the consolidation of existing metropolitan area local governments, or annexation by the central city in the region, as the best means of achieving metropolitan policy goals of reducing racial segregation, remedying inter-local fiscal disparities, and promoting regional economic development. Having one unitary metropolitan government, argues Rusk, is much better than trying to get multiple local governments with conflicting interests to act like a metropolitan government. The former is a more lasting and stable framework for sustained, long-term action.

27 This summary does not exhaust all of Frug's proposals for local government reform. He also proposed reorganizing the collection and distribution of property taxes in terms different than

local jurisdictional lines, and opening local elections to non-residents. His regional legislator proposal, however, is the most comprehensive one and stands at the center of his work.

28 There is a difference between Tel-Aviv and Jerusalem's metropolitan areas and those of Beer Sheva and Haifa. While Tel-Aviv and Jerusalem fall neatly within the classic definition of metropolitan areas as 'continuously built-up urbanized regions', Beer Sheva and Haifa depart from this model in several important respects. Unlike the classic model, they are comprised of a group of localities of various sizes separated by open spaces and bound together by highways, and were therefore defined by some scholars as 'regiopolis' or 'regional cities' instead of metropolis (Gradus & Stern, 1980). Nevertheless, a substantive definition of metropolitan areas, as self-contained regions that are characterized by high interdependence, specialization and decentralization, encompass all four Israeli urbanized regions (Florestano & Marando, 1981). Thus, the Negev regiopolis, with the city of Beer Sheva at its center, 'tends to function as one metropolis, but instead of being a continuity of built-up areas, there are islands of small and medium-sized urban communities and industrial complexes, separated by arid vacant land and connected by a network of roads' (Gradus & Stern, p. 418).

29 The proposed reform, which would presumably solve intra-regional inequalities and inefficiencies, would not resolve the problem of inter-regional inequality. There is a significant disparity in economic power among the four regions, with the Tel-Aviv metropolis at the top of the list, with some 46 per cent of the entire job market, and the southern district at the bottom, suffering from high rates of unemployment and economic deprivation. Leaving the scene to free market forces would result in the reproduction of the socio-economic hierarchies imprinted on Israel's political geography, through state policies such as population dispersal, during the formative decades of the 1950s and 1960s. Therefore, even after implementing the reform the state would still have a role in equalizing inter-regional economic disparities. The equalization efforts should take the form of differential investment in infrastructure, education and industry. The state must invest in modern infrastructure, such as airports, interstate highways and railroads, that would efficiently connect the southern region to the rest of the country. In addition, industries and businesses should be encouraged to relocate to the southern and northern regions by offering them financial benefits, such as tax reduction and subsidized land (Shachar, 1997).

30 Mazal Mualem, High Court of Justice: Kokhav Ya'ir will be Consolidated with the Neighboring Settlement, *Ha'aretz*, 21 June, 2001.

31 My proposal runs the risk that the distribution of land use powers between the regional government and the local governments, as determined by the Tribunal, would grant too much power to local governments, thus encouraging secessions based on the desire to regulate land use. One way to prevent such an outcome is to try and prescribe some ground rules for allocation of land use powers between the regional governments and the underlying localities. Such ground rules, however, are admittedly very hard to prescribe. Another issue that might arise is symbolic resistance to my voluntary secession proposal. Some might oppose it on the grounds that it would end up dividing well-established cities, particularly Jerusalem, but also Tel-Aviv and Haifa. One way to defuse such resistance is to name the new seceding entities 'neighborhoods' or 'quarters' instead of cities, while vesting in them the same powers which would be vested in local governments. In this way the symbolic entity that is the city would be kept intact, while creating as many functional local entities as local communities may desire.

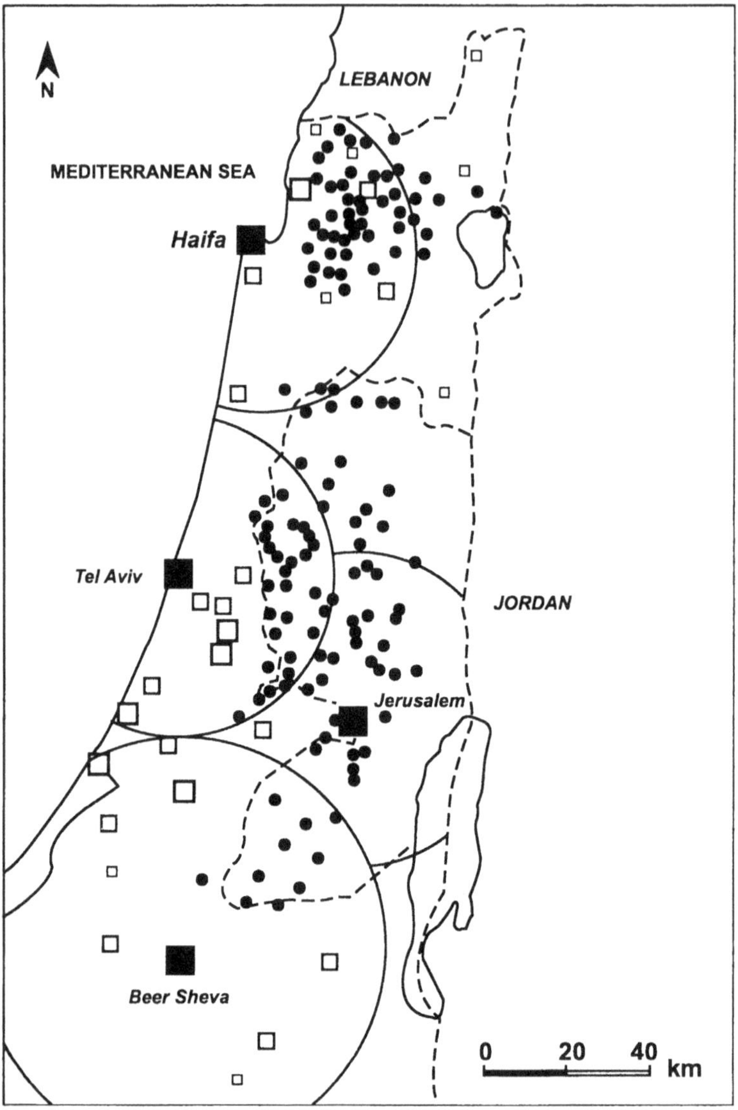

Map 2 Jurisdictional Map for the New Regional Governments

Chapter 7
Epilogue

> In the center of Fedora, the gray stone metropolis, stands a metal building with a crystal globe in every room. Looking into each globe, you see a blue city, the model of a different Fedora. These are the forms the city could have taken if, for one reason or another, it had not become what we see today. In every age someone, looking at Fedora as it was, imagined a way of making it the ideal city, but while he constructed his miniature model, Fedora was already no longer the same as before, and what has been until yesterday a possible future became only a toy in a glass globe (Calvino, 1974, p.32).

This short excerpt from Italo Calvino's *Invisible Cities* captures both the hope and the despair inherent in the attempt to rethink and restructure political space, and therefore in this study as well. The book has attempted to follow Michel Foucault's (1980) advice and write a history of spaces, which is at the same time also the history of powers. By always foregrounding the spatial distribution of hierarchical power relations, we can better understand the processes whereby a space achieves a distinctive identity. I have argued that it is impossible to understand the production of Israel's fragmented map and the unequal division of political space without taking into account the constitutive role played by Zionist ideology in their production. From this perspective, what seemed, at first sight, to be a liberating gesture, a spatially inscribed respect for distinctive cultures—is in fact a raw manifestation of subjecting powers, an oppressive production of difference that plays a critical part in nationalist hegemony. On the other hand, what was perceived initially as a tyrannical disregard of communities and their space is revealed as stemming from a desire to include these groups within the national whole, the flip side of the nationalist project.

My attempt to narrate the social history of Israel's political spaces and understand the underlying forces that shaped them is an ambitious project. It has been necessarily sweeping and has often sacrificed details for breadth. A close analysis of any of the case studies discussed in this thesis would reveal a much more complicated picture. Despite the numerous spatial mechanisms and practices employed by both state and local agents, maintaining pure homogeneous spaces is a Sisyphian task. Indeed, the very notion of homogeneous communities which supposedly occupy pure spaces is itself obscure and in a constant state of flux. As a result, examples of people pertaining to different racial, ethnic or religious groups living together in various degrees of harmony can be found. Members of an extremist ultra-Orthodox Hasidic group live peacefully at the heart of one of the most chic and trendy secular neighborhoods (Gonen, 1995). Interracial settlements serve both Jews and Palestinians who made a conscious ideo-

Interracial settlements serve both Jews and Palestinians who made a conscious ideological choice to live together. Arabs and Jews (mostly Arab-Jews) live side by side in mixed cities, although oftentimes in a tense, sometimes inflammatory, environment. Jews and Arabs, as well as European-Jews and Arab-Jews find themselves in the same classrooms in institutions of higher education. These examples are important instances of the achievable ideal of polyphonic and plural political spaces. Each of them should be carefully studied and analyzed as a liberating alternative to the current condition of segregation so endemic to Israeli society.

The primary lesson one should take from this study is that political space can never be ignored or taken for granted. We should not assume that space is the neutral grid on which cultural difference, historical memory, and societal organization are inscribed. It is precisely this kind of assumption that has enabled the power of geography to successfully conceal the geography of power. Instead, we should pay careful attention to the way spaces and places are constructed, imagined, contested and enforced. As Edward Soja (1989) reminded us, 'space in itself may be primoridially given, but the organization, and meaning of space is a product of social translation, transformation, and experience' (Soja, 1989, pp.79–80). Would a better understanding of political space and the way it is constructed produce a better society? Perhaps, and perhaps not. The least we can hope for is that such understanding would help us avoid the mistakes of past generations and help the next generation to avoid ours.

Bibliography

Abu-Rabia, Aref (1994), The Negev Bedouin and Livestock rearing—Social, Economic and Political Aspects, Berg Publishers, Providence.

Algrabli, Mordechai (1974), 'Criteria for Typification of the Social Composition of Schools and a Method for the Allocation of Special Nurturing Budgets among Schools', *Megamot*, Vol.21, pp.219–227.

Althusser, Louis (1996), *For Marx*, Verso, New York.

Avineri, Shlomo (1998) 'Zionism and the Religious Jewish Tradition: The Dialectic of Redemption and Secularization', in Shmuel Almog, Jehuda Reinharz and Anita Shapira (eds), *Zionism and Religion*, University Press of New England, Hanover, pp.9–18.

Barron, David J. (1999), 'The Promise of Cooley's City: Traces of Local Constitutionalism', *University of Pennsylvania Law Review*, Vol.147, pp.487–612.

Bauman, Zygmunt (1991), *Modernity and Ambivalence*, Cornell University Press, Ithaca.

Bauman Zygmunt (2000), *Liquid Modernity*, Polity, Cambridge.

Beck, E. M. et al. (1978), 'Stratification in Dual Economy: A Sectoral Model of Earnings Determination', *American Sociological Review*, Vol.43, pp.704–720.

Ben-David, Yosef (1989), 'The Negev Bedouin: From Nomadism to Agriculture', in Ruth Kark (ed.), *The Land that Became Israel: Studies in Historical Geography*, Yale University Press, New Haven, pp.181–195.

Ben-David, Yosef (1993), *The Urbanization of the Nomadic Bedouin Population of the Negev*, 1967–1992, Jerusalem Institute for Israel Studies, Jerusalem.

Ben-David, Yosef (1994a), 'Adaptation Amidst Crisis—Social Aspects of Bedouin Urbanization in the Negev', in David Grossman and Avinoam Meir (eds) *The Arabs in Israel: Geographical Dynamics*, Magnes, Jerusalem, pp.48–76.

Ben-David, Yosef (1994b), *The Bedouin Educational System in the Negev: Reality and the Need for Advancement*, Floersheimer Institute for Policy Studies, Jerusalem.

Ben-David, Yosef et al. (1976), *The Process of Sedentarization and Settlement among the Bedouin of the Negev*, Ford Foundation, New York.

Ben-David, Yosef and Kressel, Gideon (1995), 'Bedouin Market—Cornerstone of Beer-Sheva', *Notes on the Bedouin*, Vol.25, pp.15–25.

Ben-Elia, Nahum (1995), *Towards a Policy of Differential Decentralization in Local Authorities*, Floersheimer Institute for Policy Studies, Jerusalem.

Ben-Elia, Nahum (1996), 'Organizational Reorientation and Learning in Israeli Local Government: The Role of market Type Mechanisms', in Nahum Ben-Elia (ed.), *Strategic Changes and Organizational Reorientations in Local Government: A Cross-National Perspective*, St. Martin's Press, New York, pp.75–89.

Ben-Zadok, Efraim (1993), *Local Communities and the Israeli Polity: Conflict of Values and Interests*, SUNY Press, Albany.

Benvenisti, Eyal (1998), '"Separate but Equal" in the Allocation of State Land for Housing', *Tel-Aviv University Law Review*, Vol.21, pp.769–798.

Berman, Marshall (1988), *All That Is Solid Melts Into Air: The Experience of Modernity*, Penguin, New York.

Blomely, Nicholas K. (1994), *Law, Space and the Geographies of Power*, Guilford, New York.

Bollens, John C. (1957), *Special District Governments in the United States*, University of California Press, Berkeley.

Boyarin, Jonathan (1994), 'Hegel's Zionism?', in Jonathan Boyarin (ed.) *Remapping Memory: The Politics of TimeSpace*, University of Minnesota Press, Minneapolis, pp.137–160.

Boyarin, Jonathan (1997), 'Circumscribing Constitutional Identities in Kiryas Joel', *Yale Law Journal*, Vol.106, pp.1537–1570.

Briffault, Richard (1990), 'Our Localism: Part II—Localism and Legal Theory', *Columbia Law Review*, Vol.90, pp.346–454.

Briffault, Richard (1993), 'Who Rules at Home?: One Person/One Vote and Local Governments', *University of Chicago Law Review*, Vol. 60, pp.339–424.

Briffault, Richard (1996), 'The Local Government Boundary Problem in Metropolitan Areas', *Stanford Law Review*, Vol.48, pp.1115–1171.

Briffault, Richard (2000), 'Localism and Regionalism', *Buffalo Law Review*, Vol.48, pp.1–30.

Buchanan, James M. (1971), 'Principles of Urban Local Strategy', *Public Choice*, Vol.XI, pp.1–14.

Calhoun, Craig (1995), *Critical Social Theory: Culture, History and the Challenge of Difference*, Blackwell, Cambridge.

Calvino, Italo (1974), *Invisible Cities*, Harcourt Brace Jovanovich, New York.

Cashin, Sheryll D. (2000), 'Localism, Self-Interest, and the Tyranny of the Favored Quarter: Addressing the Barriers to New Regionalism', *Georgetown Law Journal*, Vol.88, pp.1985–2048.

Castells, Manuel, (1983), *The City and the Grassroots: A Cross Cultural Theory of Urban Social Movements*, Edward Arnold, London.

Central Bureau of Statistics (1999), *Israel Statistical Annual*, Vol.50, State of Israel, Jerusalem.

Central Bureau of Statistics (2000), *Israel Statistical Annual*, Vol.51, State of Israel, Jerusalem.

Chen, Michael (1980), 'Some Outcomes of School Reform in Israel', in Stephen Goldstein (ed.), *Law and Equality in Education*, Van Leer Jerusalem Foundation, Jerusalem, pp.61–68.

Chen, Michael and Addi, Audrey (1995), 'Community Politics, School Reform and Educational Achievement', in Reuven Kahana (ed.), *Educational Advancement and Distributive Justice: Between Equality and Equity*, Magnes, Jerusalem, pp.341–357.

Chertok, Haim (1999), 'Dances with Camels: Al-Okhbi and Rahat', in Richard Israelowitz and Jonathan Friedlander (eds), *Transitions: Russians, Ethiopians and Bedouins in Israel's Negev Desert*, Ashgate, Aldershot, pp.109–123.

Cohen, Erik (1970), *The City in the Zionist Ideology*, Institute of Urban and Regional Studies, Jerusalem.

Cooper, Davina (1996), 'Talmudic Territories? Space, Law, and Modernist Discourse', 23 *Journal of Law and Society*, Vol.23(4), pp.529–548.

Cooper, Davina (1998), *Governing Out of Order: Space, Law and the Politics of Belonging*, Rivers Oram, London and New York.

Cooter, Robert (2000), *The Strategic Constitution*, Princeton University Press, Princeton.

Dahl, Robert A. and Tufte, Edward R. (1973), *Size and Democracy*, Stanford University Press, Stanford.

Dalal, Marwan (2000), 'The Guest, the House, and the Judge', *Adalah's Review*, Vol.2, pp.44–49.

Davies, Wayne K. D. and Herbert, David T. (1993), *Communities within Cities: An Urban Social Geography*, Halsted, New York.

Denton, Nancy A. (1996), 'The Persistence of Segregation: Links Between Residential Segregation and School Segregation', *Minnesota Law Review*, Vol.80, pp.795–824.

Dery, David and Schwarz-Milner, Binat (1994), *Who Governs Local Government?*, ha-Kibbutz ha-Me'uhad, Tel-Aviv.

Dewey, John (1916), *Democracy and Education: An Introduction to the philosophy of Education*, The Free Press, New York.

Eban, Abba (1957), *Voice of Israel*, Horizon, New York.

Eisenzweig, Uri (1981), 'An Imaginary Territory: The Problematic of Space in Zionist Discourse', *Dialectical Anthropology*, Vol.5(4), pp.261–285.

Elazar, Daniel J. (1988a), 'The Local Dimension in Israeli Government and Politics', in Daniel Elazar and Chaim Kalchheim (eds), *Local Government in Israel*, University Press of America, Lanham, pp.3–40.

Elazar, Daniel J. (1988b), 'Next Steps in Local Government Reform: The Recommendation of the State Commission on Local Government', in Daniel Elazar and Chaim Kalchheim (eds), *Local Government in Israel*, University Press of America, Lanham, pp.373–86.

El-Ghoneny, M. R. (1979), 'Planning and Evaluation of Land Settlement in Newly Developed Areas in the Middle East', in Laila El-Hamamsy and Jeannie Garrison (eds), *Human Settlement on New Lands: Their Design and Development*, The American University in Cairo Press, Cairo, pp.75–90.

Eriksen, Thomas H. (1993), *Ethnicity and Nationalism: Anthropological Perspectives*, Pluto, London.

Espeland, Wendy (1994), 'Legally Mediated Identity: The National Environmental Policy Act and the Bureaucratic Construction of Interests', *Law & Society Review*, Vol.28(5), pp.1149–1179.

Falah, Ghazi (1985a), 'How Israel Controls the Bedouin in Israel', *Journal of Palestine Studies*, Vol.16(2), pp.35–51.

Falah, Ghazi (1985b), 'Planned Bedouin Settlement in Israel: The Reply', *Geoforum*, Vol.16(4), pp.440–451.

Falah, Ghazi (1989), 'Israeli State Policy Towards Bedouin Sedentarization in the Negev', *Journal of Palestine Studies*, Vol.18(2), pp.71–91.

Fanon, Franz (1967), *Toward the African Revolution: Political Essays*, Grove, New York.

Feldman, Avigdor (1995), 'The Democratic State Against the Jewish State: Space without Places, Time without Duration', *Tel-Aviv University Law Review*, Vol.19, pp.717–727.

Felstiner, William L. F. et al. (1980), 'The Emergence and Transformation of Disputes: Naming, Blaming, Claming…', *Law & Society Review*, Vol.15, pp.631–654.

Florestano, Patricia S. and Marando, Vincent L. (1981), *The State and the Metropolis*, M. Dekker, New York.

Ford, Richard T. (1994), 'The Boundaries of Race: Political Geography in Legal Analysis', *Harvard Law Review*, Vol.107, pp.1841–1921.

Ford, Richard T. (1996), 'Beyond Borders: A Partial Response to Richard Briffault', *Stanford Law Review*, Vol.48, pp.1173–1195.

Ford, Richard T. (1997), 'Geography and Sovereignty: Jurisdictional Formation and Racial Segregation', *Stanford Law Review*, Vol.49, pp.1365–1445.

Ford, Richard T. (1999), 'Law's Territory (A History of Jurisdiction)', *Michigan Law Review*, Vol.97, pp.843–930.

Ford, Richard T. (2002), 'Beyond "Difference": A Reluctant Critique of Legal Identity Politics', Wendy Brown and Janet Halley (eds), *Left Legalism/Left Critique*, Duke University Press, Durham & London, pp.38–79.

Foucault, Michel (1980), 'The Eye of Power', in Colin Gordon (ed.), *Power/Knowledge: Selected Interviews and Other Writings 1972–1977*, Pantheon, New York, pp.146–165.

Frenkel Horner, Deborah (1982), 'Planning for Bedouin: The Case of Tel-Sheva', *Third World Planning Review*, Vol.4(2), pp.159–176.

Friedman, Menachem (1991), *The Haredi (Ultra-Orthodox) Society: Sources, Trends and Processes*, Jerusalem Institute for Israel Studies, Jerusalem.

Frug, Gerald E. (1980), 'The City as a Legal Concept', *Harvard Law Review*, Vol.93, pp.1059–1154.

Frug, Gerald E. (1993), 'Decentering Decentralization', *University of Chicago Law Review*, Vol.60, pp.253–338.

Frug, Gerald E. (1998), 'City Services', *New York University Law Review*, Vol.73, pp.23–96.

Frug, Gerald E. (1999), *City Making: Building Communities without Building Walls*, Princeton University Press, Princeton and Oxford.

Frug, Gerald E. (2000), 'Against Centralization', *Buffalo Law Review*, Vol.48, pp.31–38.

Gan-Mor, Eyal and Prois, Uri (1998), *Manual of Local Authorities and Regional Councils in Israel*, Telegraph, Jerusalem.

Gavison, Ruth (1998), 'A Jewish and Democratic State: Challenges and Risks', in Menachem Mautner, Ronen Shamir and Avi Sagi (eds), *Multiculturalism in a Democratic and Jewish State*, Ramot, Tel-Aviv, pp.213–278.

Gavison, Ruth (2000), 'Does Equality Require Integration?: A Case Study', *Democratic Culture*, Vol.3, pp.37–87.

Giddens, Anthony (1971), *Capitalism and Modern Social Theory*, Cambridge University Press, Cambridge.

Gilman, Sander L. (1986), *Jewish Self-Hatred: Antisemitism and the Hidden Language of the Jews*, Johns Hopkins University Press, Baltimore.

Gilroy, Paul (1987), '*There Ain't No Black in the Union Jack': The Cultural Politics of Race and Nation*, University of Chicago Press, Chicago.

Gilroy, Paul (1993), *The Black Atlantic: Modernity and Double Consciousness*, Harvard University Press, Cambridge.

Goadby, Frederic M. and Doukhan, Moses J. (1935), *The Land Law of Palestine*, Shoshany's Printing, Tel-Aviv.

Goldberg, Ze'ev (1967), 'Fix the Body not the Organs', in Ze'ev Goldberg (ed.), *The Central Government and the Local Government: Discussion in the Central Ideological Circle*, Merkaz le-Chinukh, Haskalah u-Mehkar, Bet Berl, pp.50–56.

Goldberg, David T. (1993), *Racist Culture: Philosophy and the Politics of Meaning*, Blackwell, Cambridge.

Goldstein, Stephen (1980a), 'Forward', in Stephen Goldstein (ed.), *Law and Equality in Education*, Van Leer Jerusalem Foundation, Jerusalem, pp.1–5.

Goldstein, Stephen (1980b), 'Judicial Intervention in Educational Decision Making: An Israeli-American Comparison' in Stephen Goldstein (ed.), *Law and Equality in Education*, Van Leer Jerusalem Foundation, Jerusalem, pp.95–118.

Goldstein, Stephen (1995), 'Liberty v. Equality: Concerning Student Placement in State Schools in Israel—The Changing Views of the Supreme Court', in Reuven Kahana (ed.), *Educational Advancement and Distributive Justice: Between Equality and Equity*, Magnes, Jerusalem, pp.311–325.

Gonen, Amiram (1975), 'Locational and Ecological Aspects of Urban Public Sector Housing: The Israeli Case', in G. Gappert and H. M. Rose (eds), *The Social Economy of Cities*, Sage, Beverly Hills, pp.275–295.

Gonen, Amiram (1985), 'The Changing Ethnic Geography of Israeli Cities', in Alex Weingrod (ed.), *Studies in Israeli Ethnicity: After the Ingathering*, Gordon and Breach Science Publishers, New York, pp.25–38.

Gonen, Amiram (1995), *Between City and Suburb: Urban Residential Patterns and Processes in Israel*, Avebury, Brookfield.

Gordon, Robert W. (1984), 'Critical Legal Histories', *Stanford Law Review*, Vol.36, pp.57–125.

Gradus, Yehuda and Stern, Eliahu (1980), 'Changing Strategies of Development: Toward a Regiopolis in the Negev Desert', *Journal of the American Planning Association*, Vol.46(4), pp.410–423.

Grossman, David (1994), 'The Fellaheen and the Bedouin on the Desert Margin: The System of Relationship and Survival Strategies', in David Grossman and Avinoam Meir (eds), *The Arabs in Israel: Geographical Dynamics*, Magnes, Jerusalem, pp.21–47.

Gupta, Akhil and Ferguson, James (1997), 'Beyond "Culture": Space, Identity, and the Politics of Difference', in Akhil Gupta and James Ferguson (eds), *Culture, Power, Place: Explorations in Critical Anthropology*, Duke University Press, Durham, pp.33–51.

Gury, Israel (1967), 'The Root of the Crises of Local Government and their Causes', in Ze'ev Goldberg (ed.), *The Central Government and the Local Government: Discussion in the Central-Ideological Circle*, Merkaz le-Chinukh, Haskalah u-Mehkar, Bet Berl, pp.39–44.

Handelman, Don and Shamgar-Handelman, Lea (1997), 'The Presence of Absence: The Memorialism of National Death in Israel', in Eyal Ban-Ari and Yoram Bilu (eds), *Grasping Land: Space and Place in Contemporary Israeli Discourse and Experience*, SUNY Press, Albany, pp.85–128.

Handler, Joel (1994), *Law and the Search for Community*, University of Pennsylvania Press, Philadelphia.

Harmelekh Report (1992), Report of the Inter-Ministerial Team for the Definition of the Level of Services and Budgets in the Areas of Education and Welfare in the Local Governments, Jerusalem.

Harvey, David (1973), *Social Justice and the City*, Johns Hopkins University Press, Baltimore.

Harvey, David (1990), *The Condition of Postmodernity: An Enquiry into the Origins of Cultural Change*, Blackwell, Cambridge.

Harvey, David (1996), *Justice, Nature and the Geography of Difference*, Blackwell, Cambridge.

Hasson, Shlomo and Razin, Eran (1990), 'What is Hidden Behind a Municipal Boundary Conflict?', *Political Geography Quarterly*, Vol. 9(3), pp.267–283.

Hepworth, N. P. (1970), *The Finance of Local Government*, Allen and Unwin, London.

Hertzberg, Arthur (1997), *The Zionist Idea: A Historical Analysis and Reader*, Jewish Publication Society, Philadelphia.

Herzl, Theodore (1946), *The Jewish State: An Attempt at a Modern Solution of the Jewish Question*, American Zionist Emergency Council, New York.

Horowitz, Dan and Lissak, Moshe (1989), *Trouble in Utopia: The Overburdened Polity of Israel*, SUNY Press, Albany.

Hoshen, Maya (1983), *Migration from and to Jerusalem*, 1972–1978, Jerusalem Institute for Israel Studies, Jerusalem.

Inbar, Dan and Choshen, Maya (1994), *Decentralization of Education Authority in Local Government*, Milken Institute for the Study of Education Systems, Jerusalem.

Janner-Klausner, David (1994), 'Municipal Strategic Planning: The Reshaping of Israeli Local Government', *Progress in Planning Series*, Vol.41, Pergamon, Oxford.

Kahana, Reuven and Starr, Leora (1984), *Education and Work: Processes of Vocational Socialization in Israel*, Magnes, Jerusalem.

Kalchheim, Chaim (1988), 'The Division of Functions and Interrelationships Between Local and State Authorities', in Daniel Elazar and Chaim Kalchheim (eds), *Local Government in Israel*, University Press of America, Lanham, pp.41–82.

Kalchheim, Chaim (1997), *Local Power in the Framework of a Democratic State*, Jerusalem Center for Public Affairs, Jerusalem.

Kallus, Rachel and Law-Yone, Hubert (2000), 'National Home/Personal Home: The Role of Public Housing in the Shaping of Space', *Theory and Criticism*, Vol.16, pp.153–180.

Kaplan, A. et al. (1976), Master Plan for the Bedouin Settlement in the Negev, Ministry of Interior, Jerusalem.

Kashti Commission (1991), *Report of the Public Commission on the Status of Supra-Regional Educational Frameworks*, State of Israel, Jerusalem.

Kaspi, David (1994), *Self-Administered Local Education Authority: Between Decentralization and Centralization*, Henrietta Sald Institute, Jerusalem.

Keating, Michael (1995), 'Size, Efficiency and Democracy: Consolidation, Fragmentation and Public Choice', in David Judge, Gerry Stoker and Harold Wolman (eds), *Theories of Urban Politics*, Sage, London, pp.117–134.

Kedar, Alexander (1998), 'Minority Time, Majority Time: Land, Nation, and the Law of Adverse Possession in Israel', *Tel-Aviv University Law Review*, Vol.21(3), pp.665–746.

Kedar, Alexander (2000), '"A First Step in a Difficult and Sensitive Road": Preliminary Observations on Qaadan v. Katzir', *Israel Studies Bulletin*, Vol.16, pp.3–11.

Kedar, Alexander (2001), 'The Legal Transformation of Ethnic Geography: Israeli Law and the Palestinian Landholder 1948–1967', *New York University Journal of International Law and Politics*, Vol.33, pp.923–1000.

Kelman, Mark (1987), *A Guide to Critical Legal Studies*, Harvard University Press, Cambridge.

Kemp, Adriana (2000), 'Borders, Space and National Identity in Israel', *Theory and Criticism*, Vol.16, pp.13–44.

Kliot, N. and Medzini, A. (1985), 'Bedouin Settlement Policy in Israel, 1964–1982: Another Perspective', *Geoforum*, Vol.16(4), pp.428–39.

Kressel, G. et al. (1991), 'Changes in Land Usage by the Negev Bedouin since the 19th Century', *Nomadic Peoples*, Vol.28, pp.28–55.

Lancaster, W. and Lancaster, F. (1986), 'The Concept of Territory among the Rawla Bedouin', *Nomadic Peoples*, Vol.20, pp.41–67.

Latour, Bruno (1993), *We Have Never Been Modern*, Harvester Wheatsheaf, New York.

Lavon, Pinhas (1967), 'The Principle People', in Ze'ev Goldberg (ed.), *The Central Government and the Local Government: Discussion in the Central Ideological Circle*, Merkaz le-Chinukh, Haskalah u-Mehkar, Bet Berl, pp.45–49.

Lefebvre, Henri (1991), *The Production of Space*, Blackwell, Cambridge.

Levi, Amnon (1988), *The Ultra-Orthodox*, Keter, Jerusalem.

LeVine, Mark (1995), 'The Discourse of Development in Mandate Palestine', *Arab Studies Quarterly*, Vol.17, pp.95–124.

LeVine, Mark (1999), *Overthrowing Geography, Re-Imagining Identities: A History of Jaffa and Tel-Aviv*, 1880 to the Present, Ph.D. Dissertation, New York University, New York.

Levi-Strauss, Claude (1997), *Tristes Tropiques*, Modern Library, New York.

Lissak, Moshe (1999), *Mass Immigration in the Fifties: The Failure of the Melting Pot Policy*, Mosad Byalik, Jerusalem.

Luz, Ehud (1988), *Parallels Meet: Religion and Nationalism in the Early Zionist Movement*, Jewish Publication Society, Philadelphia.

Mandelbaum, Seymour J. (1996), 'Open Moral Communities', in Seymour Mandelbaum, Luigi Mazza and Robert W. Burchell (eds), *Exploration in Planning Theory*, Center for Urban Policy Research, New Brunswick.

Margalit, Avishai and Halbertal, Moshe (1994), 'Liberalism and the Right to Culture', *Social Research*, Vol.61, p.491.

Marx, Emanuel (1967), *Bedouin of the Negev*, Manchester University Press, Manchester.

Marx, Emanuel (1984), 'Economic Change Among Pastoral Nomads in the Middle East', in Emanuel Marx and Avshalom Shmueli (eds), *The Changing Bedouin*, Transaction Books, New Brunswick, pp.1–15.

Meir, Avinoam (1997), *As Nomadim Ends: The Israeli Bedouin of the Negev*, Westview, Boulder.

Merry, Sally Engle (1991), 'Law and Colonialism', *Law and Society Review*, Vol.25(4), pp.889–922.

Michelman, Frank I. (1986), 'Forward: Traces of Self-Government', *Harvard Law Review*, Vol.100, pp.4–77.

Mill, John Stuart (1991), *On Liberty and Other Essays*, Oxford University Press, Oxford.

Miller, Gary J. (1981), *Cities by Contract: The Politics of Municipal Incorporation*, MIT Press, Cambridge.

Ministry of Interior (1966), *Physical Master Plan of the Negev*, Ministry of Interior Planning Department, Jerusalem.

Ministry of Interior (1976), *Development Plan for the Negev Region*, Ministry of Interior Planning Department, Jerusalem.

Ministry of Interior (1977), *Report of the Commission for the Preparation of the Master Plan for the Development of the Negev*, Ministry of Interior Southern District, Be'er Sheva.

Ministry of Interior (1986), *Report of the Markovitz Committee*, Ministry of Interior, Jerusalem.

Ministry of Interior (1998), *The Commission for the Consolidation of Local Governments: Final Report*, Ministry of Interior, Jerusalem.

Mitchell, Timothy (1988), *Colonizing Egypt*, Cambridge University Press, Cambridge.

Morris, Benny (1993), *Israel's Border Wars 1949–1956: Arab Infiltration, Israeli Retaliation, and the Countdown to the Suez War*, Clarendon, New York.

Mumford, Lewis (1938), *The Culture of Cities*, Harcourt, Brace and Company, New York.

Nahon, Ya'acov (1993) 'Occupational Status', in S. N. Eisenstadt, M. Lissak and Y. Nahon (eds), *Ethnic Communities in Israel: Socio-economic Status*, Jerusalem Institute for Israel Studies, Jerusalem, pp.50–75.

Naor, Gideon et al. (1978), *The Local Government—Its Status and Roles*, ha-Merkaz le-Heker Hityashvut Kafrit ve-Iironit, Rehovot.

Newman, David (1995), 'Creating Homogeneous Space: The Evolution of Israel's Regional Councils', in Ilan S. Troen and Noah Lucas (eds), *Israel: The First Decade of Independence*, SUNY Press, Albany, pp.495–519.

Newman, David and Applebaum, L. (1995), 'Conflicting Objectives for Rural Local Government: Service Position to Exurban Communities in Israel', *Environment and Planning* C, Vol.13, pp.253–271.

Nozick, Robert (1974), *Anarchy, State and Utopia*, Harper and Row, New York.

Orfield, Gary (1995), 'Housing and the Justification of School Desegregation', *University of Pennsylvania Law Review*, Vol.143, pp.1397–1406.

Orfield, Gary (1996), 'Metropolitan School Desegregation: Impacts on Metropolitan Societies', *Minnesota Law Review*, Vol.80, pp.825–873.

Park, R. E. (1936), 'Succession, an Ecological Concept', *American Sociological Review*, Vol.1, pp.171–179.

Peled, Israel (1988), 'Legal Structure of the Local Authority', in Daniel Elazar and Chaim Kalchheim (eds), *Local Government in Israel*, University Press of America, Lanham, pp.165–197.

Peled, Yoav (1990), 'Ethnic Exclusionism in the Periphery: The Case of Oriental Jews in Israel's Development Towns', *Ethnic and Racial Studies*, Vol.13(3), pp.345–367.

Perevolotsky, A. (1987), 'Territoriality and Resource Sharing among the Bedouin of Southern Sinai: A Socio-Ecological Interpretation', *Journal of Arid Environments*, Vol.13(3), pp.153–161.

Pinsker, Leo (1997), 'Auto-Emancipation' in Arthur Hertzbrg (ed), *The Zionist Idea: A Historical Analysis and Reader*, pp.194–208.

Poindexter, Georgette C. (1997), 'Collective Individualism: Deconstructing the Legal City', *University of Pennsylvania Law Review*, Vol.145, pp.607–664.

Powell, John A. (1996), 'Living and Learning: Linking Housing and Segregation', *Minnesota Law Review*, Vol.80, pp.749–793.

Prior, Michael (1999), *Zionism and the State of Israel: A Moral Inquiry*, Routledge, New York.

Rabinowitz, Dan (1992), 'An Acre Is An Acre Is An Acre? Differential Attitudes to Social Space and Territory on the Jewish-Arab Urban Frontier in Israel', *Urban Anthropology*, Vol.21, pp.67–89.

Rabinowitz, Dan (1997), 'In and Out of Territory', in Eyal Ben-Ari and Yoram Bilu (eds), *Grasping Land: Space and Place in Contemporary Israeli Discourse and Experience*, SUNY Press, Albany, pp.177–202.

Rash, Nora et al. (1977), 'Teachers' Attitudes Towards Inter-Ethnic Integration and the Educational Goals of the Junior High School', *Megamot*, Vol. 23, pp.228–253.

Rast, Hubert (1997), 'Critical Theory and Alternate Modernities: A Partial Reading', *Journal of the International Institute* Vol.4(2).

Razin, Eran (1994), *Municipal Reform in the Tel-Aviv Metropolis: Metropolitan Government or Metropolitan Cooperation*, Floersheimer Institute for Policy Studies, Jerusalem.

Razin, Eran (1997), *Policies to Control Urban Sprawl: Changing the "Rules of the Game"*, Floersheimer Institute for Policy Studies, Jerusalem.

Razin, Eran (1999), *Fiscal Disparities Between Small and Large Municipalities in Israel*, Floersheimer Institute for Policy Studies, Jerusalem.

Razin, Eran and Hasson, Shlomo (1994), 'Urban-Rural Boundary Conflicts: the Reshaping of Israel's Rural Map', *Journal of Rural Studies*, Vol.10, pp.47–59.

Razin, Eran and Hazan, A. (1995), 'Industrial Development and Municipal Reorganization: Conflict, Cooperation, and Regional Effects', *Environment and Planning* C, Vol.13, pp.297–314.

Rose, Carol (1985), 'Possession as the Origins of Property', *University of Chicago Law Review*, Vol.52, pp.73–88.

Rusk, David (1995), *Cities Without Suburbs*, Woodrow Wilson Center, Washington D.C.

Sandel, Michael J. (1982), *Liberalism and the Limits of Justice*, Cambridge University Press, Cambridge.

Sagi, Avi and Zohar, Zvi (2000), *Circles of Jewish Identity: A Study of Halakhic Literature*, ha-Kibbutz ha-Me'uhad, Tel-Aviv.

Said, Edward W. (1979), *Orientalism*, Vintage, New York.

Said, Edward (2000), 'Invention, Memory, and Place', *Critical Inquiry*, Vol.26(2), pp.175–192.

Santos, Boaventura de Sousa (1987), 'Law: A Map of Misreading—Toward a Postmodern Conception of Law', *Journal of Law and Society*, Vol.14(3), pp.279–302.

Santos, Boaventura de Sousa (1995), *Towards a New Common Sense: Law, Science and Politics in the Paradigmatic Transition*, Routledge, New York.

Schmelz, Uziel O. et al. (1991), *Ethnic Differences Among Israeli Jews: A New Outlook*, Institute of Contemporary Jewry, Jerusalem.

Schragger, Richard C. (2001), 'The Limits of Localism', *Michigan Law Review*, Vol.100, pp.371–472.

Segev, Tom (1986), *1949: The First Israelis*, Free Press, New York.

Shachar, Arie (1997), 'Spatial Policy for Israel's Urbanized Regions', in *'Israel 2020' Master Plan for Israel in the 21st Century: General Policy Spatial, Economic and Municipal Aspects*, Technion Institute of Technology, Haifa, pp.5–41.

Shachar, Arie (1998), 'Reshaping the Map of Israel: A New National Planning Doctrine', *Annals of the American Academy*, Vol.555, pp.209–215.

Shachar, Ayelet (2000), 'The Puzzle of Interlocking Power Hierarchies: Sharing the Pieces of Jurisdictional Authority', *Harvard Civil Rights—Civil Liberties Law Review*, Vol.35, pp.385–426.

Shafir, Gershon (1989), *Land, Labor and the Origins of the Israeli-Palestinian Conflict 1882–1914*, Cambridge University Press, Cambridge.

Shamir, Ronen (1990), '"Landmark Cases" and the reproduction of Legitimacy: The Case of Israel's High Court of Justice', *Law & Society Review*, Vol.24(3), pp.781–805.

Shamir, Ronen (1996), 'Suspended in Space: Bedouins under the Law of Israel', *Law & Society Review*, Vol.30(2), pp.231–257.

Shamir, Ronen (2000a), *The Colonies of Law: Colonialism, Zionism and Law in Early Mandate Palestine*, Cambridge University Press, Cambridge.

Shamir, Ronen (2000b), 'Zionism 2000: Past, Future, and the Qa'adan Family', *Adalah's Review*, Vol.2, pp.27–31.

Shamir, Ronen and Chinski, Sara (1998), 'Destruction of Houses and Construction of Cause: lawyers and Bedouins in the Israeli Courts', in Austin Sarat and Stuart Scheingold (eds), *Cause Lawyering: Political Commitments and Professional Responsibilities*, Oxford University Press, New York, pp.227–257.

Sharkansky, Ira (1997), 'Israel: A Metropolitan Nation-State', *Cities*, Vol.14(6), pp.363–69.

Sharpe, L. J. (1995), 'The Future of Metropolitan Government', in L. J. Sharpe (ed.), *The Government of World Cities: The Future of the Metro Model*, Wiley, Chichester, pp.11–31.

Shavit, Yossi (1984), 'Tracking and Ethnicity in Israeli Secondary Education', *American Sociological Review*, Vol.49(2), pp.210–20.

Shavit, Yossi et al. (2000), 'Ethnic Inequality in University Education in Israel', in Menachem Mautner (ed.), *Distributive Justice in Israel*, Ramot, Tel-Aviv, pp.391–408.

Shetrit, Sami Shalom (1999), *The Ashkenazi Revolution is Dead: Reflections on Israel from a Dark Angle*, Bimat Kedem le-Sifrut, Tel-Aviv

Shilhav, Yossef and Friedman, Menachem (1985), *Growth and Segregation: The Ultra Orthodox Community of Jerusalem*, Jerusalem Institute for Israel Studies, Jerusalem.

Shohat, Ella (1988), 'Sephardim in Israel: Zionism from the Standpoint of its Jewish Victims', *Social Text*, Vol.19/20, pp.1–35.

Shohat, Ella (1992), 'Dislocated Identities: Reflections of an Arab-Jew, *Movement Research: Performance Journal*, Vol.5, pp.8–34.

Smilanski, Moshe (1957), 'A Social Analysis of the Structure of Education in Israel', *Megamot*, Vol.8, pp.136–144.

Smilanski, Moshe (1961), 'A Proposal for Reform of the Structure of Post-Primary Education', *Megamot*, Vol.11, pp.364–372.

Smith, A. D. (1981), 'States and Homelands: The Social and Geopolitical Implications of National Territory', *Millenium*, Vol.10, pp.187–202.

Smith, Brian C. (1985), *Decentralization: The Territorial Dimension of the State*, G. Allen & Unwin, Boston.

Smooha, Sammy (1979), *Israel: Pluralism and Conflict*, University of California Press, Berkeley.

Soffer, Arnon and Bar-Gal, Y. (1985), 'Planned Bedouin Settlement in Israel: A Critique', *Geoforum*, Vol.16(4), pp.423–51.

Soja, Edward W. (1989), *Postmodern Geographies: The Reassertion of Space in Critical Social Theory*, Verso, New York.

State Comptroller (1993), *Annual Report*, Vol.43, State of Israel, Jerusalem.

Statman, Daniel (1998), 'Offense to Religious Feelings', in Menachem Mautner, Ronen Shamir and Avi Sagi (eds), *Multiculturalism in a Democratic and Jewish State*, Ramot, Tel-Aviv, pp.133–88.

Stern, Eliahu and Gradus, Yehuda (1979), 'Socio-cultural Considerations in Planning for Nomads', *Ekistics*, Vol.277, pp.224–230.

Swirski, Shlomo (1999), *Politics and Education in Israel*, Falmer, New York.

Taylor, Charles (1985), 'Atomism', *Philosophical Papers: Philosophy and the Human Sciences*, Vol.2, pp.187–210.

Tel Aviv Department of Education (1992), *Doing it a Different Way—Tel Aviv-Jaffa Believes in Education: The Renovation of the School System in the City of Tel Aviv-Jaffa*, Tel-Aviv Municipal Department of Education and Culture, Tel-Aviv.

Tiebout, Charles (1956) 'A Pure Theory of Local Public Expenditures', *Journal of Political Economy*, Vol.64, pp.416–424.

Timms, Duncan (1971), *The Urban Mosaic: Towards a Theory of Residential Differentiation*, Cambridge University Press, Cambridge.

Tocqueville, Alexis de (1863), *Democracy in America*, Sever & Francis, Cambridge.

Torgovnik, Efraim (1988), 'Urban Policy', in Daniel Elazar and Chaim Kalchheim (eds), *Local Government in Israel*, University Press of America, Lanham, pp.83–127.

Trakman, Leon and Gatien, Sean (1999), *Rights and Responsibilities*, University of Toronto Press, Toronto.

Tute, Richard C. (1927), *The Ottoman Land Laws*, Greek Conv. Press, Jerusalem.

United Nations (1963), *Local Government in Selected Countries: Ceylon, Israel, Japan*, United Nations Technical Assistant Programme, New York.

Vinograd, Eliyahu (1998), *Local Government Law*, Halakhot, Ramat ha-Sharon.

Wirth, Louis (1998), *The Ghetto*, Transaction, New Brunswick.

Yiftachel, Oren (1992), *Planning a Mixed Region in Israel: The Political Geography of Arab-Jewish Relations in the Galilee*, Avebury Gower Publishing, Aldershot, Hampshire.

Yiftachel, Oren (1995), 'Planning as Control: Policy and Resistance in Deeply Divided Societies', *Progress in Planning Series*, Vol.44, Pergamon-Elsvier, Oxford.

Yiftachel, Oren (1997), 'Israel: Metropolitan Integration or Fractured Regions?', *Cities*, Vol.14(6), pp.371–380.

Yiftachel, Oren (1998), 'Nation-Building and the Division of Space: Ashkenazi Domination in the Israeli "Ethnocracy"', *Nationalism and Ethnic Policies*, Vol.4(3), pp.33–58.

Yiftachel, Oren (1999), '"Ethnocracy": The Politics of Judaizing Israel/Palestine', *Constellation*, Vol.6(3), pp.364–90.

Yiftachel Oren and Kedar, Alexander (2000), 'Land Power: The Making of the Israeli Land Regime', *Theory and Criticism*, Vol.16, pp.67–100.

Young, Iris M. (1990), *Justice and the Politics of Difference*, Princeton University Press, Princeton.

Ziv, Neta (2000), 'Communities, Lawyers, and Legal Strategies for Social Change', *Adalah's Review*, Vol.2, pp.39–43.

Index

www.ingramcontent.com/pod-product-compliance
Lightning Source LLC
LaVergne TN
LVHW011128300926
849160LV00008B/566
* 9 7 8 1 1 3 8 2 6 4 0 4 5 *